M000085980

303.62   664107
Sesaller, Stephen.
Invisible armies

INVISIBLE ARMIES

664107

INVISIBLE ARMIES

TERRORISM INTO THE 1990s

Stephen Segaller

HARCOURT BRACE JOVANOVICH, PUBLISHERS

San Diego   New York   London

MERCED COUNTY LIBRARY

JUN 29 1988

Copyright © 1987, 1986 by Merrill Berger

All rights reserved. No part of this publication may be reproduced or transmitted in any form or by any means, electronic or mechanical, including photocopy, recording, or any information storage and retrieval system, without permission in writing from the publisher.

Requests for permission to make copies of any part of the work should be mailed to:
Permissions, Harcourt Brace Jovanovich, Publishers,
Orlando, Florida 32887.

Excerpts from *Terrorism: The Soviet Connection*, by Roy S. Cline and Yonah Alexander, copyright © 1984 by Center for Strategic and International Studies, Georgetown University. Reprinted by permission of Crane, Russak & Company, Inc.

303.62

Library of Congress Cataloging-in-Publication Data
Segaller, Stephen.
  Invisible armies.
  Includes index.
  1. Terrorism. I. Title.
HV6431.S44   1987   909.82   86-31845
ISBN 0-15-145288-1

Printed in the United States of America
First American edition 1987

A B C D E

2143

C

For Merrill

CONTENTS

FOREWORD TO THE
AMERICAN EDITION

Any attempt to provide an overview of the international
pattern of terrorism is likely to be overtaken by events, and
the problem is more acute for the journalist than for the
historian. The revelations that were emerging in Washington,
D.C., in December 1986 swung the political interpretation
of the Iranian arms-for-hostages deal back and forth. First,
the supply of weapons parts to Iran appeared connected to
a general, if naive, initiative in Mideast policy dictated by
the White House alone; then the emphasis shifted decisively
to a crude barter for American hostages with secret military
favours to the Ayatollah's dangerous regime. Whatever its
ultimate outcome, the saga demonstrates the acute and
enduring capacity of terrorism to confront the political leaders
of democratic nations with problems that always lie in the
minefields where the margins of government activity and the
political process meet the moral grey areas of compromise,
retaliation, secrecy and covert dirty tricks.

This book argues in general terms that terrorism is not
a policing problem or a law and order problem or a military
problem. It is all of these at different times, but more important
than any it is a political problem. Retaliation by states that
fall victim to terrorism, or retaliation on behalf of the victims
of terrorism, operates in those difficult margins where decisive
actions may always turn out to be injudicious – or at least
hard to justify – by seeming excessive. Public opinion finds
a clearer justification for using limited, perhaps severe, methods
against terrorists – in effect, using terrorism against the
terrorists – than for using wholesale military might. Israel's
intermittent policy of using Mossad agents to eliminate
identified Palestinian terrorists, parallel to retaliatory air raids

on refugee camps, met with little disapproval; indeed, it was widely approved as an exercise in natural justice. But the doubtful moral result is to condone the use of illegal and murderous tactics by the secret agencies of a democratic state – a position few elected politicians can cheerfully sustain.

In the two years since work on this book began, the waters have become muddier than ever around the related issues of state-sponsored terrorism and retaliation. While the French state, a democracy, ultimately accepted its responsibility for an act of terrorism against the environmental group Greenpeace in New Zealand, the Syrian government continued to plead an implausible innocence of terrorist crimes in Britain and West Germany – despite court convictions and overwhelming evidence of links between the convicted terrorists and Syrian diplomats. Indeed, the distinction between terrorist and diplomat was far from clear. Yet neither case falls within the previous definitions of state-sponsored terrorism, which has been taken to mean the financing or arming of small terrorist groups (who otherwise would act independently) by states for covert political purposes.

Though such incidents do clearly fall within the proper definition of terrorism (see Chapter 1), they are in a sense irrelevant to the terrorist phenomenon that is now universal summit fodder and that produces from statesmen ever new, mostly cosmetic, initiatives of state cooperation. In a similar way, the US air raids on Libya in April 1986 are somewhat irrelevant to the issue of terrorism. Libya's quixotic leadership, uniquely, advocates terrorism and certainly sponsors some terrorists. Yet the basis of the retaliation was far more a matter of Colonel Gadaffi's unacceptable military and political activity elsewhere in Africa and the Middle East, and the limited consequences to the United States in carrying out such an attack on behalf of numerous allies, in a classic instance of airborne gunboat diplomacy. To use terrorism as an excuse for such actions, however, is as dangerous as the terrorism itself.

Hostages represent one of the most emotional political propositions, and it is understandable enough that the release of a country's own hostages is of concern to the government involved. However, the idea that any state should endanger the perceived integrity of its political programme and undermine the apparent direction of its whole foreign policy in any area of the world for the sake of a handful of very unfortunate individuals must be seen as the ultimate example in political terms of shortsightedness and misplaced priorities.

On Capitol Hill the buzzword of the congressional hearings investigating the Iranian arms supplies was 'gullibility'. Had anyone in the administration seriously believed that by supplying a supposedly limited quantity of arms to Iran, all hostage problems would be resolved? If anyone did, how high was the price to be? Did no one foresee the risk that if one group of hostages was released, another would be seized? And if they did, were they prepared to go on paying an escalating price for the foreseeable future?

All governments wish to protect their citizens wherever they may be in the world, within reason. Yet all Western governments have long since advised their citizens to leave Lebanon, to leave Iran, to leave any country in which there is a conspicuous risk that their mere nationality could lead them to fall victim to acts of violence, kidnapping, or terrorism. To those in the direct employment of the US government (or other Western states), the risks are very clear and an unwelcome component of the job description. No one could possibly have accused the United States government of failing to warn its citizens to get out of Lebanon, in particular, when the dangers there had become quite clear. Nevertheless, the American government, amid President Reagan's patriotic revivalism, honourably or rashly continued to assume responsibility for people who were openly gambling with their own physical safety – some of them, of course, for honourable and worthwhile reasons. Such a policy must be seen as a distorted and disproportionate gesture of national pride.

As Chapter 7 of this book demonstrates, nothing is more likely to encourage terrorists in their view that American hostages are the highest prize than the manner in which the US administration handled the hijacking of TWA Flight 847 in 1985 – as a political spectacular. The very high profile of such incidents in the United States means that the terrorists are guaranteed their first goal: namely, the attention of the world for their grievance (however unconvincing it may be) and direct communication to the top levels of government – even to the Oval Office itself – by the simple expedient of capturing a handful of unfortunate American citizens. To take a parallel example, the arrest of the American journalist Nicholas Daniloff in Moscow could only have meant two things: either that he was working as a CIA spy as the Soviet Union alleged, or that he was unlucky, the chance victim of a pre-arranged political device. The hostages on TWA Flight 847 were just unlucky. Yet by the time of their release, like Daniloff, they had become involuntary hero-ambassadors for the United States. For the Reagan administration, the well-meaning obsession with hostages finally produced positive public relations and political consequences with the release of the TWA hostages, as it did again in 1986 when three hostages (Anderson, Jacobsen and Jenco) from Beirut were freed.

More recent revelations have shown weapons capable of prolonging a war of slaughter and attrition being traded merely in the hope of rescuing so few American lives. The blinkered pursuit of freedom at any price for US hostages resulted in a paralysing blow to the credibility of the Reagan presidency and its proclaimed position of co-ordinated and effective opposition to all terrorism, state-sponsored terrorism in particular. It seems unlikely that even the most devoted American patriot could say that the prize – the release of three or four hostages – was worth the gamble. The US government – like many others, but more so than any – exaggerates the scale of the problem by risking so much in its search for appropriate responses and innovative solutions. In so doing it undermines the quality of its wider moral leadership of the West, which is, and will remain, essential.

FOREWORD

The opportunity to study terrorism at something close to first-hand, and in exhaustive detail, may be seen as something of a mixed blessing. Nevertheless, the subject lies so close to the heart of contemporary politics and international relations, touching almost every conscious citizen at least with its shadow, that no journalist could refuse such an opportunity. Such as it is, my ability to write this book derives substantially from the eighteen months I spent working as Director of a documentary series called *Terror*, produced by Krosney Productions of New York, and commissioned by Channel 4 in London, ZDF of West Germany and Global Television of Canada. I therefore owe a debt of thanks to Herbert Krosney: firstly, for employing me in such an absorbing field of journalistic enquiry; and secondly, for his permission to quote occasionally from programme material. This is not, however, the book of the series: it is based almost entirely on research and interviews conducted after the transmission of the programmes in midsummer 1985.

It seems to me that no book could ever be written without the author being able to rely upon a complex network of support: on the good advice and encouragement of friends, the expertise of literary professionals, and the love of a family – in my case, mother, father, brother, wife and son. My friends, agent, editor, publisher and family should all accept my thanks for their respective roles. In particular, I want to record my gratitude to my father, Denis Segaller, for the right words of encouragement when they were most needed; to my son's nanny, Karen Mohan, for her success at entertaining

Adam when his interest in my keyboard was likely to overwhelm us both; and to my wife, Merrill Berger. This book is a product of my labour, but of her inspiration; no author or husband could draw upon a deeper fund of love and support.

INVISIBLE ARMIES

INTRODUCTION

This book is about terrorism, the subject most certain to grab headlines into the 1990s, as it has done for twenty years. The Invisible Armies are with us for the foreseeable future.

The name 'terrorism' has been given to a new form of crime, a new departure in politics, a new danger to freedom. The use of violence and the threat of violence are not new. But what is new is the perspective modern terrorism affords on sentiments such as that expressed by Thomas Merton in his Introduction to Gandhi's *Non-Violence in Peace and War*: 'Violence is essentially wordless and it can begin only where thought and rational communication have broken down.' Those words were written in 1948; today, examining what the world calls terrorism – whatever the difficulties of agreeing on a definition – we find the opposite is true. The violence of terrorism is positively verbose: always accompanied by threats, communiqués and manifestos, and succeeded by historical argument and political reaction. First the violence, then the claim; first the blood, then the bluster. Violence is the megaphone for terrorists and their claims.

Terrorism is regarded as a uniquely offensive form of political activity by a near-unanimous majority of citizens, governments and institutions in the developed world. The use of terrorist tactics is a response to political impotence, to a position of weakness, to the inability to influence events (whether any influence is deserved or not). The developed world reacts to terrorism with understandable revulsion, and more importantly rejects the terrorists' case (whether it has any merit or none) specifically because terrorism has been

1

employed. It is a vici
uance of terrorism, e'

As a rule, terrorism
of government who
heroic about the risks
population, the very a
to win over. The reac
act of terrorism is, firsi
impotence. There are
simply revolted by th
uncomprehending of
violence in the name o
is far from new: Karl
of bloody acts of violei
of 'popular struggle'
tween the dedication of the terrorists and the mingled shock
and indifference of the people watching. As he wrote to his
friend Friedrich Engels on 14 December 1867, after the
Fenians (Irishmen fighting to be free of British rule, as ever)
had bombed Clerkenwell Prison in London, killing a number
of passing Londoners: 'The last exploit of the Fenians in
Clerkenwell was a very stupid thing. The London masses
who have shown great sympathy for Ireland will be made wild
by it and driven into the arms of the government party. One
cannot expect the London proletarians to allow themselves to
be blown up in honour of the Fenian emissaries.'

The third repercussion of an act of terrorism is the confused
clangour of stable doors being slammed, bolted, welded shut
and bricked up. But terrorists are not so foolish as to strike
twice in the same place. Like the moving finger, terrorism,
having hit, moves on: leaving enraged states with the limited
and dangerous options of vigilance, diplomacy and seeming
impotence on the one hand; or blunderbuss retaliation and
seeming barbarity on the other.

The sensation value of terrorism, however, is distinctly out
of proportion to the actual physical damage caused and the
numbers killed, and above all out of proportion to the successes achieved by the terrorists. Terrorism since the 1960s

has claimed relatively few victims in global terms. US State Department statistics in mid-1985 showed that from 1968 to 1984 inclusive, a total of 7,435 terrorist incidents worldwide had claimed a total of 4,796 lives (of whom 465 were Americans). In the same period, it might be reasonable to guess that fifty natural disasters have claimed as many lives each, if not more; without considering the infinitely greater suffering and death toll of famine and epidemics in sub-Saharan Africa.

Unnatural disasters produce more morbidity than terrorism – for example, murder and road deaths. In the two states of Texas and California together, in 1983 more people died at the hands of murderers (4, 864) than had been killed by world-wide terrorism over sixteen years to 1984. In 1981, roughly the same number of victims (4,684) died in road accidents in Texas alone. Still more (5,498) met the same death in California. And in 1983, even on a declining trend, 44,600 people died in road accidents in the United States as a whole: ten times the total number of victims of terrorism in almost two decades, throughout the world. The disproportionate anger aroused by terrorism is simply attributable to its essential illegitimacy; terrorists' victims suffer the exact moral opposite of 'accidental death', the antithesis of the *crime passionnelle*.

Terrorism has been allowed to undermine the notion that the West has enjoyed forty years of peace since 1945. What clearly the West has avoided, though many areas of the world have not, is the mass-casualty carnage of full-scale territorial war. Some insist that the existence of nuclear weapons – paradoxically so destructive that their use is almost unthinkable – has guaranteed the peace as much or more than the sheer cost and human loss of conventional war. Others believe that terrorism has also made an ironic contribution to peace – by permitting certain conflicts to express themselves at a level of loss and destruction which in the very long term can be regarded as acceptable.

There is an attractive myth that terrorism is a basic law-and-order problem, involving few people and amenable (despite all the contrary evidence) to tough, simple measures. But why should terrorism stop, when the massive publicity attending a single act of terrorism will predictably outweigh decades of peaceful representation and lobbying? Why should it stop, when concerted government actions have produced a nil effect of deterrence?

Terrorism is copiously reported in newspapers, news magazines, television and radio. But in search of truth you have to report both sides of the story. There are in effect two stories here: the story of the terrorist incident, and the separate story of the government reaction to terrorism. Every incident provokes predictable and deserved condemnation of bloodshed from government spokesmen, but such reactions rarely reveal the meaning of the event. However distasteful and offensive, there is another side to the story – the terrorists' side.

This is not to propose a friendly exposition of the terrorists' case – far from it. Modern terrorism has afflicted the world for long enough, yet the most important questions seem still to be unanswered; or more disturbingly, the uncomfortable anwers remain ignored. It is important to ask: Who becomes a terrorist? What issues seem to end in terrorism and what issues do not? What provokes an individual to shed blood in peacetime? What complex group and individual motives lie behind the emergence of a terrorist organisation? What evidence do terrorists observe for a belief in their ultimate success? Why won't they stop even when they do make substantial gains?

In the case of state policy, one has the same inquisition to perform. We know about states insisting on law and order and legitimate democratic power – but why do states not stand by their avowed principles? Why do they do deals with terrorists? support some terrorists while condemning others? seek to define terrorism narrowly to satisfy their local, political or sectarian preferences? The first, crude answer is that governments are political entities, and in politics (despite the absolutes uttered by the politicians) every issue can be fudged according to the needs of the situation. What we must learn in exposing these dishonesties is that terrorism and democratic government are at opposite ends of a continuum: government ministers and all professional politicians should be able to understand terrorists if anyone can, because they are crudely speaking in the same game, playing by different rules.

The central objective of this book is to generate a sense of comprehension and realism in the debate on terrorism, and to demonstrate that pragmatism must *visibly* replace dogmatism and grand principle as the sole viable response to terrorism. Terrorist violence has been present in the world for long enough – and growing year by year – to convince anyone that it cannot be 'defeated'. While every terrorist event provokes new debate about the appropriate response, the purpose here is to show that the debate is effectively finished; that the decision has in fact been taken, by almost all relevant powers, that terrorism is an ugly but necessary price to pay for two quite separate things: democratic freedoms whose destruction would be guaranteed by the repression which can be and has been employed to kill off terrorism; and the reluctance to address unpalatable political problems whose solution, in effect, is too low a priority.

After the decline of the major wave of Red Brigade violence in Italy, a secret service source said this: 'All we wanted was for the terrorists not to use terror. We didn't want to eliminate them as a political opposition.' This is the right approach (though many would claim that the Italian government *did* want to eliminate the political movement which lay behind the Red Brigades, and that its unprecedented legal methods were designed to do just that). If the state makes terrorists into a generalised enemy, it tends to legitimise the terrorists' belief that they are at war with the state, and thus that they have become its moral equal. If the state accepts the terrorists' right to dissent, and recognises the source of the grievance as real while opposing its criminal expression, it may succeed in marginalising terrorism.

Whenever governments can detach the politically sympathetic supporters of terrorism from the practical exponents, they make terrorism more difficult to perpetrate. If there is no willingness to make reasonable concessions to pressure groups or independence movements – even concessions as limited as low-level official contacts merely to hear a grievance expressed and a case articulated – then governments will perhaps justly open themselves to the accusation of inflexibility, and terrorism will perhaps justly be seen as the price they pay for their hold on power and its maintenance long term.

Terrorism offers governments and leaders a unique problem in modern politics. There is a crime, with victims (usually innocent), public outrage, accusations and demands. The state is attacked for some policy or other, or the absence of a policy, but it is not the state which suffers directly – indeed states are only composed of their people and their public and private property. The government must react somehow to reassure its citizens and to present an image of calm. What usually occurs is rather more, however: the Prime Minister or President promises that terrorism will not influence policy; that terrorists will be subject to justice (sometimes meaning retaliation upon other unrelated victims); that terrorism will never pay. The problem is that these claims are almost always false. Terrorism does produce results – it gets issues into the public consciousness, and draws attention to the policies which provoke terrorism as a reaction. Terrorists almost always get some kind of concession.

This book attempts to identify the meaning of terrorism by detailed interpretations of terrorist movements and their actions, of terrorist individuals and their opponents in the security services, of the declared aims of the terrorists and the corresponding declarations of states under attack, and of the grey areas between the terrorism governments oppose, and the terrorism they declare to be legitimate by virtue of their own legitimising authority. In taking as its brief the whole of terrorism in the contemporary world, the book cannot remain absolutely consistent in detailed analysis or general theory. In fact, terrorist actions can have opposite consequences according to the circumstances in which they are perpetrated, or the purposes to which they are directed. If the Invisible Armies and their terrorism were amenable to simple and consistent judgements, they might not be worthy of the overwhelming attention they attract – now and into the 1990s.

1   DEFINITIONS

Twentieth-century terrorism has come of age. In Britain, children of the age of terrorism are old enough to vote. In the USA, the firstborn of the age of terrorism can now legally drink alcohol. It was in the mid-Sixties that the word itself began to gain (or, very retrospectively, to regain) international headline currency: around 1964, when the Palestine Liberation Organisation was formed, as an umbrella organisation for the previously disparate radical Palestinian groupings.

Though the precise make-up of the PLO was of little relevance, what the world saw in its actions, and those of many other groups who began at about the same time, was the emergence of modern terrorism, a phenomenon so specifically dependent on the communications, technologies and political organisation of the times as to distinguish it from any earlier form. It is almost impossible, close to twenty years later, to reconstruct the sense of strangeness that most observers felt about these incidents. As if from the ether, violent and brutal attacks exploded into the awareness of Western nations. Almost invariably the terrorism concerned a 'quarrel in a far-away country between people of whom we know nothing', to borrow Chamberlain's 1938 stricture on a far more visible and concrete form of conflict. Here were groups and individuals from unlikely parts of the world, representing causes and minorities of which the established post-war order of NATO, SEATO and all the rest took no notice, demanding a place on the agenda of international policy.

There was something characteristic of the decade in the first flush of terrorism. The terrorists were clearly men and women of their time, who like their non-combatant contemporaries were rejecting aspects of the old order. Many modern terrorists began their careers in radical student politics in 1968 – the year of 'student revolution' across Europe. Women's liberation could not have been more graphically portrayed than by Leila Khaled, the Palestinian woman who hijacked a jet plane to London and was promptly released. Such dramatic nonconformism and rebelliousness was clearly the basis of much uncritical support from politically naive students, excited more by the superficial appeal of agitprop slogans and images than the content of their actions. But instead of taking drugs, these rebels were taking lives; instead of holding sit-ins, they were holding hostages.

Western European radicals first identified – and romanticised – Palestinians as displaced Arab nationalists who had established a novel publicity tactic: that of commandeering international aeroplanes and forcing them to fly to new destinations in the Arab world – though sometimes they boldly flew into startled Western capitals. Sometimes they blew the planes up – but international airlines were a rather faceless and quite acceptable target for the political generation of 1968. It is no mere chance that so much terrorist activity has its origins in the age of Small Is Beautiful and Do Your Own Thing.

After two decades of modern terrorism, and – equally important – of the unsuccessful efforts of every kind of government to eliminate it, there can no longer be any question but that terrorism has become, and will remain, a permanent fixture in the linked worlds of politics and conflict. The practice of terrorism is immersed in the functions of modern international relations, and there is no convincing evidence to support the great weight of wishful rhetoric, that terrorism or the terrorists can be eradicated.

Terrorism is not a uniquely isolated form of political activity, but part of a continuum that runs from conventional war at one end, through guerilla warfare, insurgency, sabotage, espionage, intelligence warfare, state repression and persecution, and torture. In this context, the principal distinguishing feature of terrorism is that its practitioners lack official legitimacy: even if terrorists do act on behalf of legitimate states, the legitimation of state sanction is always denied in public. For this reason terrorism works more disturbingly and provokes greater outrage than any other example of the political use of force.

A movement which has nothing at its disposal but terrorist tactics will fail; but with a political programme, a sense of diplomacy and relative popular support, it may thrive. The most effective terrorists are those who make the effort to combine their 'military' abilities – the willingness to act violently – with 'political' sophistication – making violence into persuasion, rather than mere brutal protest.

Until the mid-1960s the Palestinians were known by veterans of the Palestine protectorate and UN peacekeeping forces as one of the world's unfortunate refugee peoples. What has distinguished Palestinian nationalism since then has been its combination of terrorism with a multi-faceted political programme, which has for some years lent the PLO quasi-national status. For this reason, simply to call the PLO 'a terrorist organisation' – as Israel and her closest ally, the USA, invariably do – is a gross and politically loaded over-simplification. In effect, Palestinian nationalist organisations occupy several different positions on the political continuum simultaneously.

The PLO has acted at numerous levels – first, by raising massive financial support from the Gulf; then by using terrorism to put political pressure on the West; by galvanising support among Palestinians wherever they may be; and by attempting cross-border warfare and internal insurgency against Israel.

The agenda of terrorism in the contemporary world is set not only by terrorist groups and their actions, but also by the requirements of state policy, campaign trail rhetoric and strategic interests. The political dimension is no less important in sustaining the clamour of terrorism than the availability of

9

weapons and explosives. Thus the political agenda of terrorism consists simply in states failing to condemn the terrorism, inevitably, either of their allies or of special interest groups close to their strategic political interests; and in denouncing the terrorism of their enemies. But this is a dangerous hypocrisy, for as soon as moral relativism enters into the debate there opens a gap into which some terrorists are able to run for cover.

So what are the criteria which provide the basis for an objective definition of terrorism? For the lay observer, there are two contradictory problems: firstly, every intelligent or merely regular reader of the newspapers knows exactly what terrorism is, to his or her own satisfaction; secondly, for political reasons, no definition will achieve universal agreement. The difficulties are illustrated by a case in September 1985, when three Palestinian terrorists boarded an Israeli sail-cruiser moored overnight in the marina at Larnaca, in Southern Cyprus. Three Israeli tourists on board became hostages at gunpoint. The Palestinians threatened to kill them, unless Palestinians held in Israel were released from custody immediately.

This was apparently a classic terrorist act. The threat of violence was amplified by the first actual violence – the one woman on board was fatally shot in the stomach. But even as terrorism experts and journalists began to discuss the new security risks represented by the incident, it developed in quite unexpected ways.

Almost immediately, the terrorists gave themselves up and it was discovered that they had killed all three of their hostages – the two men executed by point-blank pistol shots in the back of the head. Next it was alleged that the Israeli victims had in fact worked for the Israeli intelligence services, watching marine traffic in and out of Cyprus – a well-known staging-post in many terrorist campaigns. There were also suggestions that the Palestinians were part of a mysterious 'Force 17', an élite hit squad under the direct control of PLO Chairman Yasser Arafat. Israeli agents have certainly waged a covert war on the PLO's most senior (and perhaps most dangerous) intelligence operatives – whom they regard, by definition, as terrorists. All such 'hits' have themselves looked from the outside, just like the Larnaca case, to be acts of terrorism.

Was the incident then really terrorism, or did it merely have that appearance while in fact being part of an intelligence war? The problem for observers is that everyone knows what terrorism is – until they attempt to define it. Nevertheless there *are* objective standards by which one can define terrorism – whatever claims the terrorists make for themselves as 'freedom-fighters' or 'commandos for justice'. If an act has certain features and consequences, terrorism it is. Even if a terrorist act is carried out by a diplomat or soldier of a legitimate state, the agent can objectively and impartially be called a terrorist. In short, a spade is a spade, whether the gardener calls it a shovel, or the landowner 'a gardening implement'.

Terrorist acts or campaigns have two levels of objective. Tactically, the goal is publicity, and recognition of a problem or claim. For the terrorist with a cause to promote, the advertisers' apocryphal saying holds true: all publicity is good, and bad publicity is better than none. Terrorism without publicity is a weapon firing only blanks. At the strategic level, the goal is absolute change – freedom, independence or revolution.
* Terrorism always involves a criminal act; the use or the threat of violence against the person in crimes of murder, kidnap or hostage-taking; the use of violence against property and assets in vandalism, arson and bombings.
* Terrorism presents the unique danger of a readiness to kill at random, not in anger or hatred, but deliberately to produce a political shockwave with the intention of bringing forward change.
* Terrorism is not war, subject to conventions which define the immunity of many classes of persons. Many terrorists claim a false legitimacy by asserting that they are in a 'state of war' with a government. However, they ignore those rules of war which define neutral territory and non-combatants and forbid the taking of hostages and ill-treatment of prisoners.

11

Indeed, terrorism may specifically attack the soft, civilian, undefended targets because of their normally accepted immunity.

* Terrorism involves surprise and therefore needs to be planned and structured in advance, though individual targets may be selected more for reasons of opportunity than anything else.

* Terrorism plays no part in riots – spontaneous public disorders which may share some political origins with terrorist actions. Though the violence or anger involved may have a similar effect to terrorism on the public audience, riots lack any calculating element of political blackmail.

* Terrorism presents demands for immediate action; and guarantees escalation if demands are not met.

* The terrorist is almost never a lone individual – clearly the actions of deranged individuals should be excepted, even though they may have some outlandish political fantasy directing their actions.

* The left has no monopoly on terrorism, though leftists often denounce studies of terrorism for ignoring its right-wing exponents. Terrorism perpetrated by the left consists of far more incidents, damage and victims than that of the right, but the right acts in a far less systematic, more random and more deliberately shocking way. There is no doubt that the occasional major neo-fascist attacks, for example in Italy, with as many as eighty dead in a single incident, have helped create an atmosphere of public revulsion which has in turn been directed more determinedly – and certainly more successfully – against the somewhat less murderous, though still dangerous terrorists of the left. Neo-fascist terrorists are fewer in number, more militaristically secretive and inaccessible, and occasionally subject to the protection of the co-conspiratorial state.

* Terrorists will never fail to claim responsibility for their violence. Without identifying themselves and communicating some demand or ultimatum, their act is pointless. Without political motivation, mere criminal violence would have no impact or repercussions.

* Terrorism is the antithesis of assassination in the spectrum

12

of political violence. Assassination dictates the selective killing of an individual enemy in the hope that his policies will die with him. If the target is the King, the cause is not much advanced by shooting the Palace Guards.

* The physical target of a terrorist act, the individual victim, may be unimportant, even random, in itself; the most important 'target' is the larger audience. Terrorism is designed to produce a psychological effect far wider than the concrete results of a particular violent incident. The murder of one police officer, or the bombing of one military factory, implies and intends a continuing threat to all such officers and factories – and to the society in which they operate. Bombs or other attacks on 'type-targets' have a particular resonance – against airline offices, holiday resorts, police stations, tourist beaches or facilities of multinational corporations.

Almost every campaign of terrorism will develop according to a predictable pattern of incidents and stages. The first event will probably be a bombing, causing damage but no casualties, followed by a telephone call, usually to an international news agency, either directly claiming responsibility for the attack or giving instructions on where to find a 'communiqué' which does so. The message is usually typed, and the language – almost invariably English – inflated with political jargon. The first escalation of tactics will probably come with a telephoned warning that a bomb has been placed where it will injure people, such that an evacuation emergency follows. There will be threats of more such incidents unless 'demands are met'.

By now the new terrorist group will have achieved at least the first stage of its early goal – publicity for the cause. In this connection it will almost certainly issue some longer statement of purpose and may contrive to give a clandestine interview to a newspaper or broadcasting outlet. Through its existence it will have needed finance; and bank or post office robberies may now be seen to be deliberate fund-raising efforts by the terrorists.

The next escalation will be a sign of desperation – and the more dangerous for that – probably involving the taking of hostages, and thus a siege. There the dangers to the terrorists

13

are greatly increased, which in turn threatens the lives of the hostages all the more. Some terrorist groups have deliberately avoided this route, but such actions have a high publicity profile and often help galvanise support in the community which already broadly sympathises with the group's efforts or goals. If, as is almost certain, the group is getting nowhere with these tactics, there will be two likely consequences, one external and one internal. Externally the group will begin to kill: assassination and bombs without warnings will try to pressure compromise from the state-enemy. Internally there are likely to be sharp divisions about the wisdom of such an escalation, and in extreme circumstances the killing will turn in on the dissenting faction. The single most dangerous element in a terrorist group is the member who wants to exercise restraint, for in terrorism 'you're either for us or against us'.

If the terrorists survive the security response to their use of random violence, they will begin to enjoy a grandiose sense of their power, believing themselves to be the enemies and equals of the state. The group, organised probably in a cell-structure with a central command and individual cells which do not contact each other, will be forced to live in increasing secrecy. Clandestine life ironically requires all the more support from those sympathisers who sustain the underground terrorists while not involving themselves in 'active service'.

As its victory fails to arrive, the terrorist group will often divert its attention from the obvious primary targets to secondary targets, sometimes in a spirit almost of petulance. The Armenian terrorist organisation, ASALA, for example, moved on from assassinating Turkish diplomats (and sometimes their close relatives) to attacking the airlines and tourist offices of other countries which trade and exchange air travel with Turkey. ASALA also attacked the French government because it had not supported the Armenian cause despite the substantial Armenian population in France.

This pattern of events, though by no means infallible, holds true for most terrorist organisations, even those few cases whose struggles have already lasted many years. Terrorists

14

are not politically ignorant, and they certainly see that the prospects of real success via terrorism are dim indeed. What they also see - and the sheer volume of states' security apparatus, rhetoric and reaction confirms it - is that terrorist tactics guarantee an audience. And that guarantees the future of terrorism, for anyone with a grievance has first to get a hearing; and when peaceful representation fails to provide one, violence - as the Palestinians and Armenians have shown - achieves it quickly, intensely and urgently.

Terrorism, therefore, is a subversive activity which, while close to simple, violent 'common' crime, belongs specifically to the invisible, dispossessed, powerless and unelectable fragments of political opinion in otherwise orderly states. Seizure of power by the disorderly - power of life and death over hostages, power of negotiation with police and armed forces, power of press attention and power of fear over large sections of the population - inevitably scandalizes, outrages and undermines those who lead and govern their states by consent and through electoral process.

Terrorists kill one man to threaten a thousand, or to intimidate an industry; to breed public insecurity; and to blackmail governments into reconsidering the policies which generate these violently negative consequences in otherwise orderly states. But although one might get the contrary impression from contemporary front-page leads and leaders, terrorism is not responsible for all the ills and violence in the modern world. For the purposes of definition it is particularly important to distinguish it from two close relatives of distasteful political action - on the one hand, state terror, and on the other, guerilla warfare.

Some argue that terrorism and state terror are two sides of the same coin and that to distinguish them is to discriminate against the already-oppressed political minorities in favour of an unexamined *status quo*. But state terror *is* a separate subject: the actual number of incidents and victims infinitely outweighs the toll of terrorism, and is in many ways far more important and deserving of international concern. When the

15

state terrorizes its own people, it commits an offence more intolerable even than the terrorism perpetrated by a group which is essentially powerless.

* State terror is the abuse of legitimate power, of the methods of control normally available to a state for legitimate purposes of national defence, domestic order and state security. The idea of a political state is meaningless unless its government has the right to exercise such powers in specific and reasonable circumstances.

* The methods and apparatus of state terror – false imprisonment, torture, disappearances, death squads – rarely equate with those of terrorism, except in the general sense that these acts are designed to spread a climate of fear among a wider group than the direct victims. Terrorists commit acts of public terror while concealing their real identity; the state commits acts of secret terror (not least because its repression includes control of the media) while the public knowledge of the state's guiding hand is essential. State terror acts directly against its known opponents – eliminating them, having them 'disappear', or imprisoning them on doubtful charges. The immediate targets are 'the problem', more than the wider audience. Terrorism is a war of attrition fought by an invisible – but vocal – army. The state has no need to act by attrition. It has the tools to exercise its will immediately. While the terrorist plants bombs to sow a mood of insecurity, the state acts bluntly to make political opposition very bad for the health of the opponents, and quickly.

* State terror can often be the breeding ground for terrorism – or of its military cousin, guerilla warfare: though they in turn are not at all the same thing. For some time the words 'terrorist' and 'guerilla' were used interchangeably, but inaccurately. The phrase 'guerilla war' gives the right military emphasis, and it is more aptly interchangeable with 'insurgency', a form of warfare that military men recognise while domestic police and security forces do not. While terrorism is the outgrowth of conventional political protest, guerilla activity is the preamble to civil war.

* Guerilla groups usually operate in semi-developed states or

in the less urban areas of the state, while terrorism almost always has an urban setting.

* Guerillas almost invariably hold territory within the state which they wish to overthrow, or have a secure cross-border base; they usually have the direct support of a state hostile, and probably adjacent, to the one they are opposing.

* Guerillas generally attack the state's infrastructure: its transport, communications and energy arteries (railway lines, power stations, telephone exchanges, factories); while terrorists attack the political figureheads and symbols.

* Guerillas often abduct or coerce civilians to join them and fight against the existing government, while terrorists are extremely careful to screen their recruits.

* Guerillas operate relatively openly and have a form of military command structure, engaged as they are in semi-conventional warfare; while governments usually respond to terrorist campaigns with enhanced police activity and legislation, guerilla warfare brings a military response.

It is of interest in this context to review the remarks of two men whose names are frequently invoked in reflections on terrorism and guerilla warfare. Fidel Castro, who led a remarkably successful and popular peasant revolution to overthrow the Cuban ruler Battista, argued that the place of the guerilla is the countryside and that the city 'is the graveyard of the revolutionary freedom-fighter'. Che Guevara, who fought with Castro and went on to die in combat, wrote a substantial handbook called *Guerilla Warfare*. While he did not condemn terrorism on moral grounds, he argued strongly against its efficacy:

> It is necessary to distinguish clearly between sabotage, a revolutionary and highly effective form of warfare, and terrorism, a measure that is generally ineffective and indiscriminate in its effects. Since it often makes victims of innocent people and destroys a large number of lives that would be valuable to the revolution ... many consider that its use, by provoking police oppression, hinders all more or less legal or clandestine contact with the masses, and makes impossible unification for actions that will be necessary at a critical moment.

The radical French journalist Régis Debray, who spent some time with Guevara in the Bolivian jungle, later wrote a book enigmatically called *Revolution in the Revolution?* in which he attempted to assimilate terrorism and guerilla warfare. For him, too, terrorism was specifically an urban phenomenon.

> Of course city terrorism cannot assume any decisive role, and it entails certain dangers of a political order. But if it is subordinated to the fundamental struggle [of the countryside], it has from the military point of view a strategic value; it immobilizes thousands of enemy soldiers in unrewarding tasks of protection.

By implication, Debray begs the question of the meaning or point of terrorism used alone: it is certainly true that terrorists add greatly to police officers' overtime pay by putting hundreds or thousands of them onto alert during a terrorist campaign or after any such threats. But the heightened police activity forces the terrorists underground; and the 'immobilization' of the 'enemy soldiers' is to no secondary effect – the terrorists have no second front to open up.

Having attempted to define the objective criteria by which an individual act of political criminality can be categorised as terrorism, we must now embark on the 'political agenda' of the phenomenon. In the simplest possible terms, states take sides in almost all international political arguments, border disputes, historical grievances and revolutionary uprisings. In taking sides, national self-interest too often overrides the observance of objective criteria – thus much of the agenda of terrorism in the modern world is set in the context of states' understandable, but real, biases.

In a major political shift, the incoming Reagan Administration gave a new high profile to the political agenda of terrorism in 1981. As President Reagan's first Secretary of State, General Alexander Haig, said at his confirmation hearings on 28 January 1981: 'International terrorism will take the place of human rights in our concern because it is the ultimate abuse of human rights.'

18

Identifying terrorism is not a matter of mere opinion, nor of fashion. Yet the single most widely current observation about terrorism is also the most misleading – the statement that 'one man's terrorist is another man's freedom fighter'. This should not, of course, be plausible. If terrorism can be objectively defined the definition should be applied where appropriate – but it is a sign of the political leverage the word enjoys that while some commentators have dismissed the cliché as misleading, they have simultaneously demonstrated the partiality which has given it currency.

Thus the American Secretary of State George Shultz condemned what he called 'moral relativism' in a speech on 25 October 1984, quoting the 'powerful rebuttal' of the late Senator Henry 'Scoop' Jackson. Jackson had said: 'The idea that one person's terrorist is another's freedom fighter cannot be sanctioned. Freedom fighters or revolutionaries don't blow up buses containing non-combatants; terrorist murderers do. Freedom fighters don't set out to capture and slaughter school children; terrorist murderers do. Freedom fighters don't assassinate innocent businessmen, or hijack and hold hostage innocent men, women, and children; terrorist murderers do. It is a disgrace that democracies should allow the treasured word "freedom" to be associated with acts of terrorists.'

While the sentiments are clearly sympathetic, Senator Jackson s ideas carried just the same faults as the contention he was attacking: for what masquerades as worldly realism, and underlies his moral protest, is a demonstration of the double standard which underlies the claim 'one man's terrorist is another man's freedom-fighter'. It really means 'we condemn our enemies for doing what we would excuse in our friends and allies.'

In a gesture which is equally guilty of political bias, President Reagan has twice issued official declarations listing 'Terrorist States' from the White House. No one can have been surprised that the lists named only states which were already deeply hostile to Washington's global influence and interests. By the same token, the terrorist action of an ally can be overlooked entirely. The French Secret Service sabotage of

19

the Greenpeace vessel *Rainbow Warrior* in Auckland Harbour – baldly labelled 'terrorism' by the incensed New Zealand Prime Minister David Lange – has not provoked Washington's condemnation. The attack was certainly designed to intimidate Greenpeace and its surviving activists from their course of physical observation of French nuclear testing in the South Pacific; but France has not yet appeared on any of President Reagan's lists of terrorist states, reserved as they are for purposes of political abuse rather than objective judgements.

In the modern age of terrorism, states recognise the need to define it in official publications and speeches, and not unexpectedly the definitions vary according to individual political factors. In France, where a revolutionary constitution presents acute problems in separating terrorists from political refugees, a Senate report of 17 May 1984 began its analysis of the problem of terrorism with five pages devoted to 'The Quest for a Definition'. Paragraph A was headed 'L'Introuvable Definition' – the definition not to be found.

The report's 'Analyse Descriptive' can be summarised as follows:

1. Motivation ... the first element to be taken into consideration ...
2. Terrorism is a mediated phenomenon, and in a double sense. The victim of a terrorist act is the messenger as much as the target. The victim carries the message to the real addressees who are the most numerous and widespread witnesses possible ... In a second sense the terrorist act brings into play an active pedagogy: the important thing is not the act in itself but the hold on conscience or the revelation that it involves from the spectator or the participant of the necessity and the possibility of important changes in the organisation of society.
3. Terrorism is a communications phenomenon.
4. Terrorism attempts to win hearts and minds.

The Senate report concluded in these terms:

Finally, and since one knows that any definition is practically guaranteed to fail, let us restrict ourselves to remembering that the terrorist act is an act of violence which tries in a legitimate state to impose a broadly minority will upon the authorities or on the guardians of sovereignty, that is to say upon the electors. For that purpose it makes use of the effects of surprise and mobilises reactions of fear among a public that is not very prepared for this shock treatment.

It is perhaps in the nature of the French approach to terrorism that their definition should be discursive and explanatory. In the official publications of US agencies, on the other hand, terrorism is defined coldly and bluntly. The State Department's Office for Combating Terrorism – a division with an emphatic brief in itself – carries the following definitions inside the front cover of its periodic statistical reports:

Terrorism: The threat or use of violence for political purposes by individuals or groups, whether acting for or in opposition to established governmental authority, when such actions are intended to shock, stun, or intimidate a target group wider than the immediate victims.

International Terrorism: Terrorism conducted with the support of a foreign government or organization and/or directed against foreign nationals, institutions, or governments. International terrorism has involved groups seeking to overthrow specific regimes, to rectify national or group grievances, or to undermine international order as an end in itself.

While the first definition offers great clarity, the second is a description of almost any kind of international hostility short of actual war, and lends itself to the prejudiced employment of the term against political enemies. In September 1984, the State Department's annual survey 'Patterns of Global Terrorism: 1983' carried two shorter and simplified definitions, with a disclaimer.

There are a wide variety of definitions used by experts to describe the phenomenon of terrorism, but no single one has gained universal acceptance. For purposes of recording and coding data on terrorist incidents, we have adhered to definitions that represent a middle ground within the broad range of expert opinion, both foreign and domestic.

Terrorism is premeditated, politically motivated violence

perpetrated against noncombatant targets by subnational groups or clandestine state agents.

International Terrorism is terrorism involving citizens or territory of more than one country.

But these are not the only US official definitions. Alongside the State Department's there is an FBI definition, which – predictably – focusses on the criminal aspect of terrorism: 'Terrorism is the unlawful use of force or violence against persons or property to intimidate or coerce a government, the civilian population, or any segment thereof, in furtherance of political or social objectives.' Speaking in 1984, Judge William H. Webster, the Director of the FBI, went on to point out that 'the FBI is also very cognizant of the intent of the individual'. He emphasised his particular concern at the lawlessness of terrorism in another speech on 9 July 1985 to the Corporation, Banking and Business Law Section of the American Bar Association: 'I think of terrorism as the ultimate rejection of law. In the history of mankind, war has at least been made the subject of efforts to confine it to principles of law. We have articles of war and we have covenants with respect to the treatment of criminals in time of war. But there is absolutely nothing lawful about an act of terrorism.'

Clearly the most important definition for any state which has the rule of law as its basis, is the legal definition. Until very recently, a number of terrorist acts were not properly defined under American Federal law, and terrorists could only be prosecuted under State law for the common crime aspects of their actions. The increasingly high-profile political role of central government in responding to terrorism was only reflected legislatively in 1984, when the US Congress passed into law the Comprehensive Crime Control Act. Paragraph 3077 defines terrorism as activities that:

1. Involve violent act or acts dangerous to human life that are a violation of the criminal laws of the United States or of any State, or that would be a criminal violation if committed within the jurisdiction of the United States or any State;

2. Appear to be intended (*a*) to intimidate or coerce a civilian population; (*b*) to influence the policy of a government by

intimidation or coercion; *(c)* to effect the conduct of a government by assassination or kidnapping.

This definition was itself borrowed from the existing Foreign Intelligence Surveillance Act, Title 50, Section 1801 *(c)*, while omitting subparagraph 3 of the earlier Act, which applied specifically to 'international terrorism':

> 3. Occur totally outside the United States, or transcend national boundaries in terms of the means by which they are accomplished, the persons they intend to coerce or intimidate, or the locale in which their perpetrators operate or seek asylum.

The reaction and rhetoric employed by political leaders in the aftermath of terrorist attacks is probably essential – yet almost certainly futile. Legal definitions of terrorism can improve the management of the problem for police and security agencies to a marginal degree, and give a public impression that the phenomenon has a high priority; but they rarely diminish its incidence. Nevertheless the sheer volume of state machinery, rhetoric and reaction to terrorism guarantees its future.

Nothing can be more useful to terrorists than that after their attack, which will have generated its own publicity, the pot should be kept boiling by politicians' or police and security authorities' condemnations. Given that they have made the fearful decision to proceed with violence, one must assume that they are immune to the criticism as such – what they regard as a benefit, simply, is the widening limelight for the cause.

Terrorism – both the event and the response to it – does offer a platform, it does deliver an audience, and it does communicate a message that is probably heard by no other means. That is exactly why terrorism has such a profoundly unnerving effect upon the 'governing classes'.

Studies of terrorism, and political initiatives to deal with terrorist groups, have approached the problem as a mere question of mechanics, and have been distinguished by the absence of real insight into the thinking, motivation and tactics of terrorists. Academics have studied the case histories of terrorist actions, causes and individuals as a branch of historical studies. Experts in international defence and strategic studies examine terrorism in the context of the dynamics of power blocs. Military men present terrorism as another form of military campaign – as insurgency or irregular warfare to which military tactics can be applied. Police chiefs commit themselves to defeating terrorism in the context of its criminality. Psychiatrists and psychologists debate the family history or the technical sanity of the terrorist individual. All these approaches have some interest, but none of them has much value without the essential recognition that in some (and increasingly numerous) circumstances, terrorism makes sense and offers hope to groups of people who see no other route to achievement. This proposition – apparently revolutionary in all government, political and security circles – is of course actually self-evident. But to admit that one can identify – intellectually, if not emotionally – with the terrorist undermines the received wisdom that he is beyond the pale, a kind of pathological leper. To call someone a terrorist dismisses his claim upon human sympathy.

However unpleasant the political illness may be, to diagnose it accurately must be the first step in reducing the symptoms and ultimately controlling, if not curing, the disease. The case for terrorism, for the small and desperate group, is that it is the only weapon (but a potent one) available to those for whom the political process is discredited, or too slow to deliver. Using terror is a low-tech, low-cost, high-result route to a worldwide audience. Governments prefer to explain terrorism backwards – taking the carnage and destruction as evidence of psychopathic tendencies. Instead they should regard terrorist acts as a logical step, if one that inspires revulsion, towards tangible political gains, derived from recognisable political objectives and frustrations.

Only when governments replace rhetoric with an acceptance that, for some, terrorism makes sense, will they step closer to containing or limiting it. Terrorism can work for ill-motivated states and even the superpowers, because its low-tech methods are cheap, mobile, deniable and less drastic than the commitment of conventional military force; and simply more effective than diplomacy. A world in which some states condemn terrorism while others employ it is not susceptible to simplistic formulas. Though some government reactions are a propaganda effort to marginalise the support or potential support for terrorist groupings, a propaganda war rarely ends in victory for either side. No government can protect everything and everyone, everywhere and constantly. The terrorist can strike at anyone, anywhere, at any time. Nothing will eliminate terrorism; defeating it is a pipedream.

2 TERRORISM IN THE WORLD

'I drove around with Urbach and Fritz in the VW,
along with a crate full of Molotovs, and we were
wondering what else we could do. We were too
late for the factories; it was around 2 a.m., and
from 2 on there are people in the plants. So then we
looked around at what else we could start, but
nothing really came to mind. We thought of
setting the Opera House on fire, but then went
home sort of aimlessly.'

(Michael Baumann, *Terror or Love.*)

As politicians with a bent for law-and-order policies are wont
to point out, by no means everyone with a grievance breaks
the law in order to bring it to the attention of the authorities,
their neighbours and their colleagues. Terrorism remains an
option chosen by a very small minority of the aggrieved
throughout the world. One is therefore compelled to consider
where and in what political circumstances it does arise; from
what kinds of grievance or cause; and how it proceeds from
cause to action.

Twenty years after the conclusion of the Second World War
– with its distinctly arbitrary resolution of some thorny
boundary disputes and simple overruling of the claims of some
national minorities – a generation of indignant, impatient and
marginalised people composed one of the most vigorous and
therefore dangerous elements of the peacetime world. They
were undoubtedly more ready to take up their collective or
individual fight because they had not been involved in war.

Every general prefers a volunteer army which has chosen to dedicate itself to defending a cause: in just the same way the terrorists are most effective for being the ultimate volunteers.

Terrorism is caused not least by the modern trend towards political agglomeration; as states form into groups for economic and military safety-in-numbers, so the interests of non-state minorities are much more likely to be neglected and ignored. Even the small, less powerful Third World nations feel compelled to align themselves in a Non-Aligned Movement. A minority group may be granted a special status – which may be no more than token – in such a forum, but it is unlikely to force itself on the attention of the group except by violence. The PLO achieved Observer status at the UN in the 1970s heyday of Arab power and influence; Kurds are allowed to participate in Non-Aligned events, as a reward for their years of bitter fighting against all the states in their claimed homeland.

The trend towards larger power blocs has an echo in the trend towards the dominant images of fewer and fewer world political leaders. In a sense this gives terrorists more power, at least through the media, because pre-eminent leaders can no longer devolve security concerns to deputies and responsible ministers. They have to address the terrorism issue personally (besides facing the fact that they may be the target) and this makes the terrorists' actions seem more important.

Terrorists include not only those who have been denied their homelands and national self-determination, but also the characteristic 1960s 'small is beautiful', anti-authoritarian factions and extremist revolutionaries like the Red Army Faction; besides the clandestine agents of legitimate states and powers. Old historical struggles like that between Britain and Ireland are one source of terrorism; peace treaties which end wars and fix new boundaries, like the Soviet-Turkish border in the 1920s another. Terrorism may be the chosen weapon to remedy the consequences of an unexpected war, as it was in part for the Palestinians after the Six Days' War of 1967. But equally, terrorism can be the initiative of a tiny group of

27

unrepresented yet unrepresentative radicals whose ideas could never gain currency in any larger arena than that of the group itself – as one sees in most of the urban revolutionary groups such as the Weather Underground, the United Freedom Front or the Red Guerilla Resistance of the United States; the *Rote Armee Fraktion* / Baader-Meinhof Gang and *Revolutionäre Zellen* of West Germany; the *Brigate Rosse* or *Nuclei Armati* of Italy; and so on from the Angry Brigade through *Action Directe* to *Rode Hulp* of Holland.

There are clear patterns, but for every pattern there are peculiar exceptions. As for geography, it is apparent that the leftist urban terrorists of the 1960s and 1970s vintage owed their existence to the availability of theoretical and political education in the university systems of the highly cultured West – in France, Italy, West Germany, somewhat in the USA, and slightly in the United Kingdom.

In South America and some Far Eastern countries, where severe instability often alternates with severely authoritarian rule, terrorism tends to emerge in fairly traditional settings of popular revolt, and to be met by state terror exercised through the military apparatus. Out of power, the right rarely resorts to terrorism in such countries: control of the armed forces readily provides the tools for a takeover. In those European countries with a fascist past (notably Germany, Italy and Spain), however, rightwing remnants remain which in many ways apparently steal the clothes and the methods of the left, staging individual terrorist attacks to provoke a sense of crisis and instability – to which the implicit solution is a return to militaristic, authoritarian and nationalistic 'order'.

Terrorism, for the group which graduates to using it, is an idea whose time has come. To some, like the Baader-Meinhof Gang or the Red Brigades, it is a quick process: even though they may begin as radical pranksters more than political thinkers, the direction of their political development convinces them that traditional political channels, if they are considered at all, are closed to them, and violence succeeds exuberance. Andreas Baader's first criminal act was an attempt at arson in a large Berlin department store, and heedlessness of human life succeeded a willingness to destroy bourgeois property. In Germany, the terrorists of the left were convinced that the state was beyond democratic change, imprisoned by bourgeois values and a stifling work ethic, led by politicians who – it was axiomatic – were corrupted by power.

The new right, in West Germany, had some surprisingly similar views to the leftist revolutionaries: both believed that the state had become an impotent servant of the USA's strategic interests. Both left and right displayed a clear sense of political urgency in the 1960s, one generation after the immense turmoil of Germany's national fate at the end of the Second World War. The neo-fascists felt that German nationalism had been entirely forgotten, that no one was fighting for re-unification of Germany any longer: not least because consumerism and bourgeois values had turned the nation into what one German neo-fascist of the 1960s called 'a Peter Stuyvesant democracy'. The left wanted American influence ended because they didn't like what America was doing in Vietnam. In 1968 and thereafter, students in Europe and the USA were demanding freedom for North Vietnam, freedom for the Palestinians, and freedom for themselves – though what they wanted to do with theirs was never clear.

At different times (and occasionally at the same time) German 'trainee terrorists' of both left and right made their way to training camps or secret bases of the PLO, usually in Lebanon, in the late 1960s. The left were there partly for practical training, but more so out of a sense of 'solidarity' with the Palestinian struggle. The right were there to do business: they wanted weapons and training, and they were prepared to help the Palestinians with some kind of support services in Europe; it is safe to assume that anti-Semitism played a part in the understanding that developed between the German neo-Nazis and Palestinian radical groups. The Baader-Meinhof revolutionaries, the self-appointed comrades of the Palestinians, were regarded as romantic and inefficient by their hosts, who never took them at all seriously; the militaristic neo-fascists, with their authoritarian and disciplined style, seemed far more businesslike and serious.

29

In Italy, a similar diagnosis of the domestic political situation again gave rise to varying terroristic responses by left and right. Italy has an inherent political base for mass political movements of the left – the strongest Communist Party in Europe is only a part of the picture, with its permanent dilemma of pursuing revolution through democracy. In the 1960s there emerged a range of political movements of the left – including *Autonomia Operaia*, CoCoRi and NAPAP – which desired urgent social change in a state perceived as a non-functioning democracy: that is to say, the large number of political parties, frequent elections and acutely fragile governmental coalitions made the democratic business of political change through popular political action an impossibility. Activism through the existing political parties was impossible, they thought; new political parties would only replicate existing difficulties; nothing but terrorism could have presented the same challenge to established state powers, even though the number of terrorists was vastly outweighed by the number of non-violent radicals who attempted a form of extra-parliamentary politics which banded under the banner of Autonomia. What Autonomia meant was that the common people would together decide – without reference to government – how they wanted their housing allocated, their schools run, their medical care delivered; how much they would pay in the shops, how much they would be paid in the factories, and how many hours they would work. It was organised anarchy, perfected into a political theory.

Terrorism somewhat inevitably accompanied the efforts of Autonomia – directed against the police who arrested and ill-treated demonstrators, against the bosses who resisted the workers' or unions' demands, against university professors who opposed them (the leaders of Autonomia were almost all university professors themselves), and against the politicians who tried to stop the whole thing. The left saw the whole state as discredited and obsolete, and terrorism would help to kill it off. The new right saw the same fragility of state institutions precisely as a reason to re-establish 'strong government' in the shape of a military fascist regime. The fascists and Autonomists engaged in pitched battles in the streets of Italy's major cities in the early 1970s, and to amplify the sense of chaos, which they felt would provide their opportunity to seize power, the fascists staged occasional but barbaric bombings in which the death tolls were always far higher than any similar actions by the left. Substantial evidence emerged that members of the Italian police, secret service and armed forces conspired to perpetrate fascist attacks, and to throw the blame onto the left for some of them. If violence seemed to have run out of control, it would be easier to make the case for authoritarian government.

The example of Italy serves to illustrate a more general rule of terrorism: that the right has a distinct sense of scale; the more dead bodies, the greater the impact and repercussions. The left tends to believe in selective resonant targeting, preserving at least nominally a sense that the popular support of their constituency (whether real or imagined) must not be frittered away.

If it is possible to reach some general conclusions about the political circumstances from which terrorism develops, is it possible to predict in what settings it will occur, and what targets it will choose?

Certainly terrorist incidents occur more widely in democratic, free societies: partly because of opportunity of action and partly because of the potential advantage of publicity. While terrorism does occur in the more controlled societies (and the very nature of such societies means that we may hear far less about their terrorism than might be justified by real events), the control of citizens' movements, work, political activities and media, limits both opportunity and effect. In a society which has officially abolished unemployment it is an almost impossible proposition to live 'underground' and to disappear from daily life to wage a clandestine struggle.

Terrorism in pursuit of separatist causes naturally occurs within the state in the case of a move towards regional independence: the only relevant place for the actions of Basque separatists is Spain. Where the territory is separate but not independent, as in Corsica or New Caledonia, the attacks will largely be within the disputed territory and rarely on the mainland, though the local representatives – civil or military – of the mainland power are automatically at the top of the target list. Confining the attacks to the disputed area is in part a propaganda tactic, in an effort to portray the struggle as – which it usually is not – a local territorial conflict between 'Popular Forces' and the distant state. However, these are only general trends and there are numerous and tactically appropriate exceptions. As a forgotten remnant of Dutch colonial rule in Indonesia, for instance, the South Moluccans staged a quite intense campaign of terrorism in Holland in the early 1970s. By hijacking Dutch railway trains, and even holding schoolchildren hostage, the separatists raised their cause from obscurity into the limelight in a way which no other tactic but terrorism could have achieved.

The terrorists of *Euskadi Ta Askatasuna* (Basque Homeland and Liberty), or ETA, who have no boundaries to cross between Bilbao and Madrid, succeed in occasional attacks against government targets on 'enemy' ground: their most spectacular single success was the assassination of the Spanish Prime Minister, Luis Carrero Blanco, in 1973, which has become a legend of Arthurian proportions in Basque nationalistic gatherings.

Inevitably, separatist causes arise wherever power has changed hands; or where international conferences, convened by the powers of the age, have ruled that a number of distinct regional or national entities should be agglomerated into single nations. The pre-eminent example is that of the Palestinians whose national refugee status and discontent gave rise directly to the PLO and its terrorism. While the PLO acts firstly against Israel – the disputed territory which was Palestine – its ubiquitous capacity to act, wherever targets are appropriate and available, against those whom it sees as obstructing national self-determination, gave rise to the very idea of 'international terrorism'.

It is increasingly obvious, moreover, that international

terrorism's relative efficacy in attracting public and political attention is having a 'copycat' effect upon a still wider variety of local and regional conflicts. The Indian subcontinent, which for centuries has been prey to the continuing resentments and rivalries of both a caste system and tribal competition, has only in the 1980s begun to see identifiable terrorism emerging as a medium for regional and racial separatism. The Tamil Liberation Tigers of Sri Lanka and the Sikh National Liberation Army of the Punjab have added their names to the terrorists' index. Besides staging terrorist attacks in their own countries, Sikhs in particular – who have migrated widely from India to Western Europe and North America – have been able to stage or plan attacks outside the country itself, with an assassination in England and bombs in West Germany, Canada and Japan.

Western Europe, with its preponderance of former colonial powers, consequently suffers far more direct terrorism than any other part of the world. (One excludes Lebanon, where terrorist tactics happen to be a prominent part of the format for a full-scale civil war.) The United Kingdom, France, Spain, Portugal, the Netherlands are all susceptible to angry or demonstrative attacks by disgruntled subjects on their distant or former masters. The United States suffers its very substantial share of world terrorism for the same reasons – not so much, perhaps, because it is a real colonial power, but because it is very widely perceived as a nation which dominates many others through so-called 'economic imperialism'. Just like the Kanaks in New Caledonia or the Corsican separatists, the terrorists who want to rid themselves of US oppression attack US interests in their own territory, and not as a rule on mainland USA, where the hostile backlash would be so severe as to be certainly counterproductive.

The terrorists who want instant social revolution conform to most political stereotypes: they are, by definition, anti-government; they are invariably anti-American, anti-capitalist, anti-nuclear (on both weapons and energy issues), anti-NATO, anti-business, anti-wealth. They are convinced, as an article of political faith, that multinational corporations abuse the rights of workers throughout the world, exploit them for low wages and discard them when more profitable business methods become available, and conspire to suppress individual freedom. These terrorists may be able to burn the American flag in demonstrations outside American embassies, but it is harder to tear down the banners of international business.

By definition, terrorists exaggerate: they usually subscribe to conspiracy theories which greatly over-estimate the powers of governments; in particular they take the exaggerated view that the US government can issue policy instructions to smaller, weaker and poorer nations. It is as simplistic a view as the idea that a multinational company operates without any kind of restriction or consultation: but the monster fits their myth, and the chosen ideological targets are very accessible. Every city in the world has representatives of American and Western business corporations, essentially vulnerable to attack unless they decide that prevailing political risks dictate extreme security measures. With an international business presence come the inevitable camp followers – the staff managers and their families, further support staff, and ultimately the more adventurous and wealthy tourists who are constantly searching for new territory.

In some ways, international business is a more appropriate enemy for the terrorists than government: for like the terrorists, big business wields actual power in a world set apart from the democratic, electoral process of voters and government. Arguably, business executives can have more real influence on individual lives than political executives. While terrorists envy the business community its non-governmental power, they attack it for the assumed motives and purposes for which its power is used. For the majority of terrorists profess socialist or Marxist political principles, and the embodiment of international capitalism makes a ready target.

Attacks on business are intended to cause a general sense of insecurity, and therefore to try to force a revaluation of the benefits of operating in the given territory. Attacks directed – increasingly in Western Europe in the 1980s – at defence industries have the specific intention of dissuading the companies from operating in that sector of business. They intend to blemish a glossy plate-glass-and-marble million-dollar public façade with the shock of ultra-vandalism and bloodshed. A very important secondary effect is the diverting of resources from the wealth-creating business of the corporate body into expensive and burdensome security measures, which in theory pushes the price of operating closer to the level of unacceptability. No diplomatic mission wants to represent its country behind an inner-ring security sanctum of barbed wire, computer-coded entry systems and body-checks: and no business wants to be transformed by its enemies' attacks into the stereotype that is their hostile caricature, of faceless, stateless and impersonal bureaucrats behind high walls. But the attacks are increasing, and the defences are becoming more and more necessary.

The power of terrorism to alter outcomes – which is partly a function of the sophistication with which it is employed – changes dramatically according to the political situation in which it is used. Indeed, the tactics and efficacy of terrorist groups will vary according to the underlying support they can rely on from their community, or their claimed constituency. In this respect it is useful to distinguish between 'grievance-terrorism' and 'ideological terrorism'.

In the case of urban revolutionaries like the Red Army Faction or Action Directe there is little or no external constituency. But for nationalist/separatist groups, there is usually a substantial community – Catholics in Northern Ireland, Corsicans generally, Armenians scattered through the world – with a basic sympathy for the goals of 'their' terrorists. The existence of this wider theoretical constituency often allows terrorists a (misplaced) sense of legitimacy: that they are taking up the cudgels on behalf of others whom opportunity or lack of courage prevents from doing so.

Not surprisingly, terrorists always believe they can find support for their actions from the community. Michael 'Bommi' Baumann, who was a member of the German Red

Army Faction, argues in his book *Terror or Love* that the German terrorists were originally seen by German liberals as radical pranksters who had a salutary effect on stodgy German respectability, and thus gained a degree of amused approval. The convicted Italian terrorist Oreste Scalzone, looking at the West German experience of terrorism, asserted that 'when the Red Army Faction kidnapped and killed the German Prosecutor General Siegfried Buback, millions of people approved secretly.' The French author Yann Moulier, who translated the prison/political memoir of Professor Toni Negri – a leader of Autonomia, convicted terrorist, elected Radical Party Member of the Chamber of Deputies, and Dean of the Parisian political exiles' club – makes an even more emphatic assertion. He claims that 'the killing of [Prime Minister Aldo] Moro was a very popular act – the Red Brigades became the third most popular political party in Italy!'

It is hard to see anything but self-delusion or justification in such claims. On the other hand, there is ample evidence to suggest that in longstanding and hard-fought regional struggles such as those for Basque and Corsican independence, the fighters are so widely supported – if only passively – that the efforts of police and security forces to suppress or eliminate them are in vain. In the case of the Basques in particular, there is a very deliberate effort to blur the lines between traditional celebration of folklore and festivals, political agitation, and fullscale participation. While the divisions are obscure to the outsider, however, it is apparent that community circles are very well aware who the fighters are. The *Euskaldunak* (Basques, in the Basque language of Euskara) have a specific campaign which employs their national traditions with the armed struggle. In Basque, it is called '*Alaitsu eta Kementsu*'; in Spanish, '*Allegre y Combativa*' – which one might interpret as 'Festivals and Fighting'. For both participants and spectators, the festive and cultural aspects help to make the military campaign acceptable.

Irish Catholic Republicans of Northern Ireland offer a substantial degree of at least passive support to the Provisional IRA. Here, too, the fighters have a degree of informal celebrity in the community, not least because the IRA seeks to impose a local discipline on young offenders who misbehave, in order to establish its authority as an alternative to the (predominantly Protestant) police or the British army.

The position of the community, then, always plays a most important role in the inevitable propaganda struggle which accompanies any substantial terrorist campaign. The government in question will certainly attempt to show that the terrorists represent no one by concentrating upon their violent, criminal methods; while those who support their objectives will try to emphasise the large issue, aggrandizing their role in pursuit of 'justice' while playing down the violent tactics.

Particularly during the period of the hunger strikes in 1980 and 1981, the British government and the IRA were waging a full-scale propaganda war on both sides of the Atlantic. The target was the Irish community in the United States, where supporters of the Provisionals have been able to raise substantial sums of money for weapons over the years, and a wider Irish lobby has prevented tough action being taken against those who either finance, arm or shelter terrorists within the USA.

Both sides knew how much was at stake in winning the confidence of the community for whom the IRA claimed to be undergoing martyrdom. Nominally the hunger strikes were in support of five demands which Republican prisoners in the Maze prison wanted met; but it was actually a desperate tactical reaction to the belief, foolishly articulated in public by British government sources, that the IRA was 'on the run'. The IRA found an issue on which to make the most potent possible protest, and exploited it with immense skill to revive support from its own community. As the critic Denis Donoghue observed in the *New York Review of Books* of 22 October 1981, 'The declared conflict [between the British government and the IRA] is merely nominal.' His masterful reading-between-the-lines is worth quoting at length:

The real conflict is between those Irish people who regard the

37

IRA as perverts, corrupters of a great tradition. The Provisionals have only one aim at the moment: to compel the Irish people to acknowledge them as their true, legitimate sons.

The IRA can hardly hope to achieve this aim by force of argument, definition and reason. They must transcend the terms of any such discourse. The only way to do that is by taking some mortally intimidating course of action, something that requires courage, passion and selflessness. Discourse can only be transcended by action: inside a prison, action can only take a symbolic form, all the more potent for being irrational and exorbitant. There is no gesture more compelling than the hunger strike, and ideally the hunger strike until death.

When Bobby Sands became the first to die, he gave the cause a martyr's image to sustain it. In a stroke of political genius he had, from a prison cot, been manoeuvred into the position of becoming an elected Member of Parliament for Fermanagh and South Tyrone. The Provos had their supporters painting murals throughout Republican West Belfast to portray the sacrifice of the hunger strikers. The most memorable and most photographed mural was a religiose portrait of a gaunt, bearded hunger striker holding a rosary, captioned, 'Blessed Are Those Who Hunger For Justice'.

As Denis Donoghue perceived, 'Bobby Sands's death by hunger has achieved what he could never have achieved by his prowess with a gun. And it has been achieved not by reason or argument but by the primitive force of a symbolic act.'

An unlikely 43 million Americans claim Irish ancestry, of whom a substantial majority still live on the East Coast, above all in New York and Boston. It is the belief of the British government, and its Information Service (BIS) in New York, that there are no more than 5,000 supporters of the IRA in the United States, and that all the rest of the Irish-American community (who might be or become contributors to terrorism through the supposed charity NORAID) are open to persuasion by skilful and factual presentation of the Irish realities. The objectives of the BIS are threefold: firstly, to show that the IRA are terrorists; secondly, to explain the internal political organisation and perspectives of Northern Ireland;

thirdly, to cultivate investment in the Province – which, para-doxically, is less easy if the BIS succeeds in its first objective.

During the hunger strikes, the BIS set about redressing the balance by issuing factual statements emphasising the actual crimes of which the hunger strikers had been convicted. Thus a letter from one New York resident who described them as 'political prisoners' provoked the Press Officer of the BIS in New York to fire off a lengthy and lofty rebuttal, part of which read:

> These prisoners can by no stretch of the imagination be described as 'political prisoners', a term which is reserved for those imprisoned for their beliefs, not their actions. They have not been adopted as 'prisoners of conscience' by Amnesty International, which rejects the cases of those who have used or advocated violence: and the European Commission for Human Rights has stated that they are not entitled to political status.
>
> The seven hunger-strikers have been convicted, between them, of: four murders, three attempted murders, three woundings with intent, one attempted wounding with intent, carrying firearms with intent (three counts), possessing explosives with intent (three counts), causing explosions (two counts), robbery (two counts), assault, conspiracy to intimidate, false imprisonment, causing and attempting to cause grievous bodily harm, using firearms to resist arrest, and belonging to an illegal organisation (two counts).

Similarly, the BIS did not hesitate to circulate – with a strongly negative implication – the very remarks of Danny Morrison, then Sinn Fein's publicity officer, which were to become a lasting rallying cry for the IRA's supporters. At the *Ard Fheis* (annual conference) in 1981, he asked: 'Will any-one here object if, with a ballot paper in this hand and an Armalite in this hand, we take power in Ireland?'

Examples of such propaganda contests demonstrate the importance for every terrorist group of a wider resource of support – from committed radicals on the fringes of illegality themselves, or even from legal and legitimate political parties. Alongside any small group of genuine terrorists there will be found a wider group which inhabits the margins between legal

39

political activism and illegal terrorism. While revolutionary (ideological) terrorists can never count upon the active political support of publicly identified allies, nationalists and separatists always enjoy relationship with a legal, political front: the IRA has Sinn Fein; the Corsican FLNC has the *Conseil des Comités Nationalistes;* the Basque ETA has *Euskal Iraultzarako Alderdia* (Party for the Basque Revolution). France, pre-eminently, has a great range of *Comités de Soutien* or Support Committees for 'political prisoners' of every political colour: for Armenian political prisoners – that is, for Armenian terrorists jailed by the French courts for killing and holding hostage innocent persons in the Turkish Consulate in Paris; there is a *Comité de Soutien* for Basque political refugees in south-west France, and two Irish *Comités.*

These, then, are the political mechanics of terrorism, the places, political systems, causes and grievances which give rise to the phenomenon that has marked a historical generation. They are focussed by two case histories of terrorist movements which lie at opposite ends of the spectrum of 'constituency support'. One, the French Action Directe, is purely engaged in revolutionary politics; the other, ASALA – the Armenian Secret Army for the Liberation of Armenia – is a nationalistic group, practising 'grievance-terrorism' and able to draw on substantial support and funds from the widely scattered community which it is proposing to reunite, under one flag and in one homeland, one day.

One of the most disturbing developments in terrorism in the 1980s is the New European alliance, involving French, German and Belgian groups, with sporadic parallel action from Portuguese, Spanish, Italian and Dutch comrades, apparently pledged to attack government, international agency, and business targets. The targets are united by the anti-American, anti-business, anti-military, anti-nuclear, anti-NATO themes of the terrorists' politics. The prime mover of this alliance appears to be the French revolutionary group Action Directe.

Action Directe is a second-generaton European terrorist group. Its roots do not lie directly in the student *événements* and movements of May 1968, which to a large degree gave rise to both Italian and German terrorism: but its politics lie in the same tradition. Since the group was first heard of in 1979 it has had a single leader, but the political odyssey of Jean-Marc Rouillan shows an opportunistic willingness to espouse political causes or marginalised minorities, primarily to keep the group active In this respect, Action Directe is unusual – no permanent, emphatic political objective has animated all its actions, though since 1984 its ideology has crystallised into a jargon ridden Marxism-Lenninism.

The activities of Action Directe have passed through five clear phases:

1. 1979-80 – The group first became violently operational in firing machine-gun bursts at the façades of French government ministry buildings, the offices of large companies, and the French National Police Headquarters. In 1980, a shell was fired from a rocket launcher at the offices of the Ministry of Transport – one of the twenty attacks in the same year in Paris and Toulouse.

2. 1981-82 – Action Directe took up pro-Palestinian, anti-Israeli actions, taking their cue not least from the Israeli invasion of Lebanon. They operated in tandem with a group named *Fractions Armées Révolutionnaires Libanaises* (FARL), using the same weapons and issuing joint communiqués. Together, they assassinated two diplomats – an American and an Israeli.

3. 1983 – The Italian period. Action Directe collaborated with Italian terrorists who had taken refuge in Paris. Members of Prima Linea and COLP *(Communisti Organisati per la Liberazione del Proletariat)* joined Action Directe terrorists in hold-ups to raise funds for both their purposes – in the case of the Italians, to establish a 'foreign front' for Red Brigade terrorism in Italy. In one hold-up, two French policemen were shot dead and one wanted Italian terrorist, Ciro Rizzato, was killed in the gun battle.

4. 1984 – Action Directe leaders took refuge in Belgium

41

where the CCC *(Cellules Communistes Combattantes)* existed as their counterpart. This was the beginning of a practical co-operation which brought Action Directe into the anti-American, anti-NATO Marxist camp of existing European terrorist groups, including CCC, the Red Army Faction of Germany (by now in its third generation) and even the Portuguese group, FP-25. A major theft of explosives in Belgium provided the means for more than thirty bombings in France, Belgium and West Germany.

5. 1985 – Action Directe reverted to pursuing goals inside France, related for the first time to the internal politics of the country: notably with three bombs to protest the broadcasting airtime permitted to the ultra-rightwing National Front leader, Jean-Marie Le Pen, and with bombs protesting French economic involvement in South Africa.

The leader of Action Directe, Jean-Marc Rouillan, was born in 1953 in Auch, the provincial capital of Gers. The French capacity for romanticising the most dangerous and daring criminals has already created a myth of an intelligent, cultivated art-lover, half-paranoid and half-megalomaniac, who never takes off his bullet-proof vest. Rouillan and his constant companion Nathalie Menigon, who is two years younger, were students in the 'pink city' of Toulouse, where they became involved in anti-Franco protest groups in the early 1970s – the last few years of the dictator's rule in Spain. Rouillan allegedly took part in cross-border 'missions' to strike at Spanish targets, besides many demonstrations and some physical assaults on Spanish interests in France. In 1974 he joined a clandestine organisation, the *Groupes d'Action Révolutionnaire Internationalistes* (GARI), and like many students then and now, wore his radicalism around his neck in the shape of a Palestinian *keffiyeh* headdress. His anti-Spanish actions got him arrested in 1974, and he was freed in 1977. He was re-arrested in July 1978 and spent another six months in jail. At that stage, in 1979, Rouillan, Menigon and others (including Régis Schleicher, Frédéric Oriach, and two French-Algerians, Mohand Hamami and Laouari Ben Shellal) founded Action Directe.

A former radical associate, 'Alain', analyses the political background to the establishment of Action Directe in terms of the wider political context of the radical left in France. A French counterpart of the Italian *Autonomia Operaia* (Workers' Autonomy) participated in the Paris demonstration by steel-workers from the dying industrial town of Longwy, and were surprised by the violence which occurred in the mass march. 'The problem was to find the capacity to widen these protests into a movement of mass support: with a repressive government, a mass movement is impossible, but a very radical part of the movement starts to consider "military organisation".' The irony was that the French Autonomie worked on the assumption that the state was always repressive and, 'Alain' says, 'never entertained the idea that the Socialists would gain power by election – we thought it could only come by other means. Then the government stole the radicals' clothes, and cut the ground from under their feet, by taking up the themes that radicalise people – the Third World, South African apartheid and so on.' He continues: 'There was a failure of political organisation by the radical Left, and it deepened the split between them and the people who were turning towards military force and clandestine activity – who never believed that any elected government would meet their political ideals.

'Terrorism always arises when there are no pre-eminent political issues to unite and maintain an organised public movement. And terrorists, people who support the militaristic groups, are much more efficient than radical activists – they are the other branch of the institutional form of politics.' So, according to 'Alain', the radicals who maintain legality and legitimacy are stuck in a middle ground of impotence, while the 'real' politicians and the 'efficient' terrorists slug out the real battles. That was also the view of the founders of Action Directe: 'The concept of Action Directe, and the group itself, developed from an absence of debate on the issues where they chose their targets' (i.e., defence, NATO, international monetary systems, American capitalism dominating the West). 'They were against the institutionalisation of the movement and criticised such a development as "mere words" – when they wanted literally "Direct Action".'

The political theory of direct action is mysterious: 'Alain' refers to a Maoist view that there need be no complicated political motive for a revolutionary act. 'First you act, then consider – was it well or badly done? How was it received by the people?' He makes the analogy that terrorism represents the same approach to political problems – arbitrary, dramatic, and sensational – that the media employs in relation to 'facts', claiming that the real power lies not with the participants in events, but with the editor who has the power to emphasise coverage, write headlines and change meanings.

For ideologies of the extreme left, violence in itself is not an issue; the world is full of it, they say: state terror, wars devouring human cannon-fodder, hunger, drought, disease. The only interesting question, they believe, which arises with the violence in political confrontation, is what effect it has. 'People in Autonomie used to say "we have committed an act of violence during a demonstration in order to avoid worse acts of violence occurring in isolation" – a kind of de-escalation,' says 'Alain'. Thus it is interesting to reflect on the purposes of Action Directe's leader Jean-Marc Rouillan, at least in the light of 'Alain's' description: 'He is very important, definitely the leader. He is *un baroudeur*, the kind of man who would have gone off to fight in the International Brigade in the Spanish Civil War. He was closely linked with the anti-Franco movement in the last years. He was absolutely not interested in intellectual matters, political theory, or anything like that. But he's not a mere gangster.'

Action Directe became operationally viable as a clandestine organisation of real force with a major robbery in the northern French town of Condé-sur-l'Escaut, on 29 August 1979. At five minutes to noon, five men and a woman burst into the main hall of the tax collection offices at 10 rue Notre-Dame, in the centre of town. They were all armed and masked, some of them wearing welders' face-masks, some caps, and some in bullet-proof vests. They rounded up the staff of the tax office, uttered the classic instruction 'Hands up, don't move', and cleared away 16 million francs from the safes and the piles of cash that were being counted when they arrived. They had walkie-talkie contact with other colleagues outside in stolen cars, and their militarily precise operation was over as quickly as it had begun.

According to a woman member of Action Directe, interviewed by Radio France-Inter in 1981, 'The guys who did the robbery did it for the revolutionary movement in general. So the money was used for the whole revolutionary movement, not only the French movement, but certainly in part for international solidarity, for infrastructure, to get hold of papers, weapons, and to help comrades in jail.' It was widely believed, from the hallmarks of the raid, that the attack not only served to assist 'the international movement', but had been carried out with international assistance. Both the Italian *Prima Linea* (Front Line) group and the Spanish GRAPO (Revolutionary Group of the First of October) were allegedly connected.

In France, the money raised by such robberies – 'proletarian expropriation' as Rouillan called them – enabled Action Directe to go underground and obtain the weapons used in twenty or more attacks on French government and business in 1979–80. Living a clandestine life is difficult, said Rouillan: 'We try to do these hold-ups as little as possible, only what is necessary. Stealing money from banks is justified, but we don't do it for fun. We do it out of need, in order to function, to buy apartments, cars, weapons, papers – false papers necessary for living underground.'

Like all terrorists, Action Directe depends greatly on false papers – identity cards, passports, driving licences, social security numbers, car registration and insurance documents. Sometimes these can be bought, but more often genuine, blank papers have to be stolen from the original source – either the local government offices where they are issued, or the printers where they are first produced. On 5 August 1980, Action Directe attacked the Mairie of the 14th *arrondissement* in Paris.

45

One of the participants, a young woman, told Radio France-Inter what they were after: 'It was pretty simple: basically, we needed identity papers, in fact all the papers we could get from inside. We decided to go in to the Mairie, with some of the comrades, and help ourselves. We got the thing together very quickly, we had enough cars that we had stolen already. We arrived; we got out of the cars, went in, and we warned the people inside, "We have come to get papers, we haven't had any for a long time." We made them open the safes, and we took away all the papers and rubber stamps that we thought were useful. Then we went out, got back in the cars and left. There was no violence because the people reacted very well and weren't unduly alarmed. They saw that we were calm and precise. Of course, we had our hoods up so that we could not be recognised, and the weapons were just to make an impression.'

Just over a month later, on 13 September 1980, Rouillan's secret life came to a temporary end: at 6.15 p.m. in the rue Pergolese, Paris, a metallic coloured Peugeot 604 crawled along the street. Suddenly there was gunfire, and at the entry to an apartment building Rouillan was surrounded by police officers before he could reach for his Magnum .357. A woman leapt out of the car and emptied both magazines of her pistol before being seized by police, who found a grenade in the vehicle. Her name was Nathalie Menigon, regarded by police as in some ways more radical and more dangerous than Rouillan himself. The two leaders were tried and jailed and the round-up of Action Directe continued, with most of the principal figures in jail by the end of 1980.

But in May 1981, following a traditional but controversial practice of incoming presidents, François Mitterrand declared an amnesty for several thousand prisoners whose crimes supposedly had a political element: and to the amazement of many, by no means all counted among Mitterrand's political opponents, Rouillan and Menigon, along with other leading Action Directe members were released from jail. (Mitterrand's simultaneous promise to reinforce France's traditional role as a land of exile for political refugees prompted a stream of

46

wanted, and in some cases convicted, Italian terrorists to smuggle themselves across the Italian-French border and make their way to Paris where they could evade trial, jail and extradition.) Rouillan had spent less than eleven months in custody, being released on 7 August 1981; Menigon just celebrated an anniversary of her imprisonment and was freed on 21 September.

Both Menigon and Rouillan gave secret interviews to Radio France-Inter; since their release Rouillan has given only one other interview, to the leftwing newspaper *Libération*, in August 1982. And in October 1982 he supplied written replies to questions put by the communist newspaper *Le Matin*. But neither occasion offered any guide to the overall intentions of Action Directe. Thus Rouillan's somewhat hazy description of the political objectives of Action Directe – as outlined to France-Inter in 1981 – is of particular interest: 'We want a communist society, with every proletarian conscious of his class identity – that is to say the destruction of capitalist society based on the merchants profiting from the wage-earning class. And we think that the end of man's exploitation of man will come with the destruction of this capitalist society, full of unemployment, misery, exploitation, organised murder, accidents at work in the name of profit. We are true communists.'

In late 1981 and early 1982 Action Directe went underground, disappearing into the Arab ghettoes of the 18th and 20th *arrondissements* in Paris. Here they made contact with, and recruited to their banner, radical Arabs, members of Turkish workers' groups who lived on the margins of legality, and people from the squatters' movement. All their causes were thrown into the stew of Action Directe policy. At this stage Rouillan allegedly also pursued some contacts with the 'legitimate left'. One unconfirmed story suggests that when Rouillan was arrested, on complaints from the owners of a 'squat' property which turned out to be sheltering seventeen illegal Turkish workers, he was released within an hour after pressure on the investigating magistrate by a Socialist Party Deputy. Another rumour was that some of Rouillan's

47

comrades had hijacked an official car belonging to Lionel Jospin, the Secretary of the Socialist Party, and stolen certain 'important papers' which they quickly photocopied and scattered to a number of locations, some outside France. The inference was that any effort to prosecute Rouillan could be undermined by embarrassing revelations – of an unknown nature – about the government party.

In March 1982 Action Directe published its political manifesto entitled *Pour un Projet Communiste*. As a literary work it has no merit, consisting of indigestible Marxist-Leninist jargon. Its critique of world capitalism, and the particular examples that are singled out for vitriolic political abuse, do however suggest some of the targets of later violence. One 'axis of intervention' is defined as 'French imperialism – supreme arena of decadent capitalism'; and the document specifically attacks the International Monetary Fund, OPEC and American multinationals in these terms: 'America has systematically financed the invasion of the world by her multinationals and satisfied the hamburger-eaters of the world (MacDonalds – of course) thanks to the International Monetary System sustaining her power and the continuing domination of the developed world.' In terms of domestic politics, the document bemoaned unemployment, empty housing and high rents, the difficulties of foreign workers, and the increasingly international character of French industrial corporations.

During 1982 Palestinian terrorists (largely Syrian-backed) were particularly active, not only in the Middle East but in Europe. Paris had inherited London's former unenviable position as the battlefield for Middle Eastern terrorism, yet it was in London that Abu Nidal terrorists gunned down the Israeli ambassador Shlomo Argov as he left a Park Lane reception. Israel's response to this and an accumulation of other provocations was to mount 'Operation Peace for Galilee' – the invasion of Southern Lebanon which ultimately transformed that country, drove the Palestinians out of Beirut, and lasted three years. But it was in Paris that most terrorist actions against Israeli or Jewish interests took place. Even before the invasion, Action Directe's Arab connections had mounted an attack on the Israeli trade mission in April 1982. In the same month, an Israeli diplomat was shot dead: this attack, too, was claimed by *Fractions Armées Révolutionnaires Libanaises* – as was the killing of the American attaché, Charles Ray. The FARL communiqué, later discovered to have been printed by the same equipment as Action Directe material, was distributed in French, Arabic and Turkish.

Over the following months a 'hot summer' of terrorism swept Paris, including the machine-gun attack on Goldenberg's restaurant in the Jewish Marais, which killed six people. Less publicised were three Action Directe bombings on Jewish targets, which Jean-Marc Rouillan justified to *Liberation* as 'a perfectly normal reply to the situation in Lebanon. This is international solidarity. Action Directe actually claims the paternity of its attacks.'

The wave of terrorism that afflicted France was too much even for President Mitterrand – whose amnesty of little more than a year earlier was seen by many as at least partly responsible for the bloodshed. Mitterrand went on national television to announce the setting up of special anti-terrorist forces, the appointment of a Minister for Public Security, Joseph Franceschi, and, with effect from 17 August 1982, the proscription of Action Directe. Two months later, Rouillan gave his reaction by letter to *Le Matin*:

'In 1981 we came out of prison as militants of Action Directe, and in August 1982 our situation was exactly the same. All the reasons invoked to justify our dissolution were as valid in 1981, at the time of our amnesty. I feel like a prisoner who has gone absent on parole. Dissolving Action Directe prevents it from publicising its ideas, or expressing itself, and obliges its militants to go underground.'

At the same time, one such militant supporter of Action Directe was released from jail. Mme. Helyette Besse was one of Action Directe's most unlikely luminaries – a fiftyish, swarthy and chubby lady anarchist who was the proprietor of one of Paris's most out-of-the-way backstreet 'alternative' bookshops, called *'Le Jargon Libre'*. Now she announced the reactivation of *Défense Active*, a committee of support for

'French Political Prisoners'. The committee had first been formed to protest at the omission of some names from President Mitterrand's amnesty – some 'presumed' Action Directe members, some autonomist militants from NAPAP *(Noyaux Armés Pour l'Autonomie Populaire)*, some anti-nuclear militants, some people held on suspicion of involvement in the Condé-sur-l'Escaut robbery. The revived committee, according to Besse, would 'regroup, in other respects, militants, ex-militants and sympathisers of Action Directe'. However, her personal freedom to campaign was limited by the fact that she was herself awaiting trial for possession of three blank Italian identity cards. (In August 1983 she was found guilty and fined 500 francs.)

Despite the new illegality of the organisation, Action Directe continued to try to build, by involving disparate political minorities. It also plunged into the community of Italian 'political exiles' – finally becoming implicated in a brutal shooting incident where two policemen died. This followed a robbery in the last week of May 1983, when a Parisian public relations consultant was ejected from behind the steering-wheel of his car as he left a smart restaurant in the 17th *arrondissement*. Two men brandishing pistols forced him out and drove away. On 31 May, at about 2 p.m. in the avenue Trudaine, two policemen from the 9th *arrondissement* anti-robbery squad stopped the car and asked the occupants for their papers. Both officers were shot dead on the spot. At the end of the car chase that followed, a wanted *Prima Linea* terrorist, Ciro Rizzato, was shot dead by police, but his companion(s) escaped.

By the end of 1983 (when Helyette Besse was arrested by customs officials for irregular holding of foreign currency, in the shape of $10,030) Action Directe was beginning to look towards international collaboration. A number of new extreme leftist publications appeared in radical bookshops: *L'Internationale*, *Combattre pour le Communisme*, *Ligne Rouge* (which specialised in the publication of terrorists' communiqués, claiming responsibility for attacks) and *Subversion* were among them. It was *Subversion* which published their political agenda: 'We must build a fighting Communist International, to destroy the party of war. This is the party of the capitalists, of multinationals dominated by American interests. The evolution of Western Europe is now the cornerstone of world struggle. So we must detach Italy from NATO, as that country is one of the weakest links. Elsewhere we must smash French social democracy, a traditional agent of imperialist wars.'

These unusual publications represent the tip of the iceberg of European terrorist co-operation. *Subversion* is allegedly edited from a prison cell by Action Directe veteran Frederic Oriach, who is serving a six-year sentence for attacks on Israeli targets in 1982. The magazine is published in Brussels: it has carried contributions in the name of the Red Army Faction, the Red Brigades, Iranian *fedayeen* and Action Directe. Another review, *Correspondances Internationales,* has as its publication director the advocate Jacques Verges, whose career has included defending political extremists of every complexion – Klaus Barbie was one of his clients.

Subversion was the subject of an extraordinary police incident in Brussels. Its articles, identifying the USA, NATO, and the French arms industry as legitimate targets for the class struggle, naturally provoked interest from the Belgian authorities. The first issue of *Subversion* carried two contact addresses, one (false) in Paris, the other a Brussels post office box situated a few yards from the home of a known militant, a professional printer suspected of contacts with local terrorist groups. The Brussels police sought a warrant from the authorities to open the postal box, but were refused permission; and although the second edition still carried the address (though not the one in Paris) no action was taken. The printer, subsequently, was directly implicated in terrorist attacks committed by the Belgian CCC.

From the beginning of 1984, the various component parts of the European terrorist alliance began to turn their theories into actions, waging a really substantial campaign against the kind of targets identified in their political tracts. On 25 January 1984 a quantity of plastic explosives blew up at the

Military Studies Bureau of the Aerospatiale Company at Chatillon; and on 29 January another bomb exploded at the Panhard-Levassor factory in Paris. Both attacks caused substantial damage.

Action Directe's new Belgian headquarters was almost certainly in Brussels – where Rouillan and Menigon had helped to establish the CCC, and to set up the strong alliance with German groups. The Belgian police were getting more alert to the dangers of their presence with every bomb that exploded in the name of the anti-NATO, anti-military alliance. On 13 March 1984 they came within an ace of capturing the three most-wanted terrorists in Europe, when Rouillan, Menigon and Régis Schleicher together returned a hired car to a car rental office at 176 de la Chaussée de Vleurgat, in Brussels. At about 9 that Tuesday morning, they drove up to the office in a brown metallic Toyota Camry, hired the previous Friday by a well-dressed man. He gave the name of Jacques Quériaux, a Belgian citizen whose identity card gave his birthplace as Quévy – a town near the French border which was explanation enough for his strong French accent. But Quériaux was Schleicher; and since 8 a.m. armed members of the Brussels Justice Police had been waiting for his return.

By some extraordinary mistake, a single officer – the twenty-seven-year-old Jean Marie Arnould – was sent into the office, where he went to speak to a man whom he took to be an employee of the agency. It was Schleicher, who immediately grabbed Arnould's pistol, and with another man (presumed to be Rouillan) ran out to the car. The office manager, Christian Lemmens, told the press later: 'I thought they were trying to leave without paying, so I followed them into the street. The car was parked in front of our windows, with the motor running. Inside there was a woman with long hair, wearing a wool hat and a blouson jacket. She opened the door, pointed a pistol at me, and yelled "Get lost, fast!" At that point I realised that one of the three men was being held by the others. They all jumped into the Toyota and it disappeared.'

Inspector Arnould enjoyed only a short journey with his captors – after a few minutes down the road to Waterloo they bundled him out of the car, having relieved him of his police identity card, his pistol (a GP7.65) and his radio set. But they let him keep his handcuffs, with his hands locked tightly in them. Despite roadblocks and a police hunt throughout Belgium, the leadership of Action Directe escaped *en masse*. And despite the nature of the crimes for which the three were wanted by police across Europe, the French press relished their narrow escape. *Libération*'s headline on the story said, 'Jean-Marc Rouillan smashes a mousetrap and scoots away!' *Le Quotidien de Paris*, referring to the trio's handling of their police hostage, said, 'Terrorists, yes; but conscious not to forget traditional French elegance!'

There is no clear motive, except perhaps a sense of narrow escape, for Schleicher having left Belgium that day or the next. Possibly Rouillan ordered him back to France because his face was now well-known in Belgium – at least by Inspector Arnould. But two days later he was in France – and in police custody. Surveillance had revealed that the leadership of Action Directe was planning to regroup once again – either in Italy or in the Midi – and that Helyette Besse was handling the logistics of renting houses and raising funds. On the morning of 13 March, she and a woman courier who worked for Action Directe got off the Paris-Marseilles overnight train at Avignon, and headed for a rented villa at Pontet: a house Helyette Besse had already used as a base and arsenal for her Catalan comrades. A substantial force of police kept the house under surveillance, in the belief that they would finally round up Rouillan, Menigon and Schleicher together. When Schleicher arrived alone, they did not wait to see if the others would follow – forty police officers burst into the house, fifteen of them carrying pump-action rifles, and surrounded Schleicher and Besse.

If the arrest was a setback for Action Directe, it barely halted the development of the 'European campaign'. Just as the big cash haul from Condé-sur-l'Escaut apparently sustained the European revolutionaries for several years, so another theft in

Belgium now provided the CCC-AD-RAF terrorists with the wherewithal for almost as many attacks as they had the will and the numbers to stage. On the night of 2-3 June 1984, terrorists broke into the explosives store of a quarry at Ecaussines, thirty-five kilometres south of Brussels, and stole almost a ton of dynamite and plastic explosives.

If any confirmation was needed of the uses to which such a haul was to be put, it came with the first explosion – not in Belgium, but in France – on 23 August 1984. About twenty-three kilos of the explosive blew up in a car parked outside the Paris headquarters of the Western European Union, at 83 avenue du President Wilson. This attack, by Action Directe, was closely followed by another on NATO oil pipelines in Belgium, by CCC; and a third, on a military training school in Bavaria, West Germany, by the Red Army Faction. There followed a further eight attacks on industrial, military and political targets in Belgium between October and the end of the year.

Between January and June 1985 there was a lull in Belgium: a pause in activity, however, which coincided with an escalation of attacks in both Germany and France. With the turn of the year, Action Directe devoted itself again to French political matters: that is, concentrating on the specifically French element of the familiar target areas – defence contractors, industrial multinationals and so on – and launching attacks relating to French domestic and foreign policy.

In West Germany, on 7 January 1985, the Red Army Faction raided the explosives depot of a cement factory in Geisingen, Baden-Württemburg. It was not a great haul, but they got away with 35 rolls of fuse cord and 376 detonator caps. These materials were almost certainly used in the first of a concentrated series of attacks on American military targets in West Germany on 7 August 1985, which was a model of terrorist tactics and rhetoric. A car bomb consisting of explosives and gas bottles killed two American citizens and injured more than twenty when it blew up at the US Air Force's Rhein-Main base near Frankfurt. The attack was claimed jointly by the RAF and Action Directe: their communiqué claimed the attack was a blow struck against imperialism: 'The USAF base is a centre for war against the Third World, used to transport American troops and military equipment for acts of intervention in the Middle East and Africa.'

The groups later admitted to the murder of a US serviceman whose identity card had enabled them to get access to the base. The second-hand Volkswagen car which served to transport the bomb carried US military licence plates, and had been bought in Frankfurt ten days earlier. West German police named the suspected purchaser of the car as Sigrid Sterneback, 'a veteran RAF hardliner' who has been on the wanted list since 1977, with a price on her head of 50,000 Deutschmarks.

On 15 June 1985, an apparently new terrorist group attacked the American Forces Network Pomcus depot, in Mönchengladbach. The attack was claimed by the 'Fighting Unit for the Creation of an Anti-Imperialist Front in Western Europe' – a title which neatly describes the collective aims of the AD-RAF-CCC alliance. Their letter demanded the 'immediate release' of a jailed RAF terrorist, Günter Sonnenberg, and the 'bringing together of the prisoners of the Red Army faction and the anti-imperialist resistance in groups capable of interaction'.

Yet another new name – or possibly a new group – emerged in late June. On Wednesday 19 June 1985 a parcel bomb exploded in a luggage locker at Frankfurt International Airport, killing three people. At first there was a mysterious silence – breaking the normal pattern of terrorism, where the prime rule is to make a public claim. But three days later a bomb exploded in a letter box of the Bayer Pharmaceuticals Company in the centre of Brussels. A few minutes afterwards, an anonymous caller to the police claimed responsibility for the bomb, saying it was a response to pollution of the North Sea by toxic waste, and the seizure by Spain of the *Sirius* – one of the campaign ships of the environmental pressure group Greenpeace, who promptly denied any connection with the terrorists.

Later the same day, staff at Agence France Presse in Paris

found a letter: written in English, it read 'Our brothers have just strike *(sic)* in Frankfurt Main. Congratulations'. The letter was headed, in French and English, 'The Peace Conquerors' – the same name given earlier the same day to Belgian police, and never heard elsewhere. Neither claim made mention of the other, but the letter opened by Agence France-Presse in Paris went on to warn 'Stop Nuisance – Stop Pollution – Stop Airport' (presumably the airport extension at Frankfurt). The letter added: 'Before the end of the month we'll destroy a major Frankfurt Airport building, and a Jumbo Jet.' This warning certainly evoked a frisson of shock – though little serious speculation of a link – when the next day, 23 June 1985, an Air India jet went to the bottom of the Atlantic Ocean.

Attacks continued in Belgium throughout 1985. No individual names had yet emerged in connection with the CCC. No details about the organisation had been discovered. There are many instances in the past of terrorist groups inventing new names to distract and confuse the security forces pursuing them. It was tempting to speculate that the Belgian comrades-in-arms were a fiction, a Red herring to scatter attention away from Action Directe and the RAF. The European police forces were working on the assumption that the new terrorist alliance had four leaders: Jean-Marc Rouillan and Nathalie Menigon, of Action Directe; Inge Viett, a longstanding comrade of the Baader-Meinhof and Red Army Faction ranks; and a Belgian anarchist (and former member of Action Directe itself), Pierre Carrette, aged thirty-three, the son of a policeman and a printer by trade, who had first come to the notice of the police when he championed the cause of imprisoned terrorists in West Germany. (Late in 1985, however, the concrete reality of CCC's membership was confirmed with the arrest, after fourteen months of police investigation, of Pierre Carrette and three associates: Bertrand Sasoye, Didier Chevolet and Pascal Vandegeerde. The trio had been under surveillance, and when they met Carrette at a hamburger bar opposite Namur station, police blocked all the exits and moved in. All four were armed, but they did not resist arrest: subsequent searches of safe houses revealed documents relating to the

CCC's twenty-seven bombing attacks, and police claimed they found Carrette's fingerprints on leaflets. All four had been filmed by police as they revisited the scenes of their attacks.)

By far the most dramatic escalation of terrorist attacks, however, came in France. In January 1985, the first communiqué signed jointly by Action Directe and the Red Army Faction was delivered to AFP in Paris. It discussed 'the essential tasks facing communist guerillas in Western Europe':

> We must construct a politico-military front in Western Europe, for the central project, in the present phase of imperialist strategy, is the attempt to unite European states into a homogeneous structure, into one hard block, which would be completely integrated in the noose of imperialist power – NATO.
> The new policy of NATO puts particular emphasis on the placing of Euromissiles, the revitalisation of the Western European Union, the creation in France of the Rapid Deployment Force, co-operation in weapons areas by NATO members, discussion of German participation in the French strike force, and its integration into NATO.

The production of this document has an interesting history. An Italian who was a member of Action Directe, before becoming a police informer, gave a secret interview to *Libération* in which he told of a meeting in Paris between French, Italian and German 'Euroterrorists':'I went to a meeting-place on 6 January to take part in a meeting of the Committee of Support for the RAF hunger-strikers. We were very excited because we knew that a woman militant from the RAF would be there. She was actually there with another RAF woman, and there were people from Action Directe. Afterwards I was given this draft – written by the Germans, reviewed by the French – it was agreed at another meeting the next day devoted to Franco-German links. To get this alliance, each side had made concessions: the Germans had distanced themselves from the Eastern bloc, and Action Directe was abandoning its libertarian side.'

On 25 January the US State Department – taking note of the

new 'Euroterrorist' communiqué – predicted terrorist acts against 'targets related to NATO, and persons working in the defence area'. That same day Action Directe demonstrated what it meant to drop its 'libertarian' attitude. Inspector-General René Audran, Director of International Affairs at the French Ministry of Defence, was shot dead with eight bullets from a Colt pistol at 8.50 p.m. outside his house in avenue des Gressets in Celle-Saint-Cloud. Twenty-five minutes later, AFP in Paris received a call. A woman's voice said, 'Get a pen. Action Directe claims the execution of René Audran. Signed by the Commando Elisabeth Von Dyck, a member of the Red Army Faction, executed in Nuremberg by the German police.'

Audran was one of the most senior figures of the French military-industrial complex and his murder sent shock waves throughout the French defence industry, which employs almost a million people. He had been in his post since 1983, after a long career in the arms industry, and was a technical expert of international stature; but he had no known political role.

Even though the German connection may have been a deliberate false lead, French police took the view that Action Directe almost certainly did employ a German comrade to help in making the hit: not least because the German authorities were also pursuing enquiries into a nearly identical murder of Audran's close European colleague and rough equal in the West German Defence Ministry, Ernst Zimmerman. Two terrorists had rung the doorbell of his suburban home early in the morning, on the pretext of delivering a parcel, tied up his wife, and shot Zimmerman dead in his bedroom.

On 29 July, in yet another similar incident directed at a similar target, Spanish terrorists assassinated Rear-Admiral Fausto Escrigas Estrada, the Director-General of Defence Policy. At 8.30 a.m. the admiral was travelling to his Madrid office in his chauffeur-driven car, when a vehicle ahead stopped and blocked the road. One or two men fired at the admiral's car with a sub-machine gun: the admiral died within minutes, and his driver was seriously wounded. The killers' getaway car was found in another part of Madrid, loaded with explosives, and despite an attempt to defuse the devices, the car blew up. Witnesses later identified one of the gunmen from police photographs as a member of the ETA-Militar 'Spain Squad'. Four months later, the death of yet another senior defence industry executive – in Belgium – caused yet more speculation about the Euroterrorist campaign against the arms and defence industry. The body of Juan Mendez-Playa, a senior sales executive for Belgium's largest arms manufacturer, was found dead in his car, shot six times in the body. No clues to the killer's identity were apparent.

Action Directe attacks on military-industrial targets continued through the year in France: at 5.30 a.m. on 27 April 1985 they exploded a car-bomb at the Parisian headquarters of one of the Euroterrorist alliance's principal enemies – the International Monetary Fund. The car, a red Renault 11, had been hijacked earlier and filled with explosives and gas bottles. The explosion caused every single window in the seven-storey building to shatter, besides many in neighbouring buildings.

It seems likely that a similar attack was planned for the same weekend by Action Directe, who frequently grouped their attacks within hours or at most days of each other for greatest effect; but their plans were disrupted by the arrest of the delivery man bringing the explosives for the job – once again from the Ecaussines haul – from Belgium. On 28 April, customs officers and officials of the PAF (*Police de l'Air et des Frontières*) arrested a twenty-eight-year-old Turkish courier, confirming the pattern and supply-chains of the Euroterrorist operations of 1985. Muzaffer Kacar – originally recruited before Action Directe was banned, in the Goutte d'Or district of Paris – had arrived at the Gare du Nord by train from Strasbourg – with a detour through Brussels. In his bags the police discovered four sticks (sixteen kilos) of dynamite, four detonators, eight false Belgian identity cards and eight false Belgian driving licences. Serial numbers confirmed the link to the theft from Ecaussines. Kacar's passport revealed that he had been shuttling between Paris and Brussels, where Rouillan and Menigon were still assumed to be in hiding, and lived in Mulhouse, very close to the German border, which was interpreted by police as confirmation of the theory that Euroterrorism was triangular in shape.

Action Directe's attention was also directed to French domestic politics, where one of the most divisive developments recently has been the emergence of substantial support for the ultra-conservative and racist National Front Party, led by the supposedly charismatic figure in the shape of Jean-Marie Le Pen. The level of support for his party has given broadcasters little choice but to offer him opportunites to speak on their programmes – but it was too much for Action Directe. After he had appeared on Radio France-Inter's *Face au Public,* and Antenne 2 television's *L'Heure de Vérité*, Action Directe fired both barrels. Ten minutes apart, at about 5 a.m. on 14 October 1985, bombs exploded at the Maison de la Radio, by the river Seine on Quai Kennedy, and at the offices of Antenne 2. Both places received warnings a few minutes beforehand, and a telephone call to AFP gave the location of an Action Directe communiqué.

The terrorists accused Le Pen of 'pushing the limits to see how far Capital can go in attacking the working class and dividing it with racism. While Le Pen is preaching Holy Capitalist War under the lights of radio and TV studios, the French military is carrying it out on various territories.' A third protest bomb exploded on 17 October, at the High Authority for Broadcasting; Action Directe declared that this bomb was the work of the 'Commando Ahmed Mouley' – an Algerian 'martyr' (marking the racist context) who died in the Battle of Algiers on 3 March 1957.

Finally, Helyette Besse came to trial. Described variously as Action Directe's 'Hot Mama' and its 'Good Fairy', she had been in jail charged with 'criminal association' since 17 March 1984. But the earlier charge of illegally holding foreign currency came to court on 30 September 1985. Her statement to the court summed up her predicament exactly: 'I am here because I am an anarchist, a Communist, and a militant member of Action Directe. This charge of illegal possession of currency is a side-issue.' She further claimed that France was a 'state which refuses to recognise political prisoners'. On

21 October the court found her guilty and ordered the confiscation of her illegal $10,000, a fine of 80,000 francs and a suspended prison sentence of one month. According to Helyette Besse, speaking with the unrepentant pride which guarantees the continuation of terrorism, criminality was irrelevant: 'I am neither a criminal, nor a smuggler: but an Action Directe militant.'

In the case of terrorism directed towards regional self-determination or national liberation, it is usually the rule that a violent militant fringe has existed almost as long as the cause. In the Basque country, present-day fighters talk of a fight which has lasted 150 years, and frequently there is a family tradition – almost a vocation – of 'the struggle'. The efforts to free Ireland from British influence belong to a history of seven centuries of intermittent violence. But for the Armenian people, whose nationalistic grievance is relatively recent in historical terms, the route of violence came as an abrupt and specific response to sixty years of unsuccessful efforts to have that grievance recognised by international opinion.

The Armenian Secret Army for the Liberation of Armenia (ASALA), the preeminent terrorist group dedicated to recognition and independence for the Armenian people, emerged in 1975, the diamond jubilee of what Armenian nationalists call 'the first genocide of the twentieth century', when Ottoman troops drove Armenians out of their homeland in northeastern Turkey in 1915.

In the 1980s, there are some two million Armenians in what they, like the Jews, call their 'diaspora'. They live in Syria and Lebanon, France, the USA and Australia, among many other countries. One of the leaders of ASALA, who emerged as a public figure in radical Armenian circles, is Alec Yenicomechian, an accomplished linguist and former student of economics at the American University of Beirut. His is one of the largest and most respected Armenian families in Beirut, with a particular leaning towards medicine: both his father and uncle are eminent doctors. According to Yenicomechian, and indeed all Armenians, the Ottoman authorities forced some two million Armenians to leave the towns and villages where their people had lived for a thousand years: 'During this forced deportation, specially formed armed bands attacked the deportees' caravans, to deprive them of their meagre resources and massacre them, killing several hundred thousand Armenians. Another several hundred thousand perished in the course of this long march, from exhaustion or lack of food and water which was very often denied to them. And there were several hundred thousand more, who had survived the infernal deportation and armed attacks, who were literally massacred by the Ottoman army in the Syrian desert. In total 1.5 million Armenians or more were massacred or driven to their death between 1915 and 1920.'

Although historians argue on behalf of both sides to escalate or diminish the figure, there is no doubt that a fearful death toll resulted from the forced marches. What is more important in the light of the contemporary terrorist campaigns, is whether modern Turkey is to be held responsible for the actions of its predecessor power, the Ottoman Empire. Conscious of this historical lacuna in political responsibility, Yenicomechian is quick to add this to his accusation about the genocide: 'The scenario was completed a few years later by Kemal Ataturk, the father of present-day Turkey.'

By 1975, according to him, the patience and hope of Armenian nationalists had been exhausted. 'For sixty years the Armenian people had hoped that the world's conscience would awaken, and they would recover their rights. In 1965, the fiftieth anniversary of the massacres, we redoubled our peaceful efforts: in the next ten years, Armenians knocked harder on the doors of big and small nations, the United Nations; we sent memoranda, prepared documents and legal depositions; we organised peaceful demonstrations all over the world, involving tens of thousands of people. All imaginable peaceful means had been tried. 1975 was a year of reckoning, but there was nothing in credit.'

Therefore, according to Alec Yenicomechian, a sea change occurred in Armenian thinking: 'After sixty years of waiting, sixty years of efforts and peaceful struggle, after so many years of humiliation, the Armenian people finally realised that nothing would be given to them freely, realised that if they wanted to regain their legitimate rights, it was necessary to pay with their blood. So Armenian fighting organisations saw the light of day.'

The programme of terrorist violence commenced in 1975; however, it was not the Armenians, but the modern Turks who paid with their blood. A highly efficient assassination campaign of Turkish diplomats began, conducted principally by two groups – the Armenian Secret Army for the Liberation of Armenia, and the Justice Commandos of the Armenian Genocide. ASALA, which has been by far the more active group, was based in Beirut, with significant links to pro-Syrian factions of the PLO. In that respect, they demonstrated that terrorists often benefit from the adage 'My enemy's enemy is my friend', Syrian-Turkish relations being characterised by mutual suspicion and intermittent hostility.

Yet alongside the historical evolution of Armenian terrorism there was a chance catalyst which focussed attention onto violent action and retaliation. The first Armenian terrorist was the most unlikely: Gurgen Yanikian, a much-travelled Armenian engineer living in affluent retirement in California. One summer's day in 1975 he invited two diplomats from the Los Angeles Turkish Consulate to have lunch with him in a motel, and to accept the presentation of a portrait of a Turkish national hero. Once lunch was over, he pulled a pistol from his pocket, and shot both men dead in cold blood. Then he called the police. At his trial he testified that the killings were in revenge for the death of his brother, whom he saw killed by Ottoman troops exactly sixty years earlier.

The Californian courts were unmoved by Yanikian's defence, and at the age of 76 he was sentenced to life imprisonment. On his death in 1984 several hundred members of Southern California's prosperous Armenian community turned out to pay their respects to this paradoxical emblem of the community. One Armenian newspaper editor told the mourners: 'We are gathered today to honour the memory of Gurgen Yanikian. There are those who think of him as a

murderer, an assassin; there are others who think of him as a
martyr. He could be both, or neither.' Yanikian's lawyer, still
pleading the case for his client even after his death, asserted:
'He wanted the world to know that what happened was
wrong. If we don't remember the past the future is doomed.'

In the underground Armenian press that circulates in
Britain, France, Greece, Lebanon and the USA, Yanikian is
celebrated as the first hero and martyr of the Armenian age of
terrorism. His double murder in 1975 was a catalyst to militant
young Armenians to pursue terrorist action against Turkey:
in the course of the next seven years some fifty Turkish
diplomats (and their unfortunate wives, children, or chauf-
feurs who happened to be in the line of fire at the wrong
moment) were assassinated, mostly by ASALA. The killings
took place all over Western Europe, in the USA and Canada,
and in Australia. Terrorist 'commandos', trained in Lebanon,
took over embassies and consulates, demanding the release of
imprisoned comrades. Bombs were planted, and grenades
thrown, at Turkish Airlines (THY) and Turkish Government Tourist offices. As the death toll rose, the Armenians
were unable to detect any hint of flexibility or concession;
therefore they escalated the campaign to include bloodier, but
suicidal attacks, inside Turkey.

On 7 August 1982 two terrorists, Levon Ekmekjian and
Zahrab Sarkissian, took over a restaurant at Ankara's
Esenboga International Airport. They threw hand-grenades,
and fired automatic weapons into the crowded airport depar-
tures area; they made futile attempts to negotiate with the
Turkish authorities; and when Turkish troops burst into the
restaurant, Sarkissian was shot dead and Ekmekjian captured,
and later executed. Seven passengers had been killed.

In honour of this action, three more Armenian members of
ASALA - calling themselves the Levon Ekmekjian Commando - staged a grenade and machine-gun attack in the
covered market of Istanbul on 16 June 1983. According to *Hay
Baykar*, the militant newspaper of the French Armenian community, the attack occurred 'when a convoy of military jeeps
was about to pass: the commando was trying to take three

military hostages.' The predictable firefight followed, leaving a disputed number of dead. *Hay Baykar* said the death toll was 'three according to official Turkish sources, twenty-five, including seventeen Turkish soldiers, according to ASALA'. One of the commando, Meguerditch Madarian, apparently blew himself to pieces with a grenade rather than be captured by Turkish soldiers, a gesture eulogised by *Hay Baykar*: 'Meguerditch Madarian fell as a martyr in the flower of his youth, an image of Armenian youth which despair and cynicism about the success of our cause have led to the most awful, most insane sacrifice – Madarian, dead on the enemy's soil.'

This, then, was the Armenian armed struggle, regarded by Alec Yenicomechian as the inevitable last resort for Armenian nationalist aspirations. 'Our experience and that of others have proved that the armed struggle remains the principle means of regaining our legitimate rights: and we have opted for the armed struggle. Today we are accused of being terrorists – but what does the word mean? For me, a terrorist is he who by his acts aims to sow terror. We do not aim to sow terror. We are not terrorists. We are not fascists. We struggle for our cause and for our rights. We know who is our enemy and our struggle is directed against this enemy. Our enemy is the Turkish State – this state which has flouted the rights of Armenians, which has flouted and still flouts today the rights of the Turkish people, the Greek people, the Cypriot people, the rights of all minority people who live in Turkey. This state is the very incarnation of Terrorism.'

Armenian terrorists had become adept at picking off the vulnerable, accessible diplomatic personnel of the hated Turkish enemy. In addition, ASALA started to think in a more political way and to confront one of the essential problems of their Utopian nationalistic dream – which would be farcical in a less bloody context. 'Armenia' – the nation they wish to unite under an independent flag, for the first time – lies half in Turkey, and half in the Soviet Union. While some Armenian revolutionary sentiment tends to regard the Soviet Socialist Republic of Armenia as 'already liberated', its population at least is secure and permanent. Turkish Armenia, on the other hand, has had a dwindling population for decades, and it is apparent that so many Armenians have left the Middle East for more prosperous countries, with more opportunities (particularly the United States), that soon there will be no Armenians left for 'Armenia' to unite. Armenian radicals regarded this population flow as a new form of the Ottoman forced-march tactic, and consequently began efforts to staunch the flow of their countrymen out of the homeland.

Their prime target was Italy: they believed that a substantial exodus of Armenians was being assisted by welfare and aid agencies in Rome, usually in liaison with United States agencies, as the USA was often the country of destination. In fact, by no means all of the migrants were coming from Turkey – many were from Syria and Lebanon (effectively changing one land of exile for another) and some even from the USSR. But ASALA decided to halt the exodus with relatively small-scale bombs and further threats to the aid agencies, including the World Council of Churches, and to the small Rome hotels where migrants stayed in transit. After one such bomb, ASALA issued a communiqué in broken English from Beirut, asserting their purpose:

> We declare the responsibility of this explosion and announce that our next operations are very, very soon if our here mentioned demands are not met.
> 1. Closing of all 16 immigration centers which are specially guided and kept by the American and Turkish imperialism and zionism to fascilitate the immigration of our people to the USA and other countries.
> 2. Every hotel that gives boarding to Armenian immigrants will be attacked by new methods and the casualties will be big!, and the authorities will have to take full responsibility.
> 3. The evacuation of all members of these offices as soon as possible otherwise the peoples judgement will be given against them soon.
> If our demands hereby mentioned are not met which are our rights, the continuing of the function of these offices indicates the covering up of our cause and accomplishment of the plot dictated and planned by the American and Turkish fascist-imperialistic programm.

For this we will tensify the armed struggle against these regimes and will not diffrinciate you from the imperialist zionist Turkish authorities and our struggle against you will be within your borders.

We ask our revolutionary masses to joind hand with us to overcome and distroy this America/Turkish impirialistic plans in this country.

Long live the rights of self determination of depressed people.

23th Decem. 1979 The Armenian Secret Army
for the Liberation of Armenia.

The communiqué's irrelevant references to zionism, in the extremist Palestinian manner, bear witness to the kind of co-operation that the Armenians' base in Beirut provided. The 'depressed people' finds an echo in Yenicomechian's words, in which he justifies violence with enthusiasm: 'We are accused of using violence: I accept that accusation with pride, and I add that there are two sorts of violence – that of oppressors and that of the oppressed. The violence that we use is the violence of the oppressed and humiliated.' It is possible that Yenicomechian was himself the author of the communiqué; for by 1982 he had become a public spokesman for ASALA in Beirut, organising and appearing at clandestine press conferences. But earlier he had played a direct role in the violence that he found so easy to justify.

At the time of the communiqué, the balance of death was highly favourable for ASALA. They had killed some thirty Turkish enemies without having any of their own number either arrested or killed. It was ironic, therefore, that Yenicomechian, the propagandist of Armenian terror, should have become the first such victim, blown up by the bomb he was preparing in a Geneva hotel room in October 1980. In his own words – the words of a true believer – Yenicomechian can both justify and accept what happened: 'All peaceful ways were barred to us. Only the armed struggle cannot be barred. That is why the armed struggle saw the light of day. That is why I accepted the risk of this mission. That is why I was

67

preparing three explosive devices on the night of 3 October. Bad luck, or more likely my incompetence, meant that I was not able to accomplish this mission. As a result of the explosion of one of these devices in my hands, I lost my sight, I lost my left hand, I have problems with my ears and my balance, and I am very seriously handicapped, and very conscious of it. Perhaps I should be very demoralised, should regret having agreed to carry out this mission, and regret having become involved in the armed struggle. However, my morale is very high and I do not regret having chosen this duty. Because I know why I am fighting, I have a deep faith in the cause and the justice of the cause. I am still convinced that the armed struggle is the only way to regain our rights. The Armenian people has given thousands and thousands of martyrs during its history. I am not the first, and I shall not be the last.'

Terrorism tends to be a very short-term career, and Yenicomechian is an unusual case for his surprising survival to fight, or at least to propagandise, another day. But with or without him, the violence continued to escalate over the next two years.

Armenian terrorism's worst atrocity occurred on 15 July 1982, when a large suitcase bomb exploded without warning by the Turkish Airlines check-in desk, Counter 61, in Orly-Sud Airport, Paris. At 2.11 p.m. a black suitcase, left on a baggage cart, exploded in a ball of flame, killing four people instantly in the blast. The bomb consisted of only half a kilo of Semtex explosive, but it was connected to three portable gas bottles which explained the large number of burns among the fifty-six people injured, twenty-one of them with serious injuries of which three more died later.

Within barely more than an hour, an anonymous caller to the AFP bureau in Athens claimed the attack in the name of ASALA's Orly Group: 'ASALA takes full responsibility for the attack against passengers who were destined for Turkey. We will continue to attack Turkish interests and Turkish diplomats. We call upon the rest of the world to distance themselves from Turkish institutions, for Turkey and her interests are the target of the Armenians.'

The incident provided evidence of the strains imposed on a terrorist group that is getting nowhere, despite its adoption of the ultimate tactic of sheer, illegitimate violence. Orly was not just one more attack in the calendar of Armenian violence: it represented the first attack in a new, more ruthless and more random policy of violence adopted by a faction of ASALA.

The Secret Army had been under acute pressure since its valued advisers, the PLO, had been expelled from Beirut by the Israeli invasion in August 1982. ASALA moved back to the Bekaa Valley, largely under Syrian control, in Eastern Lebanon. From there it was far harder to launch attacks into Europe than from Beirut, and tactics were under severe examination within the organisation. In effect, one of the two or three most important individuals in ASALA, who goes under a variety of false names (Hagop Hagopian/Mirhan Mirhanian/Monte Melkonian/Dimitri Giorgiu/Khatchik Avedissian) had decided that if selective violence, directed specifically at Turkish diplomats, was having no results, then random violence directed against the West would make people finally take note of Armenian grievances.

In France, the selective violence was called *action ciblée* – or targeted action. *Hay Baykar*, the Armenian newspaper which openly supported *action ciblée*, claimed that the 'gangster' Hagopian had precipitated a split in the ranks of ASALA, and then instituted an internal war in which members of the rival factions took to kidnapping, and in one instance, executing each other. The majority faction, sticking to the old 'targeted violence' tactic, emerged with a new name: ASALA/MR or Revolutionary Movement. It was to ASALA/MR that *Hay Baykar* gave its political backing: 'Every organisation has a moment of crisis sooner or later – it is a part of the way of life of revolutionary action. Nevertheless to break with a mistaken route often marks the beginning of great things in the future. This step backwards for ASALA may unveil two steps forward for ASALA-Revolutionary Movement ... Since 1975, young Armenians have experienced their nationalism through the rhythm of the armed struggle. With this generation, the Turkish State is compelled to sleep with one eye open. Has not ASALA/MR already taken the oath to continue the struggle until victory?'

The activities of Armenian terrorists in France were abruptly curtailed after the Orly operation, principally because the French police rounded up more than fifty Armenian extremists, lending credence to those critics of the government who had maintained that Armenian terrorists were known but tolerated for domestic political reasons within France. (For example, the then Prime Minister Pierre Mauroy, Justice Minister Robert Badinter, and Minister for Public Security Joseph Franceschi, all represented towns or cities which had substantial and vocal Armenian minorities among their voters.) Nevertheless, within a week of the Orly attack another incident took place which amplified fears of Armenian militancy, and revealed the existence of a new terrorist group, or the results of another split, this time within the Justice Commandos of the Armenian Genocide.

Though the Justice Commandos have rarely operated within Europe, it was from Lisbon that the news emerged of an armed assault on the Turkish Embassy compound in the suburb of Restello. At about 10.30 a.m. on 27 July 1983, five gunmen attempted to storm the Embassy: a Portuguese armed guard shot one man dead and was wounded by the remaining gunmen, who made an abrupt change of plan and rushed into the Ambassador's residence. Within thirty minutes an explosion rocked the building, and fire broke out: and when police penetrated the building they found the five charred bodies of the commando members, who at some point had killed an Embassy staff member. The wife of the Turkish chargé d'affaires later died in hospital from burns.

The first communiqué on behalf of the group was received by AFP in Paris at 1 p.m. – about the same time as the terrorists' bodies were found in the wreckage of the Ambassador's residence. It simply stated that the 'Armenian Revolutionary Army' claimed the attack – a name which had been heard only once before, in the aftermath of the murder of a Turkish diplomat in Brussels two weeks earlier – though that killing was first claimed by ASALA. Later in the day, a letter was sent to both Associated Press and United Press International, explaining that 'the operation was neither a suicide attack, nor a demonstration of madness. By exploding a bomb in the Embassy, our comrades sacrificed themselves on the altar of liberty.' In one of these communiqués the ARA declared that it was 'a new military organisation which is totally distinct from any existing Armenian organisation.'

ARA claimed to speak 'in the name of third-generation Armenians' – reflecting the sixty years, or two generations, which had passed since the massacres, and the sense that the third generation was now taking up the cudgels for Armenian nationalism after years of neglect. And in a pointed reference to the extraneous political content – usually revolutionary Marxism – which frequently infiltrates nationalist sentiment, the ARA stated: 'Our battle against the Turkish government belongs strictly in the traditional Armenian cause, to the exclusion of all other interests. We strongly reaffirm our total independence from any other powers, no matter who they may be.' Finally, the ARA revealed its probable origins by encouraging supporters of their parent group to break away: 'We exhort other clandestine organisations, and in particular the Justice Commandos of the Armenian Genocide, to come and join us in order to proceed in united combat.'

Some interpret the whole exercise as a smoke screen put up by ASALA to evade both their internal and external problems; but whoever the Armenian Revolutionary Army are, their existence does not represent a reduction in Armenian terrorist fervour or firepower. Since 1983 fatal attacks have continued against diplomats and Turkish interests; the ARA have been involved in attacks in Brussels and Vienna, and, on 12 March 1985, three ARA gunmen stormed the Turkish Embassy in Ottawa. There is no reason to believe that they and their comrades will stop. Their cause apparently endures, however recondite the world beyond Armenian nationalist sentiment may regard it.

The Armenians maintain a claim on an island which the tide of history has already swept away. Despite the fact that the

Treaty of Sèvres decided in 1929 that an Armenian State should be established, consisting of six provinces including Van and Trabizon (on the Black Sea), most political realists regard the continuing claims for Armenian nationhood as fanciful. They bear in mind that about one third of the 'homeland' is in the Soviet Union, and that the whole straddles the only border in the world between a NATO country and the USSR.

For Armenian militants, just as for the Palestinians on whom Armenian terrorists (among many others) have modelled themselves, there is no role for 'passive resistance'; there is no one for them, as it were, passively to resist. The Turks can be deliberately attacked, to provoke attention and the remote hope of 'justice'; or the issue can be forgotten, and the Armenian communities of the world – in France, the USA, Australia and elsewhere – can confine ideas of their heritage to folkloric nostalgia. All Armenians in the world are united by remembrance of the events of 1915, and it is a function of the militant groups to remind their own people of the justifying power of the 'genocide' as they themselves act violently. One of the world's most prominent Armenians, the Governor of California George Deukmejian, makes a point of speaking at anniversary rallies to commemorate the massacres. On 24 April 1983, he told several thousand Armenian-Americans that they 'must not forget the killings of as many as 1.5 million people in 1915'.

Most will continue to observe the traditional date of remembrance, but shun and deplore the militancy which answers injustice with rough justice and bloodshed. Yet there will remain a tiny minority unwilling to comply with the overwhelming weight of history, and prepared actively to resist. A minority of one, with a pistol, can make his voice clearly heard – as Gurgen Yanikian demonstrated. An elderly French Armenian declared, after the outrage at Orly Airport, that the existence of people willing to fight for Armenia meant that he could now die in peace: 'We have been given back our history,' he claimed. 'Well, even if we obtain nothing, we will slam the door on our way out and the world will have to remember us!' The Armenians are only one of many groups and movements, whose motives range from the comprehensible to the insupportable, who have learned to use terrorism by example. But the suitcase bomb left at an airline's check-in desk kills just the same number of innocent people if it explodes in the name of a just, or an unjust, cause.

3   MIND AND MOTIVE

'Qu'importe les victimes si le geste est beau?'
The reaction of Laurent Tailhade on hearing that
an anarchist bomb had been thrown in the Chamber of Deputies in Paris.

Meeting terrorists is not an alarming or disturbing experience;
face to face, outside the crisis or drama which is taken to be
their natural milieu, it is easy enough to see them as comprehensible individuals. Their humanity and their experience
are not different in kind from that of every other kind of
participant in political struggle. They are far from being
stereotype radicals; they are usually intelligent and copiously
well-informed in political affairs; they are rarely unbalanced.
   What distinguishes terrorists from their peers and com-
petitors is the willingness to pursue their struggle beyond the
limits which constrain the overwhelming majority of citizens
from protest or direct action, whether they are malcontents or
not. It is not true, of course, to suggest that the terrorist is
unable to see the limits; for it is the very conscious violation of
the barrier of acceptability which gives terrorist violence its
impact. Thus the psychological study of terrorist motivation,
personality and character is a very proper area of inquiry in the
overall effort to understand the phenomenon of terrorism,
despite the view of some traditionalists that it may come
perilously close to finding 'excuses' for grotesque acts of
cruelty and bloodshed. Indeed, the results of clinical analysis
can be of equal value to governments trying to discourage
terrorism by appropriate political programmes, and to police

74

officers negotiating on the ground in individual hostage situations.

The FBI is clear about the potential value of 'profiling' terrorists; and yet the comprehensive interview techniques used in compiling its voluminous database on social deviants such as serial murderers, child molesters and rapists, have proved relatively unproductive with terrorists, whose ideological motivation makes them generally unwilling to participate in any dialogue with representatives of the state.

The FBI's experience is not exceptional, and there is no doubt that the database on terrorism specifically is relatively small. Most studies of the psychology of terrorism have been conducted within the confines of a single group, where a researcher has gained local access; while others have developed theories – in particular of the group psychology of terrorism – without firsthand access. But the world's most eminent terror-psychologist, without any doubt, is the remarkable Professor Franco Ferracuti of the University of Rome (Professor of Criminology) and the Catholic University of San Juan, Puerto Rico (Professor of Forensic Psychiatry). Benefiting from his position as a psychological adviser to the Italian Secret Service during the 1970s, the high volume of arrested terrorists and radicals available for study in Italy, and a taste for radical and ironic argument, Ferracuti combines abstract theory and concrete case histories into by far the most substantial body of research on the psychology of terrorists.

Professor Ferracuti has analysed the careers and personalities of Italian terrorists in two distinct ways. Firstly, he has assessed the demographic, sociological and life-history detail of the cases to observe the social trends towards terrorism; secondly, he has applied detailed psychological tests, to attempt a 'typology' of the terrorist. His observations are in some ways all the more useful for being bathed in skepticism. Ferracuti refuses to exaggerate the substance of his findings, and his approach to terrorism is tempered by a realistic understanding of the rhetorical use of the word in the modern world: 'Terrorism is an *ex post facto* definition,' he says. 'Half the members of the United Nations got there by using what others would have called terrorism. You're only a terrorist if you lose.' This slightly exaggerated attitude nevertheless requires Ferracuti to make an important destinction, which is often ignored in the efforts to diagnose the 'terrorist condition', between radical political dissent, which is ubiquitous, and the specific use of violence, which is not.

Terrorist violence, with its readiness to inflict physical harm on unknown victims at random, manifests a ruthlessness of such apparent inhumanity as at first sight to defy understanding. The terrorist murder is the antithesis of the *crime passionelle*, or the spontaneous violence of an angry riot. It is calculating, callous, cold-blooded. What we require of the psychologists is to tell us how this squares with ideological commitment, or a pride in national destiny, or a political theory that claims to direct itself towards the common good. Our general assumption, in the civilized twentieth century, is that these things are incompatible; in the face of such horrors it is more comfortable to believe that the people capable of such acts are crazy, anti-social, and cruel.

However, this conventional and dismissive assumption requires careful examination. As Dr Jerrold Post, an American psychologist and one of the most acute contributors to the international debate on the psychology of terrorism, observes: 'We may consider that the more repressive the society, the healthier are those who rise against it, or, more properly, who go underground against it. Yet, no matter how justified the cause, no matter how repressive the society, there are some who join and some who don't. Not every son of a Basque joins ETA. Are those who join the true patriots, and those who don't cowards? Or are those who join more conflicted and driven psychologically, while those who don't are psychologically healthier?'

Professor Franco Ferracuti addresses the same issue with the rhetorical question 'Are terrorists crazy?' and offers the equally blunt reply that 'the simple answer is no'. He insists that 'you can't avoid the issue by labelling terrorists insane. At the same time, you can't solve the problem by calling them criminals.'

Ferracuti's point, which is both philosophical and political, is based on research into revolutionary rather than separatist groups; but it is supported by the evidence of psychologists who have observed the latter. Thus Robert P. Clark of George Mason University, Virginia, concludes from his study of large numbers of ETA activists (or *etarras*) that ETA members are not 'alienated and psychologically distressed', but rather 'psychologically healthy persons for the most part, strongly supported by their families and their ethnic community'.

Ferracuti's efforts to establish a terrorist 'typology' have been conducted through a variety of psychological tests. As an adviser to the Italian Secret Service, SISMI, he employed the technique of 'psychobiography', in which anything written or uttered by a terrorist is analysed for its linguistic clues about the degree of aggression, conciliation, violence or instability likely to be encountered during a crisis. The psychological test which proved the best discriminator of different types of terrorist was a widely used personality test called the Adjective Check List. Devised by an American psychologist Alison Gough, the ACL is a list of 300 adjectives ('from adventurous to zany' according to Ferracuti) which is given to the subject for him or her to mark those which describe himself or herself. These results, compared with the results from control groups of 'ordinary' people of the same age and background, produce a sketch of the dependence, aggressiveness, masculinity or feminity, instability and deviance of the subject.

Ferracuti tested four groups of people: leftwing terrorists (called 'Reds'), rightwing terrorists (called 'Blacks'), drug addicts of comparable age, and leftwing 'politically-involved non-terrorists' (called 'PINTs'). Though the results are still being assessed, Ferracuti did reveal the most significant results of the study. Firstly, the personality tests revealed that the four identified groups were quite distinct, with little or nothing in common with each other. In Professor Ferracuti's words, 'we got four very separate, discriminate groups.' Of the 300 adjectives in the test, 'there were only four adjectives common to all groups.' Of those, two were 'adventurous' and 'aggressive' – somewhat predictably. As to pathological tendencies, the test produced results which demonstrated distinct differences between the four groups, but no common 'terrorist personality'. The rightwing neofascist terrorists were portrayed as the most psychopathic of the four groups – 'the most deviant are the Blacks, the least deviant the PINTs,' said Ferracuti. 'There are personality differences, not always amounting to psychopathology.'

What this means is that an ACL test on a teenager who is beginning to behave anti-socially might reveal a tendency to move on towards terrorism. Particularly anti-social behaviour might demonstrate more of a likelihood of his getting involved in an extreme-right group. Although the groups are distinct from each other in their personality profile, no profile amounts to being 'crazy'. Perhaps the most unsatisfactory aspect of Ferracuti's findings, from the point of view of its government sponsors, is that 'it became clear that for a PINT to become a "Red" terrorist was a matter of chance – simply a matter of who your friends are.'

Ferracuti's results, then, are descriptive rather than prescriptive; as Dr Post says, 'There is no one terrorist "mindset" – for many it's really hard to distinguish the kinds of activities they become involved in from common criminality, and the expression of aggression from a need to strike out against the "someone" who is responsible for their inadequacy.'

In the absence of a consistent 'mindset' for the terrorist or proto-terrorist, Post proposes a pattern based on family psychology. In doing so, he draws attention to one of the most important distinctions in terrorism, between those groups seeking national independence or secession in an effort to separate from the existing state structure, and political revolutionaries who fight to overthrow the existing state and its political system, to replace it with a preferable alternative. One of the most forceful psychological aspects of the terrorist character is highlighted by this distinction; because the Basque nationalist (to refer to the former type) is fighting within an existing tradition whose goals are widely supported within the community, while the Red Army Faction terrorist has few on whose moral or physical support he can rely in his campaign. In the first case, the terrorist is fighting to build the Utopia of his people (though most of them would dispute his tactics); while in the second case, he is fighting to destroy the social and governmental system which the majority of its inhabitants broadly accept.

Dr Jerrold Post expresses the alternative types thus: 'The "anarchic-ideologues", such as the Red Army Faction, committed to destroying the world of their fathers, and the "nationalist-secessionists", such as ETA of the Basques, who carry on the mission of their fathers.' He argues that acts of terrorism by the 'anarchic-ideologues' are 'acts of retaliation against real and imagined hurts against the society of their parents', while the nationalists 'are retaliating against society for the hurt done to their parents. Thus, at a symbolic level, the terrorist acts of the "anarchic-ideologues" are acts of dissent against parents loyal to the regime; for the "nationalist-secessionists" they are acts of loyalty to parents damaged by the regime.' This analysis allows Post to generalise further about the combination of factors which may produce terrorism; a person who is loyal to his parents, who are loyal to the regime, will be unlikely to become a terrorist; a person who dissents from his parents, who are loyal to the regime, may become a terrorist (anarchic-ideologue); a person who is loyal to his parents, who dissent from the regime, may also become a terrorist (nationalist).

In support of his theory, Post offers the observation that 'there is a tendency for marginal, isolated and inadequate individuals from troubled family backgrounds to be attracted to the path of terrorism, so that, for many, belonging to the terrorist group is the first time they truly belonged, and the group comes to represent family.'

The evidence of research into the backgrounds of terrorists, however, is in fact extremely inconsistent: not least because of the extremely wide range of cultures, nationalities and ideological causes from which terrorists emerge. On the one hand, for instance, Dr Post quotes the findings of West German sociologist Gerhard Schmidtchen, who studied the life histories and careers of twenty-three rightwing and twenty-seven leftwing German terrorists. The leftwing members of the Red Army Faction and the *Bewegung 2 Juni* (Movement of 2 June) offered instructive data. There was a pattern of incomplete family structure, with some 25 per cent having lost one or both parents by the age of 14 (a figure well above the average among their peers); 79 per cent reported 'severe social conflict' – with the parents in one third of all cases, and with authority, leading to conviction in juvenile court in another third of cases. The terrorists were disproportionately likely to fail at school or at work, and Schmidtchen categorised them as 'advancement-orientated and failure-prone'.

On the other hand, the evidence of Robert Clark in the Basque community offers no such trends; though the focus of study illustrates the different prevailing concerns in West Germany – a highly developed, industrial, urban society with a high premium on achievement, conformity and prosperity – and the Basque provinces – a rural, largely agricultural, traditional society with the Catholic and Southern European emphasis on family structure and continuity. Clark finds that 'the overwhelming majority of *etarras* are well within the range of functioning and sane human beings ... members of ETA suffer from no greater levels of stress than are observed across Basque society generally, and certainly their stress level does not exceed the bounds of what is manageable by normal, functioning men and women ... *etarras* have relationships with loved ones that are normal to the point of being mundane ... *Etarras* are not alienated persons ... '

The only evidence suggestive of psychological insecurities, in the Basque context, is the intriguing fact that forty per cent of *etarras* (or of the 500 case histories that Clark studied) are of mixed parentage – one Basque, and one non-Basque parent – while a mere eight per cent of the overall population belongs in that category. It would appear that at least some *etarras* feel the need to prove their Basque credentials; in Dr Post's interpretation (in relation to the world of their fathers) 'an act of ETA terrorism may be carried out for superficially ideological reasons, but it really says to the real parents or the quasi-parent "See what a loyal son of the cause I am".'

In Italy, the general trend is for terrorists to come from the middle class and lower middle class; from broken families, or circumstances where the father was usually absent; occasionally from migrant families who had moved from the rural, Mediterranean culture of the South to the more urban and industrial culture of the North. The leftwing terrorist is over eighteen, up to about thirty-five. He or she will be educated up to and possibly including university, in the humanities, political science or law. Contrary to the assumption that leftist terrorists would have avoided compulsory military service on ideological grounds, they have absolutely average rates of participation.

Rightwing terrorists are male. They can be in their teens or middle-aged. The rightwingers have usually failed to complete their secondary education. They are prone to weapon-fetishism, and infrequent acts of spectacular bloodiness; while the left regard their weapons as tools, rarely make use of mass-attack weapons or very large quantities of explosive and tend to have a targeting strategy. Women appear very frequently in leftist groups on a basis of apparent equality, even to the point of carrying weapons, planting bombs and killing; while the rightwing attitude is that women don't count. (The implication here is that the leftist revolutionary terrorist is breaking with a prevailing cultural pattern through political principle. The traditional position of women in Mediterranean and Catholic societies is also largely maintained, for example, within ETA - where one *etarra* told Clark that the place of women was in the home, and that they were no use to the armed struggle, 'because they talk too much, especially to the parish priest'.)

Despite the largely revolutionary nature of terrorism in Italy, there is one surprising detail about Red Brigade members which seems to belong far more to the context of Basque nationalism. Ferracuti observed that the first generation of Red Brigade terrorists 'were in many cases the children of fathers who had fought against the fascists for the

Partisans', and saw themselves carrying on the mission of their parents. An alternative explanation, which Ferracuti offers half in jest, is that they had become 'fed up with hearing how their fathers had fought. They had to overcome the Oedipus somehow – and you don't have to *kill* your father – merely to *shame* him.'

The evidence, then, on the typical 'terrorist personality' is that there is no such thing. Some terrorists appear to be stable members of the community with relatively untroubled personal histories; others, according to research assembled by Dr Post from various countries, manifest a variety of symptoms of inadequacy: 'histories of childhood deprivation and narcissistic wounds ... with a deficient sense of self-esteem, and inadequately integrated personalities ... loners, alienated individuals who did not fit ... extreme extroverts – the self-centred individual with little regard for the feelings of others ... neurotic hostility ... projecting the person's own hostility onto the social environment.'

Dr Post presents a formidable and convincing argument that group psychology offers more insight into the ways that terrorists operate, where evidence of the individual psychological pattern leaves many questions unanswered. He notes that 'what is particularly striking is the uniformity of terrorist behaviour', despite the very widely differing circumstances of the individual terrorists. Post attributes this to the dynamics of group psychology, and above all to the fact that the new recruit to terrorism is someone who very likely finds himself or herself feeling as if they fully 'belong' for the first time. He arrives at this judgement effectively in a negative way: by dismissing the ostensible 'cause' of terrorism as an insufficiently convincing motivation: 'The group cause – the ideology – is of great importance. We do not believe "the cause" is the basic underlying psychological motivation for joining. Rather it serves as the rationale for the espoused, consciously acknowledged motivation for joining.' He continues his argument as follows: 'The idea of the ideology as a rallying point is strange, because the ideology is really vapid. Some of the members of a group chant (the ideology) as slogans, and it reminds me of the mantras of various religions. I don't believe anyone does anything for ideological reasons – people do things for personal reasons which have been given ideological shape.'

So why are these people in terrorist organisations at all, rather than fringe religions? Post specifically accepts the analogy, in pointing to the Unification Church of Rev. Sun Myung Moon as a very similar refuge for the 'lonely, rejected and sad' or 'depressed, inadequate, or borderline anti-social youths'. The key concept in the psychology of recruits is 'relief at joining'. Post quotes a study of the participants of a mass arranged-marriage ceremony of the 'Moonies': taking place in the USA, this represents a socially unacceptable proposition. The study found that 'the greater the relief the sect members associated with their membership, the more likely they were to accept this deviant social behavioural norm.' Post proposes that the attraction of terrorist-group membership operates in the same way, to the marginalised individual: 'If the only time you have really felt good about yourself is when plotting the destruction of the establishment, then however you get in – youthful adventures, the drug culture, or real aggressive/paranoid bent – the group takes over, and individual differences melt away.'

When the group's importance has thus been established in the minds of the members, the priorities of the individual and the collective are established, too. But they vary from the assumptions of outsiders quite sharply. Jerrold Post's view is that for the member who has found a 'home' in the group, 'the primary goal is to feel that you belong, and to be fighting the good fight: the assumed goals of publicity and ultimate victory for the cause come second and third on the list'. For the group, there is an equivalent primary goal – 'simply to ensure that it survives as a group'. Post's analysis is that for the alienated individuals – which is his assessment of those who join, though it is not accepted universally – 'joining a terrorist group represented the first real sense of belonging after a lifetime of rejection, and the terrorist group was to become the family they never had.'

In a paper delivered to a US Department of Defense symposium on 'Outthinking the Terrorist' in April 1985, he developed the theme: 'In joining a terrorist group, the member tends to break off all previous affiliations, to become dependent upon the group for emotional support. The move from outside to inside the terrorist group means a profound alteration in lifestyle. For the group member, especially one who has committed a criminal act, the group literally becomes a protection against danger. The member needs the group for protection against the hostile outside world. When the group's existence is threatened, it increases group cohesion, as individuals find their own source of security threatened.'

The prevailing 'need to belong' not only explains the strong similarities between the behaviour of quite widely different groups; it also paradoxically explains the sense of solidarity that exists between separate groups. It is a two-stage process: because by definition the terrorist group is hostile to the state and almost certainly has the status of 'wanted criminals', an atmosphere of all-out conflict is cultivated. In Dr Post's words: 'The "us against them" framework (or "fight-flight") is a very powerful mechanism that dissolves differences and makes the group feel that all the establishment is out to destroy you, so you must destroy them to bring justice in the world.' It is an all-or-nothing attitude which permits no half measures, no grey areas: 'you are either with us or you are against us' – which greatly increases group solidarity. The second stage is the recognition that other anti-establishment groups are 'with us'; Post says that 'the links found between different groups adds evidence to the idea that "the Cause" is not the "*cause*" – the links lie between those who feel they must strike against authority'.

The acute hostility to everything and everyone outside the group is taken by some psychologists as the most revealing evidence of unstable or deviant personalities being prone to terrorism. It is a manifestation, according to one theory, of 'narcissistic rage' – defined as coming from 'the need for revenge, for righting a wrong, for undoing a hurt by whatever means, and deeply anchored, unrelenting compulsion in the pursuit of these aims'. Another commentator, John Crayton, writes that these are 'individuals who have a stunted empathic capacity. They do not understand the wishes or frustrations and disappointments of other people. At the same time, their sense of the legitimacy of their own wishes and their sensitivity to their own frustrations are intense.' In similar vein, Dr Post explains that 'a healthy individual takes the negative and positive parts of himself and relates to the whole: a borderline or narcissistic personality takes all or nothing, in a totalitarian mind-set: the parents are seen as evil, the terrorist leader takes on a god-like status.' This is splitting: the good self is opposed against the evil world, and nothing lies in between. As Dr Post expresses the conflict, 'There is the me and the not-me, the good and the bad, and if things are not going well, it is not me, it is their fault. And having projectively identified society as the source of problems, it follows that the way to cure the problems is to destroy their source, is to destroy society.'

The irony of this anti-establishment, anti-authority position is that the terrorist group is usually an extremely authoritarian unit in itself. There are both psychological and tactical reasons for this: as we have seen there is immense pressure within the group to maintain a consistent, predictable, and stable emotional environment; for reasons of survival and security it has to remain united and single-minded about both its goals and its tactics. 'There is nothing more authoritarian than the terrorist group,' says Dr Post. 'Any deviation or questioning is to touch on the member's own doubts – there's a total incapacity to tolerate ambivalence.' Evidently, the group cannot afford to risk internal doubt, and the risk of betrayal by the doubter: a strong leader will repeatedly threaten expulsion (or death) in order to enforce continuing compliance by all concerned. But for the group member who represents the pattern proposed by Dr Post, 'it is psychologically very attractive to find a group where certainty is the rule and doubt is unacceptable'.

An equivalent pressure also acts on the group to force it into action as an outlet for the tension and pressure of the usually clandestine existence of the terrorists. Rivalries may emerge which endanger the unity of the group, often between those who are seeking an outlet for violent aggression and those who have a more genuine ideological purpose in their actions. Those who favour action will find a sanction for it in the ideology – 'if the group members don't act out they will act in', according to Post, risking the group's unity of purpose and very often leading to splits which create new terrorist groupings whose ideological programme is indistinguishable from the parent group. It is probably true to say that no one outside the Palestine National Council could clearly define the precise doctrinal differences between the individual factions and fragments of the PLO; and their energies are substantially dissipated on fighting each other rather than pursuing their real objectives.

For the same reason, a cautious, tactical leader may well be deposed in favour of one who argues for more direct action. Dr Post expresses it in these terms: 'If you have one wise counsel of caution and another who says "Are we mice or men, if we don't take action to destroy our enemies, what good are we?"', unless the first goes along with that sentiment he is likely to be deposed from his leadership role.' Those responsible for considering the tactical response to terrorists pay close attention to the question of why groups stage attacks at particular times, and what political factors appear to have provoked them. Half of the answer is that successful terrorism (like successful anti-terrorism) depends upon varying the pattern of movement and activity, so that the terrorists with the longest survival rate are often the greatest opportunists, who strike when chance circumstances present a moment of vulnerability. The other half of the answer is the dynamics of the group. In Post's words: 'If the terrorist group does not commit terrorist acts it has lost its meaning.'

From a quite different context, Post quotes a member of the wartime Polish underground resistance, who 'describes the most unbearable tension produced by inaction in the underground group, a tension which threatens the group's integrity'. Extrapolating to the circumstances of terrorism, Post continues: 'The perceptive leader will sense the group's need for action in order to discharge such tension. He will direct the group to attack the enemy before its members attack him.'

Although the theoretical and psychological analysis of terrorists, and of the dynamics of terrorist groups, is genuinely useful in offering guidance as to likely behaviour, tactics and development, there remains a central question which relates to the most important distinguishing feature of terrorism: the willingness to shed innocent blood. Professor Ferracuti places particular emphasis on the idea that the terrorist espouses, that he or she is in a state of war with the enemy/state – and that in war there are bound to be innocent casualties.

The nationalist fighter can be convinced of the state of war by the existence of 'a heritage of struggle which blinds the individual to changed realities; there's a family and cultural tradition, perhaps of generations who have fought. Look at the Armenians, who are fighting to avenge the events of two generations ago which no one even knows to be historical fact – the important thing is that they believe it to be true.' This belief can form the basis of the kind of justification offered by Basque militants who argue that Spanish Guardia Civil members are only dying 'because they are in a place where they have no right to be'. It is axiomatic that the terrorist group which 'claims responsibility' for an act of violence or a murder almost invariably seeks to shift the real responsibility elsewhere.

For the Red Brigades, the Red Army Faction and similar groups, there can be no doubt that the victims of their actions are ultimately their own constituents: violence in these circumstances therefore demands a kind of 'objectification', by which the victims become mere objects in a political process. Ferracuti describes it as 'an emotional detachment – the victim is seen as an object, and is probably unknown to the terrorist who causes his death. There's no personal element in the violence. What justifies it is the strength of the political credo.' But whatever the individual motivation to commit an act of violence or murder, terrorism remains essentially a group

87

process; as Ferracuti says, 'There's no such thing as an isolated terrorist – that's a mental case.' Thus group pressure pushes the individual towards compliance in the belief that 'if you don't participate in violent actions, you may lose the respect of your group which will no longer accept you as a member'.

One of the critical issues in every terrorist group is whether, having got in, the group member can get out. The pressure of the idea that acts of violent terrorism are the *raison d'être* of a terrorist group tends to make all the members feel a sense of complicity – whether positive or negative – and a strong leader will exploit his personal reputation for ruthlessness by threatening to use the same violence against dissenters or potential traitors. Andreas Baader, of the Baader-Meinhof Gang (or Red Army Faction) was quoted as saying 'Whoever is in the group simply has to be tough, has to be able to hold out, and if one is not tough enough, there is not room for him here.' A former member of the RAF, P. J. Boock, confirmed that the pressures of the group 'can lead to things you can't imagine . . . the fear of what is happening to one when you say for example "No, I won't do that, and for such and such reasons".' Michael 'Bommi' Baumann, who moved around the West German terrorist organisations but was principally involved in the Movement of 2 June, explained the dynamic: 'The principle is – to join costs nothing, to get out is impossible. This was made clear to every new member. "Exit is possible here only via the cemetery".'

Nevertheless, it is hard to find any evidence of remorse among terrorists for their actions. In counterpoint to their self-justification, however, comes a predictable torrent of condemnation and outrage at the violence and casualties from the state and its leaders. A very prominent element in this is the public commitment to 'stand firm' against terrorism, to use 'every means available to bring the terrorists to justice' and 'redouble the commitment to democratic processes'. It is worth considering the effect of such public reassurances on the psychology of the terrorist group.

For the terrorists, government threats are as empty as government promises: they are already entirely discredited, by definition, in the eyes of the handful who have attempted to destroy or replace that very government authority. There is no doubt, as demonstrated repeatedly both by ideological revolutionary groups like the Red Army Faction and Action Directe, and by separatist-nationalist forces like ETA or the IRA, that government assurances of having the terrorists 'on the run', and public statements that they will be brought swiftly to justice, are seen by the terrorists as something of a challenge to their ingenuity. The simple tactical advantage that the terrorists retain is that they can choose their targets from an almost unlimited range, while governments can only protect selectively. This forces government onto the defensive, so that it appears able only to react to what the terrorists initiate. As Professor Ferracuti observes: 'Terrorists are not at all deterred by "firm stands" taken by the state. Governments have made two mistakes in responding to terrorism – firstly the political handling has been very naive, such that there often seems no real leadership. If your policy changes from incident to incident, then you have lost. Secondly, they never have any planning on how to react to a demand to "release our comrades"; and the terrorists know that they retain the initiative.'

At the end of the process of terrorism there lies the question of success, of real progress by the terrorists towards their goals. There is no evidence of anything other than counter-productive results for the ideological revolutionary groups: the Tupamaros destroyed democracy in Uruguay; the Red Brigades and Red Army Faction caused substantial infringements of civil liberties and repressive new laws to be introduced in West Germany and Italy; the Weather Underground and its successor groups like the Red Guerilla Resistance and the May 19th Communist Organisation only discredited the liberal student political movement which swept the United States in the 1960s.

But for separatist and nationalistic groups, fighting on their own territory, there are advances which are sometimes quite concrete and sometimes politically vague. In Northern Ireland, severe waves of terrorist activity are usually followed by new political initiatives, though the connection is played down. In Corsica, the bomb-per-day cycle of violence has brought the appointment of special French government envoys and committees to investigate problems. Above all, in the Basque country since the death of Franco, there has been a vigorous movement towards regional political autonomy, though stopping well short of national independence. The question that arises is, when so much has been achieved, why will the terrorists not stop their terror and claim a moral victory?

The answers seem to apply to all forms of terrorism, for the very political and personal commitment demanded by the decision to join a terrorist group has to be sufficiently strong to blind the individual to realities. There has to be a black-and-white political view of the world in which anything conceded by the state is a cynical trick – thus regional autonomy is called a sham, specifically because it bears so many of the features of the full independence that the Basques, for instance, seek. The personal commitment to terrorism submerges the individual in a milieu where he or she never hears an opinion different from the collective policy or view; efficient terrorism requires inflexibility.

Franco Ferracuti ascribes the blindness to progress to three factors: isolation, tradition, and timescale: 'Whether in a student commune or a Basque village, the terrorists are among people who exclusively share their own view, never even reading a dissenting opinion. In regional situations, like the Basque case, there is a tradition; for example, a family where the son feels he has to emulate his father's actions to prove his worth. And the community tends to know, to protect and to respect the fighters. Time changes the circumstances more than superficial political changes: in the Basque region, the economy will change the situation in the end, as pressure for improvement through political change dies away.'

An entirely psychological explanation of why terrorists don't give up is provided by John Crayton in his study 'Terrorism and the Psychology of the Self'. Crayton's argument is that terrorism represents a possible outcome of exaggerated group narcissism, portrayed by terrorists' impulse to acquire power, to idealise their goals, to operate in groups, to have an absolute conviction about the cause, and to develop from deprivation, disenfranchisement or prejudice. His conclusion, based on a comparison between terrorists and other 'individuals with narcissistic rage' whose acting-out emerges in different forms, is that 'We may infer that a terrorist enterprise will not stop until the omnipotent grandiose strivings are given up. The narcissistically motivated terrorist would not stop if confronted with efforts to attempt to satisfy his grandiose aims through a policy of appeasement. Rather the terrorist challenges us to modulate effectively his narcissistic rage and channel it into constructive and useful ways. It is essential that terrorists "escape" from the crisis situation without further humiliation.' That may be the psychological optimum for the terrorist-patient, but in the real world humiliation would be the mildest outcome for the terrorist at the hands of the state.

Under the entry for terrorism in *The Encyclopedia of the Social Sciences*, one reads that 'the psychology of terrorism is that of romantic messianism'. It is a particularly relevant observation, in that the terrorist group's romanticism may be the only barrier to the realism that would clarify their ultimate failure; while the goal of future justice has more than a hint of Judgement Day. Nowhere are these aspects more obvious than in the case of the Basques. For those who remain committed to the armed struggle – in the French *Pays Basque*, or Northern *Euzkadi* – the progress towards ultimate independence is irrefutable and inevitable. Whatever the likelihood of gaining final independence from the Spanish government – approximately nil – the militant Basques have no intention of stopping there. Alongside the longterm campaign of ETA in Southern *Euzkadi*, there is a limited, and more recent terrorist initiative on the Northern side of the border. 'Popol', who lives in Northern *Euzkadi*, argues that this is the prerequisite for continuing the battle for justice to its proper conclusions: 'There is an armed struggle in the North; the group is called, in

Basque, *Iparretarak*, or "Those of the North". The South goes first, but it's a global strategy, and the North will follow. It's a matter of time; when the parents of our people in the South [i.e. Spain] were fighting against Franco, our parents in the North were fighting for France.'

His certainty is echoed by 'Yosu' – a supporter of the armed struggle North and South, and one of the leading figures on the inevitable 'Committee of Support for Basque Political Refugees'. His commitment and confidence, that the armed struggle will bring ultimate victory, are absolute; and consequently offer little hope of an end to the violence which is the principal expression of his cause: 'Our freedom will come sooner or later; what are they going to do? They can't kill us all, they can't commit a genocide. It's inevitable that we will win.'

In the last days of October 1985, a ragtag group of about fifty young men and women began a week's protest march through the towns of the French Pays Basque – the foothills of the Pyrenees, and the province regarded by Basque nationalists as the northern half of their future nation. The march was intended to draw attention to the plight of Basque refugees in France who, according to their Committee of Support, had become subject to expulsion by the French government, or assassination by a cross-border hit-team known as GAL (the Anti-Terror Group) which Basques unanimously assert is a Spanish police front. The statistics seem to confirm the claim: of the 800 or so Basque exiles (who do not have refugee status), twenty-five have been assassinated and thirty have been expelled by the French government to such varied destinations as Venezuela, Togo, the Cape Verde Islands, Santo Domingo, Cuba and Panama. In March 1984 the government also proscribed any new applicants for political exile from living in the seven *Départements* in the southwest of the country, and later added seven more. About sixty Basques have consequently been forced to leave their 'Basque homeland', and another seven were in October 1984 notified of their imminent expulsion from France.

It was these latest developments which prompted the

marchers to set off from Bayonne on ten days' hard walking through the rural land of the southwest. Although it is hilly country, it has a domestic, agricultural atmosphere; across the landscape, the muted autumn colours seemed to have been extended to the pale soil, the pale cattle, and the muddy pink-and-grey pigs which graze on the browning hillside bracken. Where it can be reached, the bracken is gathered and heaped around a rustic spear of weathered timber into the character-istic thimble shape of the Basque haystack – the same shape as the mountains – ready for the winter. Small farms are flanked by great flat walls of corn-cobs, the winter feed giving the impression that stone and brick have been exhausted, and a new construction material is being tried out. Cattle trample and graze in the cornfields after the harvest, and above the hairpin bends of the Cols d'Osquiche, which the marchers resolutely tackled, hawks hover and dive.

The march in itself changed nothing: it merely demon-strated that the cause of Basque nationalism is very profoundly felt by its adherents, and entirely irrelevant to the rest. When a cause fails to attract unanimous support from its intended beneficiaries, how can it expect to gain concessions from its enemies? The armed struggle is one of the ways to bridge the gap. After three days the marchers arrived at the small town of Mauléon, where brief speeches in front of the town hall were followed by a short ride into the hill villages to unveil a commemorative statue and pay homage to 'Tigre' – Eugenio Gutierrez, who had been shot dead a year earlier by a precision rifle from a range of 100 metres outside the door of the farm where he and his young wife lived. The oration by a bearded marcher addressed 'Tigre' directly: 'We are marching as a part of the same struggle in which you fought: we will continue until we reach our goal.'

Once back in Mauléon, the marchers were rewarded with a celebration feast of consommé, chicken stew, fruit tart and plenty of contraband Basque wine, smuggled across the border from 'Spain'. The fruit tart, of redcurrants, black-currants and gooseberries, was arranged to represent the Basque flag, and was greeted by a massive cheer. The Basque

liqueur Pacharan flowed, and patriotic songs about the homeland set the room shaking in an atmosphere as festive as a
rugby club dinner. The highpoint of the singing came with a
rousing chorus of the song which immortalizes ETA's assassination of the Spanish Prime Minister Carrero Blanco in
1973. To simulate the explosion – which blew the prime
ministerial car up and over a five-storey building – everyone
in the hall leapt to their feet and threw a bread roll in the air
with a wild whoop.

The armed struggle is never far from the minds of the
advocates of Basque nationalism, and in this company it was
natural to ask about the attractions, the tactics, and the outlook
for the Basque nationalist struggle. There are no self-confessed
'terrorists', as the philosophy of armed struggle is that the
supporters and the fighters are as one. Tactically, one of them
admitted, 'We deliberately conceal the real targets within the
community, to distribute the risk of GAL's attacks.'

'Elena' is an attractive twenty-four-year-old teacher who
left Southern *Euzkadi* in 1981. Anywhere in Europe, her dress
and manner would identify her as some sort of radical. She
says that her open involvement in both student and feminist
groups led her to being identified as a radical by police, who
threatened to rape her, as she claims they have done to other
women. 'Support for the armed struggle is much wider than
just from the people directly involved in it. It is a social,
popular, mass movement. I was a known militant – not
with arms, but with crayons. But it's all part of the same
struggle.'

Another young woman, 'Miren', recalls her militant involvement in Basque politics from the age of fourteen; she
joined ETA Politico-Militar in 1979, when she was twenty-
one. Her explanation is simple and full of conviction: 'Under
Franco everyone in *Euzkadi* was aware that we were oppressed
as a nation, from children to adults: the problem was so big
that everyone wanted to join ETA, or rather ETA was the
only organisation that was ready to fight. There was no other
way.'

'Miren' became a full-time militant from 1979 onwards; in

the language of the organisation a 'liberated person', meaning, in her words, 'that I worked full time for the organisation, and had no other work; going home only for some weekends, bank holidays, and Christmas'; in other words, living underground. Although ETA operates very specifically in the context of the community, such a decision is not necessarily applauded by the militant's peers – or family: 'My parents told me not to join ETA but they said "If you have decided to do so then you certainly will. You know what you're doing."'

A former leader of ETA's Strategic Command, who joined the organisation at the age of eighteen in about 1960, expresses exactly the same motives: Manuel Pagoaga or 'Peixoto' explains that 'at that time ETA was the only group talking about the Basque problem – and doing so clearly and publicly. And I say talking because at that time ETA had not even used bombs. All its activity was for cultural and propaganda purposes and setting up.'

ETA's peaceful methods were rapidly succeeded by armed organisation. In 'Peixoto's' words, 'For 250 years not a single generation of Basque people has been able to carry on living without taking up arms sooner or later. And if we have done that it's precisely so that our children don't have to go through what we have been through. For me it's very simple. When political action is impossible, there is nothing but the armed struggle as a means of moving forward ... If you look at history, there has been no people which has gained its sovereignty without using force. So the Basque people have conducted an armed struggle; and there is a solution without having an armed struggle – to let us go the way we want to go, and give us our freedom. I don't believe the armed struggle is necessary; it has always been imposed on us.'

One of 'Peixoto's' supporters on the Committee for the Support of Basque Refugees, 'Josu', takes the same view of the political context, despite the fact that the politics of Spain have been transformed in the last ten years since the death of Franco and the end of dictatorship. He attributes the existence of the armed struggle to the fact that 'the Spanish government doesn't accept the need to negotiate. It's the only solution, a political negotiation between . . . the parties who can guarantee the peace: on one side ETA, and on the other side the Spanish Army.'

'Peixoto' claims to be pessimistic about the ending of the armed struggle in the near future: 'I don't believe the Basque people have arrived at the point where they believe there can be a peaceful solution. We have to have a dignified peace, for both sides; we can't have peace imposed upon us.' Josu echoes the sentiment: 'It has to be an honest peace, with neither side feeling it has been humiliated. We don't want the peace of the cemetery, of torture and of silence.'

'Elena', the schoolteacher, regards the armed struggle as a part of the political process, rather than an alternative to it. In her view, 'The role of ETA exists because there is a political route also. There has been a role for the struggle for twenty-five years, which has been supported by many Basque people who will go on doing so. An armed organisation is required to oppose the enormous force of the state.'

When 'Miren' joined the armed struggle, she was required to undergo some weapons training, which she describes as 'minimal'. She was brought to a house in Northern *Euzkadi* and taught by colleagues how to handle a Browning pistol. 'You are in an armed organisation, so you are forced to carry a weapon, in order to defend yourself. It's a strange sensation, you don't feel fear or pleasure . . . You are conscious of being a member of an armed group, and that you may sometime have to use this weapon.'

While 'Miren' claims her weapon was for self-defence, the record of ETA's attacks on Spanish police and military personnel is second to none for fatality. The armed struggle has its political content, but in reality its most recognisable feature is killing people – the fellow citizens of the self-appointed militants. The idea that there are problems of acceptability with this tactic seems relatively foreign to those who support the Basque armed struggle as a whole. Thus, according to 'Peixoto', the killing is not random, or wanton: 'The purpose of the armed struggle is not to kill, but to liberate; but you can kill the person who denies you that liberation . . . it's necessary to execute the people or the entities who exercise this oppression.' 'Elena' is quite sanguine about the bloodshed: 'When there's an attack on a policeman there's always a protest demonstration, but the demonstration will be far bigger when it's a Basque victim of the Spanish police.' She insists on the point that the police are not Basques, implying that their lives therefore scarcely matter. 'Anyway, they say they are Spanish first and Basque second. We are Basques, entirely, and that's all. They would not be killed if they weren't there.'

'Peixoto' prescribes the same simple solution – complete capitulation by the Spanish government – to stop the killing: 'As a journalist I am aware that nationalistic struggles always try to make the price of loss of life unacceptably high, so the enemy will give up its oppression. There comes a time when a nation says "Too much – we have to leave". It happened with France at Dien Bien Phu, with the USA also in Vietnam, it might even happen in Spain. We have offered a cease-fire, an armistice, there's an open offer of peace.'

'Josu' simply places the responsibility for the deaths on the Spanish state which counts its victims: 'The Basque liberation movement has always said that it is ready to negotiate, ready to arrive at an accord, to sit down and say "We are ready" – but it is the Spanish government which reneges on all such possibilities. For that reason the war goes on. There is an enormous responsibility on the Spanish government which refuses to see that the sole situation is a simple renunciation of their authority in our land.'

An odd sideline of the Basque struggle is the story of the Lemoniz nuclear power station on the Atlantic coast near Vizcaya. The plant is still unfinished, and six years behind schedule, because of terrorist disruption. The utility company Iberduero has suspended work, not least because three successive chief engineers of the project have been assassinated by ETA. After the second killing, in April 1981, all civilian workers refused to go on with the construction. The third casualty was Angel Pascual Mujica, killed in April 1982. At that point Iberduero suspended all work until the Basque regional government took over responsibility for the construction programme and security on site. Construction delay was estimated to cost Iberduero $1.2 million a day, in addition to the cost of terrorist attacks on their conventional 160 electricity sub-stations. By 1982 these were believed to have cost the company $260 million, and had put an almost unbearable strain on electricity supplies throughout the region. ETA militants are clear in their view that obstructing the construction of the power station, by sabotage and assassination, was a proper channel for their activities.

According to 'Elena', 'All the Basque people are against Lemoniz being built. A hundred thousand people went out to demonstrate against it, but for the government it's just a matter of economics and power. If it's stopped it's a popular victory. You can't say that the armed organisation did it alone, or that they did it to get popular sympathy. They took the view that it would help them in their mobilisation against other targets. Popular movements and armed movements are inseparable and complementary.'

'Josu' rejects the suggestion that attacks on industry, and in particular the efforts to stop Lemoniz, are an attempt to destroy the economic base of the region. 'The targets of our armed struggle are above all the repressive institutions of the Spanish government. We have succeeded against Lemoniz, and for me it's a much more important victory than the assassination of Carrero Blanco. A nuclear power station, ninety per cent finished, ready to go into service, stopped. It was being constructed without anyone having asked the Basque people whether they wanted to have it or not, without doing any studies, and in a place surrounded by one million people, wrecking the ecological environment – it was rejected by the great majority of the population.' 'Peixoto' argues that the popular victory of Lemoniz represents a useful strategy of blackmail against the government: 'After stopping the power station we can say to the government, "If you try this nonsense, you know we will be there".And that's that.'Josu' adds that the episode portrays ETA's genius: 'ETA knew how to interpret popular feeling ... There was a total identification between the people and ETA's actions.'

For almost six years, the Basque region has had an autonomous regional government, with purely Basque political parties (including extremists who openly support the armed struggle), and many other concessions including a Basque-language television service, *Euzkadi Telebista*. In real terms, the Basque nationalist cause has been conceded very many of the functional aspects of the independence for which it has fought, though still there is no Basque flag flying in San Sebastian, no Basque passports are shown at the French border, and Spanish police still patrol, nervously, in the region. The fact is that Spain has already conceded more than most states would dream of conceding to terrorism, and it is clear that nothing more is on offer. Yet, to the majority of terrorists, the concessions are a powerful reinforcement to their behaviour; they believe, with a good deal of justice, that their armed struggle has been the crucial factor in delivering this progress. One more push will surely bring the final victory.

Alongside the political concessions, however, the Spanish government has tried to open the door to terrorists, offering an effective amnesty to those who renounce terrorism and confess to their own crimes, while being granted an automatic pardon. 'Miren', after four years in ETA, decided to take the opportunity, principally because the political transformation of the region had convinced her that the armed struggle had outlasted its usefulness. 'Politically, the party system now works,' she says. 'We have an Autonomy Statute as a referendum from the Basque people, we have a Basque Parliament. The armed struggle was in fact backfiring on the struggle for liberation. It has lost popular support, which before was absolutely total.' The armed struggle, she believes, is now counter-productive: 'It is leading nowhere, and if anywhere into a blind alley. We don't want ETA to become the minority grouping which practises armed combat, and that Basque society turns against ETA.'

For the true believer however, 'Miren's' diagnosis is all

wrong. 'Elena' is convinced of the merits and the tradition of ETA's role, which is interwoven within Basque society at every level. To her, 'The people in ETA are human and ordinary. The person who participates in the armed struggle is no different from the worker, the person in the anti-nuclear or social movements. You can take part through the armed option, or as a woman in a feminist group, or as a teacher in school, or as a worker in a factory. The people involved in the armed struggle in Southern *Euzkadi* are men and women engaged in a complete and comprehensive struggle, but they have taken a more absolute option.'

Furthermore, there is a substantial minority that is able to convince itself that the political gains already achieved are a sham. Thus Imanola, a Basque teacher refuged in the North, argues that, 'The degree of autonomy that we have achieved has only made people more supportive of the armed struggle. We may have autonomy in three regions but we don't have it in Navarra. It's a case of divide and rule.' Ultimately, then, the only hope for an end to this particular region's contribution to the bloody toll of terrorism is that 'Miren's' view will prevail, that terrorism – or the 'armed struggle' – is an idea whose time has passed: 'Nowadays there is no need for ETA's existence. *Euzkaldunak,* the people of *Euzkadi,* are more mature and I believe that they don't need saviours to come and tell them they have to go in a particular direction. They already know where to go, and they have a place – a political forum – in which to fight.'

Despite 'Miren's' view that the fight should now revert to politics from armed struggle, there is ample evidence to show that ETA's activity is being maintained at a fairly constant level. The death toll continues to mount. It might be possible to attribute the continuation of activity to only one of the groupings under ETA's umbrella, as there are three separate groups: ETA-Militar, ETA-Politico-Militar, and the Co-mandos Autonomos. However, there seems no obvious reason to believe that political change in the region has convinced any of the hardline groups to give up the struggle, though some individuals like 'Miren' have.

664107

The excellent portrait of ETA provided by Robert Clark presents a number of powerful factors in Basque community and family life which lead one to the conclusion that armed struggle has become permanently endemic within Basque society, irrespective of political reality. The critical factor in sustaining and preserving the ETA cause is its organic relationship with the community from which it springs. Clark's evidence demonstrates that from family tradition, in childhood and adolescence, in recruitment and organisational systems, through family support and community prestige, the Basque community enables ETA and the *etarras* to endure.

Although Clark argues that the families of most *etarras* 'were supportive of Basque nationalism but opposed ETA's violent tactics,' he cites one case of 'the widowed mother of an *etarra* [who] encouraged her sons to join the Resistance to avenge their father's death.' 'Peixoto's' claim to belong to a 250-year-old tradition confirms the sense of historical inevitability. Clark goes on to observe that 'once the youth joined ETA and was caught, killed, or driven into exile for his actions, the family rallied around in a solid show of support for their son or brother.' 'Indeed,' he remarks, 'one of the sources of ETA's great durability over the past two decades has no doubt been the ability of *etarras* to seek refuge and solace (as well as material support) from among those whom they love and cherish.'

An indication of the community-camouflage, and the deliberate blurring of distinctions between militants and sympathisers discussed earlier, emerges in Clark's study of ETA recruitment. 'The process by which new members are recruited into the organisation is usually a slow and gradual one, and it is difficult to say exactly when a young man crosses the threshold of ETA membership.' Further, there are different categories of membership: from *Liberados* (like 'Miren') through *Legales Enlaces* and *Apoyos,* to *Buzones,* 'each of which has a specific role to play in the maintenance and support of the organisation'. During the years of Franco's dictatorship, when Basque cultural identity was severely repressed, youths were forced 'to take their folkloric celebrations to distant

MERCED COUNTY LIBRARY

JUN 29 1988

mountain tops where they could not be observed by the police or the Guardia Civil. In earlier years, Basque mountain climbing clubs ... had been used as a cover for clandestine meetings ... And it was during the excursions of these clubs to their remote mountains that ETA chose to make many of their initial contacts which later led to recruiting activities in earnest.'

The clandestine organisation of a terrorist group requires absolute trust among its members, and Robert Clark observes that the culture of male social life in small Basque towns lends itself readily to the intense, secret cell structure that ETA employs. The basic unit of male society is the *cuadrilla* – which begins as a gang of four to six boys of perhaps no more than ten years old. By their early twenties, Clark argues, 'Basque men may have stronger ties to the *cuadrilla* than to their own families' – very much parallel to the *comando* organisation of ETA. They have 'already spent as much as a decade in which the dominant social factor was a small group of intimate friends bound in tight cohesion against strangers from the outside'.

Terrorist operations invariably need far more people to carry out general support functions than to make the occasional spectacular attack, and in the case of ETA this role – of gathering and passing on surveillance information, offering food and shelter, producing propaganda materials or carrying messages – can be performed either by recruits who have not graduated to the most dangerous work, or sometimes by older supporters whose moral support of the cause takes practical shape. The blurring of degrees of complicity again has great tactical advantages in protecting the most militant activists behind layers of support from legal political activity, through minor misdemeanours, to criminal conspiracy with ETA activities.

Life inside ETA, even for the fully committed terrorist, is considerably less stressful and demanding than the totally underground, on-the-run existence of the West German Red Army Faction, because of the degree of community tolerance. The RAF, too, could not sustain its activities without quasi-respectable supporters; but even they are on the extreme margins of political and legal acceptability, and consequently under suspicion. In the ETA, on the other hand, as Clark observes, 'One gets the impression ... that service in an ETA *Comando* is rather like working at a temporary part-time job, one that requires supremely dangerous and stressful tasks, but assigns them in such a way as to interfere minimally with the daily life of the perpetrators.' With that considerable easing of the pressure, ETA *comandos* are less likely either to make mistakes that expose them to the danger of arrest, or to take undue risks. But more important, the wide support for their actions means that – as Ferracuti observed in another context – questions about the ultimate objectives of the campaign, and its likely success, are not considered. Clark describes how 'they lived and moved about in a sort of hermetically closed compartment where one simply did not raise depressing questions or challenge the ultimate victory of the organisation.'

The evidence of the interviews given by the Basque refugee marchers in Northern *Euzkadi* demonstrates how blinkered, or idealistic, such people can be. Whichever is the right judgement, their conviction guarantees the continuation of nationalist terrorism – in the Basque region, or in Northern Ireland – for much longer than the much less deeply rooted terrorism of the ideological political revolutionary.

If one is to differentiate between the dominant prevailing source of nationalistic terrorism on the one hand, and of revolutionary terrorism on the other, one identifies the essential community base of the former and the centrality of political theory in the latter. Consequently, firsthand interviews with terrorists of the far-left, ideological revolutionary groups (largely in Western Europe) have the very pronounced flavour of esoteric tutorials in Marxist or Trotskyist theory of social science.

The terrorism of the 1970s in Italy was largely born on the North Italian university campuses of Turin, Bologna and Padua, though Rome was also significant. One of the leaders of the largest 'extra-parliamentary movement', Autonomia, was Oreste Scalzone, a professor of politics and philosophy at the University of Padua. He was one of the many alleged terrorists to be rounded up in the mass arrests of 7 April 1979, all over Italy, but after seventeen months in jail he was released on the grounds of ill health. He then absconded from Italy to France, where he now lives in a slightly precarious state of political exile, the question of extradition between the two countries being delicate and contentious. While France preserves her traditional reputation as a country of political exile, Italy insists upon the fact that those charged with terrorist crimes are far from being persecuted for their political beliefs. Since his arrival in Paris, Scalzone has been sentenced to a total of thirty-six years' imprisonment on convictions for orga-nising armed bands, and complicity in a series of terrorist acts including woundings, hold-ups and extortion.

Scalzone predictably rejects the idea that he is a 'terrorist': as he himself declares, 'There is almost no so-called terrorist group ... engaged in an armed struggle, that is ready to be identified by this word terrorism.' He defines terrorism in four ways: 'Firstly, the period of the French Revolution, 1791-3. Secondly, all the methods of government built on violent repression, etc. Thirdly, all the methods of violence and coercion applied in political struggle. And in fact there's a fourth definition that one should add, that in present-day language in the democratic countries of the West, when Reagan says "terrorists" he means the Palestinians, the Red Brigades, the government of Cuba or Nicaragua; but he ignores the US government's actions in Central America. Politicians are changing the meaning of the term.'

Scalzone casts himself instead as someone who has become implicated by doing the hard philosophical work of consider-ing where the limits of legality lie in a democracy. 'I have thought about confronting and smashing the powers, and I do accept going past the point where legality ends and illegality begins. But I was a rather public person, a propagandist: there were others who made a much more radical and ideological choice, leaving their social life and their families to plunge into the clandestine life of the movement. Theirs is an extreme form of morality, it's a total personal sacrifice.'

The idea that a commitment to underground terrorism is 'an extreme form of morality' is an obvious challenge to intellectual tolerance and flexibility. At its heart, Scalzone's view of the world overturns accepted values, and in particular the idea that the state wields a broadly legitimate authority, that political representation can peacefully bring democratic change, that those who break the laws deserve the condemnation of the majority. On the issue of the legitimate use of violence, Scalzone's argument emerges amid the mist of political jargon: 'Clandestinity involves ... a process of slipping and sliding so that political opposition becomes a confrontation between a group, which is a sort of counter-state or counter-power, and the state and powers that be. People say that they are at war with society, with the state, with the constituted order. Well, given the disproportion of forces, one cannot remain at the mercy of repression!'

The 'disproportion of forces' means that the state has power while its internal opponent does not; a truism which by *reductio ad absurdum* implies that anarchy is a viable and arguable alternative to democratic order. Indeed, Scalzone rejects as naive the idea that non-violent political methods are a viable alternative to the use of force: 'If someone calls himself non-violent and he accepts the social system as it is, and thus the state monopoly on violence, that is a very gullible non-violence.' As is always the case in such hypotheses, it is possible to find legitimacy, somewhere, for the extreme view. Many people in liberal, democratic Western circles, would accept that in contemporary South Africa the 'disproportion of forces' between the oppressed majority – throwing stones when provoked to the most extreme anger – and the élite minority – exercising constant repression with all the costly hardware and military tactics of a police state – justifies some form of 'resistance'. But Scalzone's argument is not about South Africa, but Italy, and the mostly free, mostly democratic, and largely tolerant states of the West, or the First World.

Scalzone's conversation is almost impossible to edit without fears that one may be misrepresenting him. It therefore is advisable to quote his remarks at some length, though clarity does not come in direct proportion. On the moral issue of the use of violence for political ends, he observes 'You could argue that violence is legitimate when there is a consensus of the masses, but that's a dangerous criterion. I'm talking as a devil's advocate: the pogroms in the Slav countries were very popular, and there are a lot of totalitarian regimes that are sustained by popular support – so what does the game of consensus mean? It could well mean that you can justify violence against minorities, because there is a sort of modern savagery that passes in the name of consensus – you know lynchings were very democratic, very popular, so there's a paradox. Is that a criterion of legitimacy? I would say not.'

Scalzone accepts the disapproval of violence from the victim's point of view: 'Obviously on an ethical plane if one speaks of life and death, from the point of view above all of the people who become the objects of a violent action, well violence is never justified.' But Scalzone's central point about violence seems to be the playground concept that 'You started it'.

'One cannot pretend to forget first of all that violence exists, everywhere in the world, enormous systematic violence ... I am not referring to the hidden violence, which exists in the profits of production, violence which is crystallised in all our society, in all our wealth, in all our assets; it's a fact that there are billions and billions of drops of human blood in all our current life, because there have been centuries of human exploitation, of domination and oppression ... The history of human society is a history of incredible human violence, enormous violence, in famines, in the fact that people go on hunger strikes, in the fact that people are exploited, etc. ... I am saying that obvious violence, in the sense of killing people, is everywhere in broad daylight, practised by states, often monopolistic regimes. It is as if one was discussing war – okay, war exists, but there's no world war, there's no nuclear war, there's no war in the First World, none in Europe ... but war exists everywhere. So it is a bit bizarre that the current dominant ideology rediscovers all these dramatic problems of violence, only when it is a question of terrorism. 'The question of violence is always ruled by concepts of realpolitik, that is, when it is a matter of violence exercised by states or by the agents of states or by various groups sustained by one state or another. So if French secret agents provoke a death on the *Rainbow Warrior,* people talk about the whole thing, they talk about the lies, and the cover-up, everything except the death. The ethical problem of violence is only posed when the violence is exercised in one way or another by people without power.'

Scalzone's argument, reduced to its essence, is that the essential character of terrorist violence – that it is wielded by the illegitimate, unauthorised, and probably unrepresentative minority – is irrelevant. He argues that in a world of violence, the rules and distinctions between legitimacy and illegitimacy are false and discredited. The horror that state leaders and their citizens feel seem to him to be a hypocrisy which only serves to consolidate the injustice and repression which already characterise 'the State'.

In keeping with his abstract and highly philosophical interpretation of the nature of terrorism, Scalzone discusses the decision of the individual terrorist, or the group, to go underground as a matter of perceived political signs, rather than mere tactics. He argues that 'clandestinity in itself is a technique at first, though obviously a technique with symbolic content also – it's like the Spanish conquistadors burning their boats so that they could never retreat in future. Clandestinity is a very ideological, principled choice. It certainly makes it more effective to launch attacks, and to even up the disproportion of forces between state violence and a small opposition force. So it has a military effectiveness, but it is limited in political terms.'

One of the many euphemisms for terrorism in Italy – of the Red Brigades, *Prima Linea* and others – is 'social transformation'. Scalzone believes that a campaign of social transformation inevitably involves 'a minimum of defensive violence, to defend the offensive'. But he claims that the *raison d'être* of the clandestine armed group is in fact the maximum of violence possible. In his view, the invariable violence of the clandestine group means that 'they are condemned to a single hypothesis, and to go on repeating it ... clandestinity carries the risk of becoming omnivorous'. He further argues that 'the group that is dominated by militant action and preparations for it may be more effective in the short term, but in the long term will be easier to eliminate. The more linked they are to normal life, the longer they will be able to resist in the long term.'

Scalzone takes a politically pessimistic view: that terrorism gave the state in Italy and elsewhere the opportunity to consolidate its power at the expense of channels for dissent. He observes, *'Ex post facto* one can say that terrorism has produced the raw materials that governments and state institutions have used to build up and legitimise the "State of Emergency" concept. That's indisputable, in my view. National constitutions have been transformed in the process.'

Oddly enough, for someone who sees terrorism as a misnomer for mass movements of social transformation, Oreste Scalzone believes the effects of media coverage of terrorism to be counter-productive, in the sense that they offer the state grounds for justifying suspension of civil liberties, and the introduction of special laws and extra powers (of repression). 'One wants a free press which can report anything that happens,' he says. 'But when an incident is spectacularised by the media there is a boomerang effect, a contagion in society. The problem of Action Directe in France is real, evidently a murder is a tragic and horrible thing in itself, in human and moral terms; but statistically Action Directe is absolutely nothing, and if you create a hyper-problem out of it, and create this type of psychosis about the problem, you create a trap for the people who create the myth, and for society.'

Equally, in the case of firm threats by government ministers to eliminate and quash terrorist activity, Scalzone perceives an irony: 'The good sense of the man in the street tells us that a

threat merely encourages. One of my colleagues wrote in
Metropoli [an Autonomist review] that terrorism can never
win, but it can never be eliminated. The state has to examine
the roots and the reasons for it. States' threats examine the
consequences instead of the cause. Even the most fragile,
fantastic, ephemeral terrorism is a kind of a virus, it can't be
eliminated in societies which have the dynamics of ours. One
might say that it can be eliminated as a major problem, as is the
case in Italy, but as an endemic possibility which emerges
sporadically, I think it's completely false to say "We will
eliminate it, sterilise society of this sickness!" It's just as useful
as saying in our present society "We will eliminate prosti-
tution!" The result produced is always different.'

Professor Scalzone, credited by a number of prosecuting
magistrates in Italy with having planned and originated
substantial terrorist campaigns, still lives freely in Paris,
revising his radical political philosophy and reflecting on the
highly disruptive period of social transformation which gave
Italy the worst experience of political terrorism in any of the
Western democracies. He employs a biological analogy to
explain the correct or desirable relationship that a terrorist
organisation needs to develop with the social fabric, for the
greatest efficacy of its activity:

'One can make a rather rough comparison. In biology
there's an elementary distinction between bacteria and
viruses. Bacteria are relatively large organisms, with independent metabolisms, while viruses are much smaller, more
elementary organisms, which have no independent metabolisms but are symbiotic with the nucleus of the cells. So antibiotics can kill bacteria ... but are not capable of killing
viruses because they are symbiotic with the cell. The error of
clandestine armed organisations is to try to become bacteria –
large and independent – but when you succeed in becoming
bacteria, they research the antibiotics to kill you. If you
remain a virus, that is to say something which is very
connected to the cell, and the organism in itself, it's not
possible to eliminate you just like that.'

In the end, Scalzone's leftist credentials seem outweighed by his anarchist sentiments; he sums up his view of violence in these terms: 'The conjunction that seems to me to be the most horrible is the conjunction of power and violence.' His political position is anti-state, but only in a provisional sense: for the moment that the enemy state structure is replaced by another, the former opponents come-to-power become the new, formal, inimical state. Thus, Scalzone described his attitude as an example to the armed struggle of Basque nationalists, and hence to the whole idea of armed struggle and its ultimate results:

'I am on the side of the Basques for the fact that they are anti-state. But there is always a question mark ... are they in their turn going to reconstruct a state form? That's a perverse mechanism that one has seen played out in every known revolution. Obviously today the struggles of a local charac-ter – asymmetric to the national state – give some guarantee they won't end up in another state form, but the thing which intrigues me now is to understand that outside the anarchist mythology of the nineteenth century, and generic Utopian-ism, what can be the path of the movement which will not end in the re-formation of a state, a leadership group? Until one has overcome this problem – and one doesn't know if it will ever be resolved – it's okay to have all the forms of revolt, struggle, resistance, offensives, but I dread the victories. The most terrible thing that I find sadly in all revolutionary experiences, is that victories, that is what are called revo-lutionary victories, aren't much better than defeats. Defeats are not better, but I tend to prefer heresy to orthodoxy ...'

In his abstract argument, jargon and heresy, and in his absent-minded professorial air, in the academic confusion of his Paris apartment, and in his physical slightness, Oreste Scalzone strikes an unlikely figure as a major convicted terrorist. Yet the convictions stand against him, as they do against several dozen Italian radicals who have taken refuge in the political principles of France. Another such refugee is Lanfranco Pace, who emerged in much the same political tradition as Scalzone, but is a physically imposing, direct and rather humorous man, now earning his living as an economic journalist – having taught the subject at the University of Rome.

Pace was distinguished by being extradited from France to Italy to face charges of involvement in the kidnap and murder of Italian Prime Minister Aldo Moro – the spectacular height of drama and challenge that the Rome column of the Red Brigades posed to the Italian state in the 1970s. As Pace was acquitted on the charges for which he had been extradited, he had the right to choose whether to stay in Italy to face the remaining charges against him – forty-two counts of complicity in all Red Brigade activities in Rome, including murders between 1976 and 1978, organising armed bands, and insurrection against the state. Or he could choose to return to his exile in France: as Scalzone describes it, 'Pace was physically in Italy but formally in France.' Perhaps unsurprisingly, Pace chose France, and although he was technically limited to forty-five days before he returned there, it was more than a year before the Italian government gave him his passport, enabling him to leave the country.

Pace was among the leaders of an extraparliamentary leftist organisation called *Potere Operaia* (Workers' Power) which dissolved itself in 1973 under internal stresses and strains, one of which was the issue of whether to employ violence to achieve its goals. According to Pace, 'The illegality being considered was banal – comparable to the street demonstrations against Springer in Berlin, but not to the assassination of Schleyer.' Pace maintains that PotOp were intellectuals, while it was the Red Brigades who were the 'soldiers'. After the dissolution of PotOp, he admits to having spent about four months on the fringes of the Red Brigades in Rome – more through personal friendship with one of the leaders than direct militancy. 'The Red Brigades don't like to theorise and discuss,' he says, 'they want to act. If you live in clandestinity in a dictatorial regime, that's one thing: in a democracy it's different. You become cut off from reality. Your world revolves around the concrete, matters of survival, your cars, and the police. There was one person in the Red Brigades who had the sole job of moving cars around for security. You

111

formalise all daily life to the war – it's a form of regression.'

In his reflections on Italian political violence, Lanfranco Pace is detached and neutral, talking with an objectivity which belies the assumed drama of the idea of terrorism. Pace incidentally confirms a number of Professor Ferracuti's conclusions about the 'biography of terrorism': 'I didn't accept that the dissolution of PotOp meant returning to the Italian Communist Party and regular party activity. I remained on the margins, though at that point I did eighteen months of National Service.' Pace is rare in that he does not seek to excuse all forms of violence committed in the name of extraparliamentary politics: 'There were social struggles, but also, for example in 1977, there was hooliganism. In Italy there were a lot of bad revolutionaries, because in Italy there are a lot of bad reformists. The violence was being committed by people between twenty and thirty years old, who saw there were a lot of new things knocking at the door – in the schools and universities, on minimum wage reform, on homelessness. It was the decay of the system which brought the violence upon itself. What the State has to do is to pay attention to certain fundamental human rights, and see the energy of terror before it arrives, and prevent it. A repressive system and violence are in relationship.'

Pace, unlike Scalzone, does not attempt to conceal the concrete nature of his involvement with a fog of political justification and obfuscation. He speaks quite concretely of the psychological component in terrorist violence, from firsthand observation: 'The terrorists have a negative relationship to authority. Often they had bad relationships with their fathers, and no restraining influence – so they really believed they could win.' Pace further confirms the view of all the psychological studies, that terrorists in tightly knit and clandestine groups experience no challenge or dissent to confront their world-view: 'In clandestinity, they live without authority, and they come to believe it doesn't exist – although it does exist. These are people who have made a decision of which they did not know the meaning.'

Pace advances the psychological argument one step further,

to the point of capitulation by the terrorists, once caught; he suggests that the awful realisation that authority does exist, forced upon the captured terrorist, causes a complete collapse of the theory of terrorism. As he describes it, 'They could change within twenty-four hours when confronted with a recognisable authority – or a father figure – like a police officer or a judge. It's a psychological break, from total power to annihilation.'

In addition to his impeccable extreme-left credentials, Lanfranco Pace became, he claims, inadvertently involved on the fringes of the kidnap and murder of Italian Prime Minister Aldo Moro – but only, he insists, in the role of an intermediary. 'The Socialist Party contacted me and another person to get some idea of the thinking of the Red Brigades, and to see if we could negotiate, during the Moro affair. We couldn't do much more than speculate. However, a communist magistrate made that initiative the basis of accusation of my complicity in the Moro case.'

The received wisdom about the purpose of kidnapping Aldo Moro is that it was to prevent 'the Historic Compromise' – Aldo Moro's decision to bring the Italian Communist Party into coalition government for the first time. The extreme left was worried that its support would wane, and support for the newly-legitimate communists would grow; and thus Moro, who was very specifically the architect of 'the Compromise' became the terrorists' target. His five bodyguards were shot dead in an ambush that became known as the Via Fani Massacre, and he was abducted and held prisoner for a month before being shot in the head and dumped, with pointed irony, in a narrow street half-way between the offices of his own Christian Democratic Party and the Communist Party.

The Red Brigades' flair for political theatre was apparent, but according to Pace their political purpose was not as complicated as the mythology suggests; he argues that for the Red Brigades, 'war' was simple and hard. 'If you make war, you don't ask questions; that is for politics. War is a matter of two people – me (and those with me) and the enemy. Killing Moro was a challenge to the powers. The Red Brigades' leadership didn't care about the Historic Compromise. To kidnap and kill Moro was an act of simple power (i.e., in a separate arena from national parliamentary politics). Their target was known as SIM – *Stato Imperialista delle Multinazionale* [The Imperialist State of the Multinationals].'

Pace, reflecting on his political career, argues that revolution has been tried, tested, and found to fail in its confrontation with the existing powers. His perspective on the past and present is this: 'My lifetime has seen the decline of Communism in the West – in France, Spain, and Italy. But it has been an epoch when revolt has been more and more difficult, and one has touched the outer limits of democracy – like an elastic band that can't stretch any further. In Italy there were any number of committed people, in every walk of life, pushing at the limits inside the institutions of democracy. It's all disappeared. It doesn't function. Democracy is returning to authoritarianism and meritocracy. The non-violent extreme left still lives, but the symbols, imagery and messages of Communism have been discarded; and it has changed its flag from Red to Green.'

Ideological, revolutionary, 'Red' terrorism has been distinguished by its persistence; while neo-fascist, authoritarian, 'Black' terrorism is notable for its randomness. Despite Lanfranco Pace's regretful sense that 'revolt ... doesn't function', it is the strength of the political credo and ideology that has sustained leftist terrorism in Italy for so long – and which gives reason for constant fears that the Red Brigades or others are 'regrouping' for new campaigns. Professor Franco Ferracuti, in studying the 'Reds' and 'Blacks', observes that one of the most striking differences is the existence of 'a rather structured ideology...something that exists in the literature of the left'.

The favoured authors of 'Red' terrorists are 'predictable and consistent', he says: Hegel, Heidegger, Marcuse and Toni Negri (another former leader of the Italian Autonomia movement, whose career from university campus to terrorist trial, to jail, to Member of Parliament, to exile in Paris is one of the most colourful footnotes to the story of Italy's terrorist experience). Ferracuti suggests that 'there are no major writers for the right wing ... their shallowness is appalling. The only authors read with any degree of consistency are the Spaniards Ortega y Gasset and Evola – really the only ideologues of the right. Thereafter, the 'Blacks' were as likely to be readers of Tolkien's *Lord of the Rings* [which Ferracuti describes as 'celebrating an élite group, to whom all other beings are inferior'] as of Hitler's *Mein Kampf,* which celebrates the use of force.'

Ferracuti has argued that the utter certainty of ideological value is the motor that drives a terrorist to justification of morally repugnant acts. In the case of the Islamic fundamentalist terrorism of the Middle East, which causes more concern in the late 1980s than any other branch, the ideology takes the form of faith.

Since the overwhelming drama of the suicide bombings of the French and American Marine compounds in Beirut in 1983, a natural but excessive emphasis has been placed upon the Islamic theology of martyrdom. Scholars have attempted to pin down the precise rules which – it is alleged – establish that the martyr to Islam is guaranteed a place in Heaven, especially so if he takes out some of the enemies of Islam at the same time. This convenient analysis permits the West a racist view of Islamic fundamentalist feeling – attributing attacks on Western interests to eccentric, robed foreigners, thereby disallowing any sense of a political cause worth evaluation and toleration. Whatever the psychological motivation, however, the most relevant issue raised by the new Islamic terrorism is the fact of its apparent acceptability to the militant fundamentalist regime of Iran, which has significant outposts of influence in Lebanon. The Shi'ite branch of the Muslim faith regards foreign influence as automatically bad (just like those Europeans who view their countries as the tools of multinational corporations or of American military policy), so that the objectives of the terrorists correspond closely to the principles of their religious leaders.

Sheikh Muhammad Hussein Fadhlallah is a Lebanese Shi'ite leader whose career neatly encapsulates both aspects of the issue. While he is a senior mullah at a mosque in Bir Abed in Southern Beirut, he is also widely alleged to be the spiritual leader of *Hezbollah* (God's Own) – the most fanatical and extreme of the Shi'ite groups, apparently under the indirect control of Ayatollah Khomeini, and determined to spread the Islamic Revolution through Lebanon and beyond.

Fadhlallah's office and home is on the fifth floor of an apartment building in Bir Abed, a Shi'ite suburb which the civil war between the militias has reduced to smoke-blackened ruins. The remains of buildings are plastered with posters of Ayatollah Khomeini and of the Imam Moussa Sadr, the Lebanese Shi'ite cleric who disappeared on a visit to Libya in 1980. The nearby Green Line which divides Muslim West Beirut from Christian East Beirut (in much the same way that a net divides a tennis court, providing something to fire across) allows one to hear the occasional snipers' gunfire from relative safety. In the apartment there stands a steel strongroom door which would do justice to an arsenal, or a bank vault. In Arabic, a large scrawled notice instructs: 'Absolutely no entry – under any circumstances.'

The Sheikh, in brown robes and a black turban, gives no hint of passion, no anger, no violence in his speech or manner. But his remarks on the role of Islam and political violence suggest a relatively uncomplicated view on the validity of what those on the receiving end are bound to call terrorism. He explains the aims of Hezbollah: 'I work with the common people in Lebanon and in the larger Islamic world, to implement Islamic ideas in the social, political and economic areas; to raise the status of Moslems, and to liberate them from any foreign rule. But if we are challenged and have to go into battle, we will fight back.'

The issue of terrorism is automatically raised by such a determined threat: 'We don't see ourselves as terrorists, because we don't believe in terrorism,' says Fadhlallah. But he concedes the efficacy of terrorism for certain limited purposes: 'We don't believe that terror can achieve a general aim. Terror can achieve very specific aims, but not general goals such as changing a social structure.' And he employs the traditional tactics for evading any accusation of involvement in terrorism: 'We don't see resisting the occupier as a terrorist action. We must differentiate between violent terrorist actions to achieve small aims, and violence as one system among others which defends freedom in the war of liberation.

'We see ourselves as mujahideen who try to fight a Holy War for the people,' he continues. It should not be forgotten that Islamic 'Holy War' or 'Jihad' is the name of the organisation which has claimed a long series of terror attacks on American, Western European and Israeli targets, including the flurry of kidnaps and murders of Americans and other Westerners in Beirut, besides occasional attacks on American military interests in both Spain and Greece. Fadhlallah defines Islamic Jihad thus: 'The Islamic Jihad is a political action which sometimes becomes military in nature to protect the freedom of the weak elements among the Moslems, to protect their honour and their right to live with freedom and dignity. We don't differentiate between Islamic Jihad and any action against imperialistic plans in any country in the world.'

Indeed, despite their utterly different political settings, Fadhlallah shares with the urban terrorist groups of the West the same analysis of who is ultimately responsible for this 'imperialism': 'You will find the real terrorists in the United States,' he argues. 'You will find them in Israel and the other countries that are trying to interfere with our just cause ... The American Administration policy operates to control the Islamic world, in order to benefit from its natural resources, and in order to turn it into a market for its own goods, and try to prevent us from self-sufficiency in economic and non-economic areas.'

The American psychologist John Crayton argues that even in the foreign context of Islamic fundamentalist 'resistance', evidence exists of both the group dynamics and narcissistic damage that he finds relevant to terrorist experiences everywhere. In his paper 'Terrorism and the Psychology of the Self', he argues that ' with respect to the Iranian situation, for example, various sources of humiliation can be identified. The Shi'ites in Iran have traditionally been considered outsiders and

a disadvantaged group among the Moslem people as a whole
... in concrete ways ... disenfranchised by other and more
powerful sects ... It can be argued that the Shi'ite people have
developed a powerful chronic narcissistic rage in reaction to
their disadvantaged condition ... clearly indicated by noting
the Iranian reaction to [Khomeini's revolution] of nationalistic
pride and a feeling of power, in contrast to the previously held
self-image of chronic helplessness and shame.'

In terms of the concrete action, Crayton suggests that 'the
object of terrorism clearly is one of humiliation. The special
sense of outrage and terror evoked by acts of terrorism can best
be understood as arising from their assault on our sense of
"self", a concept closely related to our self-esteem ... The
takeover of the American Embassy in Teheran, a symbol of
the group-self of the United States, is a good illustration of the
way in which terrorism attempts to inflict narcissistic injury.
The Iranians occupied the Embassy, which presumably is the
inviolable territory of the United States.' Crayton further
makes a telling point about the reaction to such terrorist acts,
which holds true for many more instances than the Teheran
Embassy affair: 'The intensity of the affective response of
Americans to this action stems from the extent to which it is a
narcissistic blow to the self.' Anyone who was in the United
States during the 444 days of the hostage crisis will recall the
force of public reaction, which ranged from the sentimental –
yellow ribbons tied to trees – to the recklessly macho – 'Nuke
the Ayatollah!' America's domestic attitudes rivalled the
excess of the Ayatollah's, for whom America was 'The Great
Satan'.

Faith – whether religious or political – is all. To the individual
terrorist, or supporter of terrorism, a murder can be an
expression of the defence of freedom: a car-bomb which kills
civilians can be a blow struck in a war of liberation; a
kidnapping and murder can be a step towards justice. The
intensity of conviction that justifies one man's justice at any
price almost inevitably means that the freedoms and justice of
others will be ignored, or at worst trampled and destroyed.

118

The more acute and purposeful investigations into the psychology of terrorism, some of which have been presented and interpreted here, have as their objective the identification of the gap which lies between law-abiding radicals and law-rejecting terrorists. The essential difference might be described as the inability to see the dynamic relationship between 'my justice' and 'your freedom', to understand that liberty and justice depends on a network of interconnecting compromises. The terrorists reject compromise and set about their purposes with the traditional directness of the fanatic. Their wiser opponents do not play them at their own game, but seek to comprehend the original problem, gain insight into the mentality, and draw the fanatic back into the network of often unsatisfactory, but humane compromise.

4 STATE-SPONSORED TERRORISM

Those who have power, and those who do not, are natural opponents: and circumstances can easily provoke them into actual conflict. States and terrorists are thus natural enemies, once rational political process has degenerated and only violence seems to have a voice. While states and the powerful – both elected leaders and appointed instruments, like military and police services – are self-evidently the targets of terrorism, there has been an increasing tendency during the 1980s to see the hand of states behind the terrorists as well. America in particular, during the years of the Reagan Administration, has identified 'state-sponsored terrorism' as the most substantial new threat in the spectrum of terrorist dangers – and most of the Western allies have joined in the chorus of disapproval.

In this chorus, however, the important questions to ask about state-sponsored terrorism have been largely overlooked. Firstly, is state-sponsorship increasing the overall incidence of terrorism? Are states *creating* new terrorists, or merely giving assistance and support to those who would inevitably find some outlet for their violent protests anyway? Is 'state-sponsored terrorism' merely a new name for an existing problem? And is the accusation fairly made against only a handful of renegade states, or are the accusers equally ready, given the right provocation or political 'justification', to act in ways which others will see as terrorism?

The methods of terrorism commend themselves to some states for the very reasons that states find such great difficulties in combating terrorism. It requires only a handful of people to make an impact; it costs little; it requires a minimum of equipment or training; and above all it is deniable – provided links between the state and the terrorists are kept to a minimum. Terrorism provides a third alternative to diplomacy and outright hostility, in particular when a state sees fit to interfere in the affairs of another – via the destabilising influence of that state's own terrorist enemies.

Operations of this kind have been well defined by the former Israeli Ambassador to El Salvador and Mexico, and former Commissioner General of the Israel State Police and Border Guard, Shaul Rosolio. His career gives him ample experience on which to base the assertion that 'once conventional war is impossible, futile, or inconvenient, state-sponsored terrorism is used instead as a proxy war, without the inconveniences of declared hostilities. The state can maintain diplomatic relations, embassies, trade and overall relations while completely disregarding the conventions and agreements pertaining to this kind of situation ... As long as countries fostering terrorism can enjoy the luxury of holding both sides of the stick, this kind of terrorism will not only continue, but increase.'

Which, then are the states that sponsor terrorism? For many people in Washington, in government and near to it, it is axiomatic that international terrorism is more or less the product of a Soviet conspiracy. In the first days of the Reagan Administration in January 1981, General Alexander Haig, the incoming Secretary of State, made the accusation: 'Moscow continues to support terrorism and war by proxy with a conscious policy – programs, if you will, which foster, support, and expand international terrorism ... When you get to the bottom line, it is the Soviet Union which bears a major responsibility for the proliferation and haemorrhaging of international terrorism as we've come to know it.'

The State Department quickly issued chapter and verse for the general accusation, citing 'Financial support, training, and arms given to such groups as the PLO: surrogate use of Cubans and Libyans to assist terrorist organizations;

Moscow's propaganda effort aimed at energizing national liberation movements; propaganda supportive of the hostage-taking of Americans in Iran; and general Soviet advocacy of armed struggle as a solution to regional problems, such as in El Salvador and Namibia, promoting the use of terrorism and impeding the peaceful resolution of conflicts.'

It does not require a very fierce sceptic to take the view that as a detailed accusation on *terrorism* – as opposed to generalised ideological conflict – the statement demonstrates an acute lack of specific evidence. Indeed, there is little. Hearsay and extrapolation – as is the case with every general argument about terrorism – overshadow the minimal amount of concrete detail which could be offered in court. But this is puzzling, because in the vast majority of cases where terrorists are arrested by police or security forces, they are shown to be remarkably careless about covering their tracks. They are repeatedly captured in physical possession of large sums of cash, maps with clearly marked targets, manifestos and communiqués claiming their attacks, weapons and ammunition. Yet only very rarely – and usually ambiguously – has any clue emerged to connect European terrorists, for example, to any Soviet or East European source.

The one major exception is weaponry. Many terrorists throughout the world are found in possession of the automatic-fire Kalashnikov rifle, made either in the Soviet Union or manufactured under licence in the Warsaw Pact countries. However, American weapons are almost certainly as well represented in terrorist arsenals as Soviet weapons – for example in Ireland, where confiscated weapons represent a comprehensive history of the American obsession for the right to carry arms – yet the suggestion is not made that the USA thus foments terrorism by making weapons available.

The absence of very concrete evidence for the Soviet connection to terrorists can sustain two counter-balanced interpretations: the sceptical theory and the super-conspiracy theory. The former embraces the view that, evidence notwithstanding, it is perfectly legitimate to suppose that the Soviet Union is not blameless in the matter of terrorism, that its political objectives can be enhanced by the actions of some terrorists, and that its agencies or surrogates will give some occasional assistance, but that an integrated global plot is neither feasible nor useful. The latter view is that the absence of evidence simply proves how cleverly and deceptively the conspiracy is organised – and that mugs and dupes who claim intelligent scepticism are the unconscious partners in the plot.

For the dogmatist, the conspiracy theory is bound to be a self-fulfilling prophecy. Evidence of this is contained in a book published in 1984, entitled *Terrorism: the Soviet Connection* by Ray S. Cline and Yonah Alexander, free copies of which the US State Department was sending out in June 1985 in response to general requests for information on the subject of international terrorism. (The authors' affiliations are revealing. Dr Cline, a former Deputy Director of the CIA, is Professor of International Relations at Georgetown University and Director of the World Power Studies Program at the University's Center for Strategic and International Studies. Professor Alexander is Director of the Institute for Studies in International Terrorism at the State University of New York, as well as being a member of the senior research staff at the Georgetown Center.)

The book's theme – the Soviet connection – depends on an unambiguous acceptance of the PLO as 'terrorists' and nothing more. Eighty pages of text are followed by almost sixty pages of translated 'PLO Documents, Found in Lebanon, June 1982': which means that they are documents the Israeli intelligence services saw fit to release from their enormous haul in the aftermath of the invasion of Lebanon and the assault on Beirut.

The PLO documents prove what is publicly acknowledged: that the PLO and the Soviet Union have a warm and established formal relationship, extending to military training both in the Soviet Union and East Germany. After Beirut, the PLO's fighters withdrew to a variety of Arab states, including the Soviet client-state of North Yemen. However, the documents offer no evidence whatever that the Soviet Union specifically approves terrorist campaigns. Indeed, a close reading of 'Document 1: Protocol of Talks Between PLO and Soviet Delegations in Moscow', offers some surprises. On 13 November 1979, Soviet Foreign Minister Gromyko was saying to PLO Chairman Arafat and his colleagues:

> Here I wish to ask you a question: Are you considering certain tactical concessions in return for getting recognition from the hostile camp (Israel)? Are you considering recognising Israel's right to exist as an independent sovereign state? I remember my conversation with Yigal Allon, who told me: "How can we (Israel) talk with the PLO when they do not recognise Israel's right to exist as an independent state, and when the PLO does not even recognise the UN resolutions (concerning the establishment of the state of Israel)?" He also told me that if the PLO recognised Israel and the UN resolutions, the situation would be different, and in that case "We (Israel) would have dealt with it in a different manner".

These are the words of a diplomat, and it is no exaggeration to say that they could equally have been spoken by the representative of almost any government with which the PLO has either open or secret contacts. In the case of Britain, the PLO's representative does not have diplomatic standing, and thus only holds talks with senior civil servants and junior ministers in the Foreign Office; in the case of the United States, political sensitivities mean that contacts are held in secret between special ambassadorial envoys or Deputy Secretaries of State and PLO officials on friendly Arab territory. But the conversations differ little from what Comrade Gromyko was diplomatically setting out.

The Soviet Union's open support for the PLO is an investment against the day when an independent State of Palestine emerges in the Middle East, grateful to the Soviet Union for support, and willing to maintain an alliance which would effectively diminish the US–Israeli axis (which operates in much the same way). Cline and Alexander's thesis, however, is not merely that the PLO 'helps weaken and restrict US ("imperialist") influence in the Mideast', but that it performs 'in the capacity of a Soviet-manipulated external base and transmission belt for the export of revolutionary violence'. In fact, since the expulsion of the PLO from Beirut, and despite its gradual return, its capacity to do more than fight its own battles – with a clear tendency to revert to the terrorism with which it began twenty years earlier – has largely evaporated. But throughout the 1970s, Palestinian training camps, whose chief purpose was the military training of Palestinians as a propaganda exercise within the Arab world, were rumoured to be offering training to members of terrorist groups from Europe, Latin America, and Asia.

One document of those Cline and Alexander reproduce offers convincing evidence to this effect: 'Document 16: the "European Base" at Shatila, 1981.' (A year later, the Palestinian refugee camps Shatila and Sabra, in the southern suburbs of West Beirut, became internationally notorious as the scene of Phalangist mass-murder, in turn at least partially the responsibility of senior Israeli military commanders.) The document reads:

1. The 'European Base' is located in the Shatila Refugee camp (Beirut). The commander of the base is Aref Khateb, his codenames are 'Abu El Abed' and 'Masara El Kahal'. His deputy is Nakib (Captain) Hassan Maz'al.
2. The base serves as a place of instruction and training for various terrorist groups such as the 'Red Berets' [probably the Red Brigades], 'Baader Meinhof', 'Turkish Liberation Army', Indians, Pakistanis and Irishmen.
3. The duration of a course is 45 days during which the terrorists study demolition materials, small arms operation, karate and military tactics.
4. The training week was from Monday to Saturday afternoon.

Paragraph 5, however, reveals that this is not a captured document, but the notes of a statement given by a 'captured terrorist', presumably interrogated by Israeli intelligence officials. As a PLO document it is obviously inauthentic, if only because of the explicit use of the word 'terrorist' – unknown in the circles of all genuine terrorists. But this is the only concrete piece of evidence in the whole Cline/Alexander book of the

'Soviet Connection' to terrorism – though it is not the only evidence of a 'Soviet Connection' to the PLO. The latter, however, is not a secret, any more than the 'British Connection', the 'Italian Connection' or the 'Chinese Connection'.

For conspiracy theorists, of course, the Soviet plot does not stop at support for the PLO: the Soviet Constitution declares that all 'national liberation movements' will be supported as a matter of course, both in political and concrete terms. The first hand evidence of Soviet intelligence defectors in this regard is of value to both sceptics and conspiracy theorists: on the one hand, there is testimony that the Soviet Union won't touch terrorists because they don't behave in ways that the world's most rigid bureaucracy can understand and control; while on the other hand there are accounts which claim that deniability is guaranteed by arm's length, secondhand contacts which can never be traced back.

According to a former senior officer of the GRU (Soviet Military Intelligence), terrorism in the West is approved of, given both ideological and practical encouragement, and specifically assisted by military training – not of terrorists themselves, but of intermediary or surrogate groups who deal with the terrorists in turn. This is his eyewitness account:

> Ideological sympathy with the Soviet Union is unnecessary: anyone who helps to destabilise the West is our friend: no-one is excluded, even if they are anti-Russian or anti-Soviet. There are no limits on policy or ideological grounds: they are all useful. An Irishman who is anti-British, an Arab who is anti-Jewish, or a Jew who is anti-Arab. The Québécois wanted to split Canada – they were bourgeois capitalists who hated Russia ... but we liked them.
>
> The decision to make support for national liberation movements more active, in particular to give military training to Palestinians, seems to date from 1968. Such a decision would have to be taken absolutely at the top – that's how the power structure works.
>
> The Palestinians had their training in formal Red Army facilities. Members of Angolan, Mozambican and Cuban forces had training in the faculty of my military school which

later became a full training school for resistance movements. The liberation movement people had far tougher conditions and exercises than us: they had to crawl under barbed wire while officers fired live ammunition just above their heads; they had to jump through smoking firepits, and jump off twenty-metre towers into a swimming pool; they trained in hand-to-hand fighting, and learned to throw sharpened spades at a target. They had survival exercises where they had to kill and eat rabbits – generally living in an atmosphere of stress and violence so they would be ready to use violence themselves.

They also received some specific training for other useful skills: one was bomb-making. They were taught to produce home-made explosives, and as a result they always used large amounts of explosive, producing far bigger explosions than in our own training. They were also shown how to use basic radio equipment.

The Soviet Union exerts very little influence on how those groups fight. You have to fight for yourself, for your land and your cause. But the Soviet Union blows the spark into the fire – or puts the germ of a disease into the body of the enemy. But when we train them, we also infiltrate, by recruiting members of a movement to work for us – to find out everything they are going to do. In the Tenth Chief Directorate there's a special department which controls liberation movements.

For the Soviet Union, the Red Army Faction in West Germany was a liberation movement: so are the Red Brigades, the IRA, the Japanese Red Army, and so on. But the Soviet Union doesn't have contact with them – but training given by the PLO to others made no sense for the Palestinians. It was done at the behest of the Soviet Union. If I give you millions of dollars' worth of weapons, or cash, I have a small right to expect you to help me. I won't tell you where to place the next bomb, but I do expect to have a little influence on your spheres of action. And if someone later arrests an Irishman, he can honestly say that he has never trained in the Soviet Union – but he has been trained at the wish of the Soviet Union. And he still believes he is fighting for himself.

Supplying finance and arms to national liberation movements is done through diplomats and diplomatic bags, front companies and dead-letter-boxes. I have personally buried weapons and sums of money while on family picnics and walks in the country. We used DLBs all the time – people later tune to

Radio Moscow, to hear a coded message to make a pick-up. It's a cell structure: each person has his own part, but no-one knows the place and the sum and the purpose – the whole story.

This is powerful evidence for the conspiracy-theorists: most importantly in its revelation that the USSR extracts, as a price for training the PLO, the commitment of the PLO to train in turn other terrorist groups. It is this sinister *quid pro quo* which distinguishes Soviet behaviour, in the eyes of ideological opponents, from that of all the other nations for which military training and hardware are an important foreign-currency earner. The United States, Israel, and Britain all sell military equipment and expertise to countries which may or may not pass muster on grounds of moral conscience – but there is little that anyone can do to ensure that the customer does not in turn train other unsavoury outfits to commit acts of terrorism, possibly against the original source of the expertise.

A second defector, this time from the KGB, confirms a number of the assumptions about attitude, but is more sceptical about the Soviet Union's support for terrorism in the West: 'National liberation movements don't have to be communists: the Soviet view is "Let them take power first, then they can get into line with the ideology." The Soviet Union doesn't make any distinctions about the methods used – it rejects Western "bourgeois morality". Any method used to bring Marxism-Leninism is justified, with no moral reservations whatsoever. The ends justify the means.

'Groups like the Red Brigades and Japanese Red Army are not accepted by the Soviet Union as national liberation movements. They are called "terrorists" by official Soviet propaganda. The Soviet Union would never have had contacts with, for example, the Red Army Faction. They are just terrorists. They might recruit one of their members just to know what's going on, what their plans are, and if they are a real threat to their region. But they can still authorise the Palestinians to deal with them.

'There is a difference between liberation movements and terrorists: there is the Salvadorean Liberation Movement which is advancing Soviet state policy: in Nicaragua it is the other way round – it is American terrorists fighting with a legitimate government. What is the difference? But the Soviet Union would not openly use groups like Baader-Meinhof or the Japanese Red Army. They don't want to get caught in open contact with them because officially they condemn them.'

A third account, again from within the KGB, is clear about the lack of evidence: 'If you say the Soviet Union supports small terrorist groups you can't prove it. It is so cleverly done, you won't see any connections. There may be an invisible relationship – there could be. But no direct contact. You can speculate endlessly but there is no proof. It could be that the Soviet Union orchestrates Palestinian training for terrorists, but I doubt that it would be expressed straightforwardly. There are no documents, no signatures, nothing on paper. They are not that stupid. The Palestinians provide a very good cover for the Soviet Union to be involved in training other groups. But they can't be seen: no one can prove anything about it.'

Despite the testimony of defectors, relentless investigations by Capitol Hill Congressional and Senate Committees and Sub-Committees on Foreign Relations, Defence, Intelligence and Justice; despite a political climate offering substantial encouragement to the anti-Soviet point of view; and despite flurries of leaks from intelligence services providing the best detail available – despite all efforts, the real evidence that the Soviet Union employs a concrete overall strategy to sow terrorism throughout the world is still lacking, and the picture remains ambiguous. The absolute sceptic is ignoring realities, but the conspiracy-theorist is protesting too much: the plausible reality is that the Soviet Union has a pragmatic policy which allows events to run their course, with a little (deniable) help at arm's length when possible.

Perhaps the last word should lie with one of the defectors, who states the case most clearly by putting it into negative

terms: 'If the Soviet Union didn't like the training of secondary groups, it would be stopped immediately. There's no
doubt at all.'

It is America's absolute conviction in the moral superiority of
its own political system that permits the US government to
stand in judgement on the activities of those nations which it
declares are responsible for 'state-sponsored terrorism'. In his
celebrated 'loony-tunes' speech before the American Bar
Association in July 1985, President Reagan updated the list
of 'terrorist nations' as defined by the USA. Iran, Libya,
North Korea, Cuba and Nicaragua were identified as 'a new
international version of "Murder, Incorporated" . . . united by
one simple, criminal phenomenon – their fanatical hatred of
the United States, our people, our way of life, our international stature.'

The accusations are far from being without foundation, and
no one would seriously question the President's assertion that
'in 1983 alone, the CIA either confirmed or found strong
evidence of Iranian involvement in 57 terrorist attacks' – or
that 'we have strong evidence which links Libyan agents or
surrogates to at least 25 incidents last year [1984]'. But the
problem with the public blacklist is twofold: firstly, there
simply is not enough concrete evidence to support precise
casebook proofs of direct state responsibility for acts of
properly defined terrorism; secondly, the names on the blacklist can change according to political circumstances. Thus the
White House and the State Department stretch the definitions
– to include the kind of international political activity by
America's enemies which it justifies for itself; and to use the
public condemnation as a threat, or the lack of condemnation
as an encouragement, thereby undermining the list's objectivity.

Until the TWA hijacking in June 1985, for instance, Syria
had sufficiently irritated Washington with its support for a
variety of terrorist groups and factions, that it was among the
nations listed as 'terrorist states' in an earlier version. One of
the key elements in the deal which finally released the thirty-

seven American hostages, however, was the pressure Syria was able to bring to bear on her Lebanese friends; as Reagan conceded in his Presidential broadcast, announcing the release of the hostages, 'Syria has had a central responsibility'. The first consequence of this successful intervention was that Syria was dropped from the list of 'terrorist states', replaced there by Nicaragua, the latest *bête noire* of the Reagan Administration.

A former Assistant Secretary of State in the Carter Administration simply describes the 'terrorist nations' list as 'a bit of a fraud', citing the alterations on political grounds as a crucial weakness. Far more seriously, former President Carter himself broke with precedent to differ publicly with President Reagan's assertions. In response to his successor's claim that 'The growth in terrorism in recent years ... is part of a pattern, the work of a confederation of terrorist states', Jimmy Carter said that he disagreed with the 'basic premises of an international conspiracy, of collusion in terrorism between nations and whole peoples.'

However, in its assertion that Libya is a 'terrorist nation', the United States is on safe ground. The erratic and often flatly contradictory statements of Colonel Gadaffi, the vocal support specifically for 'terrorism' (the only contemporary example of the word being used without a critical implication, indeed with belligerent pride), and the domestic state security organs which organise a tight and effective political repression; these things all promote public acceptance of the proposition.

The Libyan example – not least because of the extremity of American irritation it evokes – most clearly illustrates the types of 'state-sponsored terrorism' which have developed in the 1980s. Firstly, there is Libyan state support for the Palestinian cause – something it shares with most other Arab states to a greater or lesser degree, though Libya tends to favour the least conciliatory factions of Palestinian opinion. It is in this context that Gadaffi provokes American Wrath by publicly offering training and logistical support 'in terrorist and suicide missions' for Palestinian national goals. He states, for example, that he will 'allocate trainers to train them and place at their disposal all the necessary weapons to carry out these missions'. In April 1985 Gadaffi claimed he had established a 'Pan-Arab Command for Leading the Arab Revolutionary Forces' to carry out acts of violence against the United States and other Western countries, and against moderate Arab regimes. Speaking at the conclusion of the Command's first meeting in Tripoli, Gadaffi praised the suicide attacks on American interests in the Middle East, and asserted: 'We want every one of us to say – "I have decided to die just to spite America". If we could bring this nation to the point where it possesses this determination it will definitely win.' The response of the State Department was blunt: 'The world cannot tolerate the lawlessness and terrorism which Gadaffi so openly advocates. He should know this and be aware that Libya will be held accountable for its actions.'

The second area of Libyan sponsorship of terrorism is seen in an extension of 'state terror' – the persecution of domestic political opponents of every kind, outside the borders of the country and on other nations' sovereign territory. Not only opponents, but also Libyans who have simply left the country to live elsewhere, are regularly threatened that they must return to Libya to accept Gadaffi's 'Green Revolution', or face dire consequences. Gadaffi's warnings are regularly broadcast by the Voice of Libya radio station, and more widely dispersed by British, American and other monitoring services. Those 'stray dogs' who decline to return to Libya by now know that they face the prospect of summary execution, even in the assumed safety of a London square or a private home in Colorado.

Thirdly, and lastly, there is the far less clear area of Libya's secret contacts with terrorists – either revolutionary-political, or regional and nationalistic, groups – who have nothing obviously to do with the internal or external political interests of Libya. It has been widely suggested that Libya has assisted the IRA with cash and weapons, that Libya has helped with the training of Red Army Faction and Red Brigades members, provided a refuge for the rump of the (pro-PFLP) Japanese Red Army - or at least its erstwhile leader Fusako Shigenobu - and organised terrorist hit squads ready to spring into action in the United States when activated. As National Security Adviser Robert McFarlane said of Libyan activities in April 1985, 'until we can stop the training by Libya of other terrorists, the graduates of whose camps are spread from the Philippines to Ireland, Libya remains a menace and a risk to us, as well as our friends.'

However, when asked to substantiate the accusation of state-sponsorship, the State Department does not provide detailed factual evidence, but a document which accurately reports the 'stray dogs' campaign of murder and assassination, and otherwise concentrates on Libyan domestic human rights violations. There has only been one 'stray dogs' assassination in the United States, out of a total of around thirty-five of which the vast majority have taken place in Western Europe. The unfortunate individual was Fisal Abulaze Zagalli, a prominent dissident, who was shot dead at his home in Fort Collins, Colorado, on 14 August 1981. There have, however, been indications of at least two further plots: the first, in May 1984 was described by FBI Assistant Director 'Buck' Revell as 'an example of intelligence analysis leading directly to prosecution'. Revell reported that 'two Libyan nationals were in the United States attempting to purchase weapons . . . Against the backdrop of previous intelligence indicating the likelihood of Libyan nations [sic] targeting anti-Gadaffi dissidents in the United States . . . an undercover Agent was introduced into the situation. He developed information that the Libyans wanted illegal silenced weapons and intended, indeed, to carry out retribution against an opponent.'

A similar incident arose just a year later when Farhat Teebar, a Libyan diplomat attached to the United Nations in New York, was expelled by the US government. On 4 June 1985, the State Department reported that Teebar was ordered to leave because 'he has been identified as being involved in a Libyan-directed plot against Libyan dissidents in the US . . . There are at least four known incidents overseas this year in which Libyan opponents of the Gadaffi regime have been killed or wounded in terrorist attacks.' The State Department spokesperson added: 'The pattern of Libyan terrorist activity is clear, and we do not intend to let it get to this stage in the US.' In September 1985 a Grand Jury was investigating an alleged 'stray dogs' plot which involved some twelve to fifteen Libyans resident in the United States.

At the same time, press reports suggested that the US government had uncovered what had been widely feared ever since the suicide bombings in Beirut of Octoer 1983: 'a radical Islamic infrastructure of terror' involving Libyan and Iranian dissidents. This may or may not have been the same connection as was described the previous October, again by Buck Revell of the FBI, with the assertion that 'Libya has established liaison with black extremist, American Indian, and Puerto Rican radical groups', and Iran 'has links to a black extremist group, the Islamic Guerillas of America (IGA)'.

What is clear is that despite the fears of America, and whatever the loud claims by Libya and its eccentric Colonel Gadaffi, Libyan sponsorship of real terrorism is in fact either brilliantly concealed from US intelligence services; or it is relatively limited; or both. (It was no great boost to confidence in American detective work that the international clamour for evidence to link Libya with the 1986 New Year bombings in Vienna and Rome – and thus to justify the USA's punitive air-raid on Libya – resulted in evidence which convincingly demonstrated *Syrian* involvement.) The most obvious form of Libyan terrorism, in the shape of the 'stray dogs' assassination campaign, barely fits the proper definition of terrorism, as the killings are purposeful, the victims specific, and the threat confined to a relatively small and individual group. It is an extramural extension of a state terror machine which operates internally in much the same way in a number of countries which are regrettably allies of the United States. Amnesty International's reports of state terror and violations of human rights are not quoted and republished by the US State Department with such approval, however, when they concern

Chile, Turkey, the Philippines under Marcos, or El Salvador.

In short, for his own political purposes Colonel Gadaffi and his state broadcasting services tend to exaggerate the extent to which Libya gives real and concrete support to real terrorists. By claiming that he is the host and quartermaster of international terrorism, he judges that he can gain credit from some of his allies, and bolster domestic support with tough talking, while hoping to avoid paying the price of actions which will outrage the international community. There is a remarkable irony in the fact that the very same capacity for exaggeration – for political ends – is what has distinguished the reaction to terrorism of President Reagan, at least in the eyes of his critics. There is a 'credibility gap' whenever a politician promises much and delivers little – and it is precisely the accusation that tough talking must be followed by tough action which makes some advocates of vigorous retaliation so dissatisfied with the Reagan record on terrorism.

The US government gets a great deal of propaganda mileage out of its attacks on state-sponsored terrorism, but its position is complicated by more than the political flexibility of its list of 'terrorist states' and the lack of demonstrable proof for its assertions. In effect, the world's self-appointed moral policeman is an Aunt Sally living in a glasshouse. For all its innocent indignation on such matters, America is quite as capable of behaving with the same disregard for its own stated standards of justice and democracy that it condemns in its enemies, and it is this contradiction that undermines both the credibility of the American stance and the integrity of its responses.

In this context it is worth quoting the definition that Cline and Alexander give in *Terrorism: the Soviet Connection,* of the value to both terrorists and state of a supportive relationship:

> Terrorism, guerilla warfare, insurgency and revolutionary war are part of the vocabulary of international violence. These terms are often used interchangeably. The most serious situations develop when the stability and welfare of nations are threatened by domestic revolutionary forces encouraged and supported outside the national borders.

If such terrorist units receive training, arms and ammunition, money and political guidance from safe sanctuaries outside their own nation, they can more readily succeed in threatening economic, social and governmental stability. They are thereby engaged in the front line of an international war for political control of a national government and hence the resources and people of the nation. A nation supporting terrorist violence in another nation is engaged in low-intensity warfare in support of expansion of its own sphere of political influence.

Does this description of state-sponsored terrorism (approved and circulated by the State Department) not equally apply to American policy in funding and arming the Nicaraguan Contras? The United States is not blameless in such matters, least of all in Central America.

There is a good case to be made – which most Western citizens would probably accept – that American policy objecives are usually pro-democratic, anti-totalitarian, humane rather than corrupt, and to be preferred to the Soviet alternative. But many Western citizens would also argue – though no doubt fewer in number in this case – that the standards of freedom, democracy, humanity and plain honesty which we collectively aspire to require of our governments a greater attention to justice and justification in all their actions. We can applaud tough statements from Whitehall and the White House which deplore the spread of terrorism by states cynical enough, or individuals desperate enough, to employ it as a form of political action. What we must beware is any delusion that because we are on the side of justice, our use or encouragement of such tactics can be justified.

The difficulty of defining terrorism is great enough for authors and academics, but for a government with citizens' lives, political interests, strategic alliances and a commercial economy at stake, public declarations about the nature of terrorism, and rhetorical threats to erase it from the face of the earth, are, at the very least, hostages to fortune. When President Reagan states, for example, that the Nicaraguan Contras 'are the modern moral equivalent of the Founding

Fathers', he is entering a moral quicksand: 'More taxpayer money to fight for freedom? Why sure – for a moment I thought you were a terrorist!' says the factfinding Congressman to a Central American jungle gunman in Oliphant's 1984 cartoon.

For the US government, however, the potential treacheries of the quicksand are escaped by adopting a simple position on the moral high-ground that it defines in its own terms. As Secretary of State Shultz put it in June 1984, 'How tragic it would be if democratic societies so lost confidence in their own moral legitimacy that they lost sight of the obvious: that violence directed against democracy or the hopes for democracy lacks fundamental justification. Democracy offers mechanisms for peaceful change, legitimate political competition, and redress of grievances. But resort to arms on behalf of democracy against repressive regimes or movement is, indeed, a fight for freedom.'

There is no question that the American involvement in the Nicaraguan 'fight for freedom' is an adventure that closely matches the description from *Terrorism: the Soviet Connection*. When, on 12 November 1981, Secretary of State Alexander Haig was asked by members of the Congressional Committee on Foreign Affairs if he would give an assurance that the US would not become involved in attempts to overthrow or destabilise the Nicaraguan government, he replied: 'No, I would not give you such an assurance.'

The catalogue of American budgets, training and military liaison with the Nicaraguan Contras is largely a matter of public record. As the Majority Leader of the House of Representatives, James Wright, said in July 1983 – in words that echo those of Cline and Alexander – 'Those whom we have recruited, trained, financed, equipped and sent into that country state unequivocally that their purpose is to overthrow the government of that country. For us to say that it is otherwise really is to evade the fact ... because what we have done, quite frankly ... has been to finance an invasion from outside of a sovereign country.'

Nevertheless, Shultz's statement of the moral legitimacy of

actions that would elsewhere be condemned as terrorism permitted him to dismiss all idea that the US supported terrorism in the shape of the Contras, both by insisting that as *freedom fighters* they could not be *terrorists*, and that as they did not commit terrorist actions, they *were* not terrorists. 'Once we understand terrorism's goals and methods, it is not too hard to tell, as we look around the world, who are the terrorists and who are the freedom fighters. The resistance fighters in Afghanistan do not destroy villages or kill the helpless. The Contras in Nicaragua do not blow up school buses or hold mass executions of civilians.' If they did, one must suppose, Secretary Shultz would concede that they were terrorists, and argue for the withdrawal of US support. Unfortunately for Shultz, there is considerable evidence that they are.

Unsurprisingly, it is the view of the Nicaraguan government that the FDN (Democratic Nicaraguan Forces, the largest grouping among the Contras) is a terrorist organisation, designed, built up, financed and directed by the CIA. On 19 July 1985, President Daniel Ortega addressed a crowd of up to half a million people on the sixth anniversary of the Sandinista revolution. He claimed that since 1982 the number of killed, injured and kidnapped had reached 12,000; that Contras had murdered 199 children under the age of twelve, injured 166, and kidnapped 303; that 7,582 children had been orphaned in the war; that 134 women had been killed; and that 321 schools had been destroyed.

In August 1985, in an embarrasing development for the Reagan Administration, Edgar Chamorro, a spokesman and leader of the FDN, spoke out against the FDN and the CIA's control of the organisation in a detailed and well-documented article in the *New Republic* magazine. Chamorro's principal points were that 'the CIA had brought the groups together with money and unequivocal promises of support'; that 'the Americans liked to make all the crucial decisions'; and that 'the CIA was talking with other anti-Sandinista groups in Miami and Central America but they ... wanted to keep us apart ... They were using us for their own purposes.'

Chamorro also describes how he was woken one night at

2 a.m. and told to read a statement on the clandestine radio station 'before the Sandinistas broke the news'. The statement took credit for the Contras' mining of several Nicaraguan harbours; but as Chamorro points out, 'Of course, we played no role in the mining of the harbors ... The CIA [had] employed its team of "Latino assets" to bomb the Sandinistas' petroleum tanks at Punto Corinto in October 1983. When I protested to "George", asking why the CIA didn't simply give us the money and let patriotic Nicaraguans do the job, he sighed, "This is the way they want us to do it in Washington."'

Nicaraguan authorities have claimed repeated instances of actions by Contras which go well beyond the boundaries of irregular guerilla warfare into pure terrorism, such as the bomb planted on a Nicaraguan passenger plane in Mexico, and another which exploded at Nicaragua's Sandino International Airport, killing four airport employees. Twice in July 1985, passenger ferries making the daily trip between the port of El Rama and Bluefields were ambushed by Contra troops. The ferries, the *Rio Escondido* and *Bluefields Express*, both carried soldiers to protect the vessels – though this may have made them the more attractive as a target. In the first attack, four soldiers were killed and in the second, one died. On 27 July 1985, Contras ambushed two trucks which were carrying the relatives of Nicaraguan soldiers at Mulukuku military school. According to the Defence Ministry, eight mothers were killed, and one young recruit, with a further eighteen wounded, of whom nine were women. The Nicaraguan Embassy in Washington claims that the US National Security Council gave explicit permission for a further attack, again on a civilian boat, which killed five people, adding that 'If the NSC approves such a small operation, the US must be held responsible for the wider campaigns.'

In April 1985, two Washington-based organisations, the International Human Rights Law Group and the Washington Office on Latin America, published the findings of a survey of human rights abuses in Nicaragua. The report, produced by Donald Fox, the senior partner in a New York law firm, and

Michael Glennon, a professor at the University of Cincinnati Law School, did not shrink from listing what it identified as abuses perpetrated by the ruling Sandinista government. But its conclusions – based on a substantial collection of sworn affidavits from eye-witnesses, and to the maximum degree gathered without the assistance of any intermediaries with political bias – concentrated principally on the actions of Contra forces against civilians:

> Substantial credible evidence exists that Contra violence is also directed with some frequency at individuals who have no apparent economic, military, or political significance and against persons who are *hors de combat*. It is important to emphasise that these are not persons caught in crossfire between Contra and Sandinista units. These are unarmed civilians who have no connection with hostilities and who have been the targets of deliberate attack by Contra units.
>
> What is abundantly clear, however, is that many acts of the Contras that were related to us cannot be justified under any accepted doctrine of conventional or customary international law. They include the torture of the Barredas ... kidnappings ... the machine-gunning and burning of persons reasonably identifiable as non-combatants ... murder ... the slaughter of unarmed civilians merely driving along a highway ... and the rape and murder of a woman in the militia ... These acts, by any standard of civilized conduct, are beyond the pale.
>
> We believe, for three reasons, that it is reasonable to infer that terroristic violence is directed with some frequency at individuals who are not, or who are no longer, taking an active part in hostilities ... The abuses described often were committed by groups of Contras numbering in the hundreds, leading to the reasonable inference that these acts were the work of supervised military personnel, not 'free agents' acting beyond the scope and course of normally expected operations ...
>
> It suffices to say that all probative evidence, taken together, indicates that serious Contra abuses against non-combatants occur far too often to justify any American support – public or private – of a sort that might enhance the ability of the Contras to commit these acts ...
>
> To the extent that it is reasonably foreseeable that they will continue to engage in such acts, any provision of aid to the Contras, directly or indirectly, by the government of the

United States would render our government indirectly responsible for their acts.

The essential conflict in the American position has been most acutely and embarrassingly focussed by the revelation in late 1984 that the CIA had produced and distributed a *Manual del Combatente por la Libertad* (Freedom Fighter's Manual) for use of Nicaraguans opposed to the elected Sandinista revolutionary government. Helpfully published in an English translation by the Grove Press of New York, it is subtitled a 'Practical Guide to liberating Nicaragua from oppression and misery by paralysing the military-industrial complex of the traitorous Marxist state without having to use special tools and with minimal risk for the combatant.'

The Manual is a simplistic but effective and dangerous handbook of ideas for disruption, sabotage and political trouble-making. The student radicals of Berlin and Paris in 1968 would have recognised most of the suggestions – and would-be radicals anywhere would find useful advice in it. Illustrated in comic-book style, the book is designed to give suggestions which do not require dangerous conspiracies or the use of serious weapons. The introduction points out: 'These measures are extremely safe and without risk for those who use them, as they do not require equipment, skill or specialised activities that can draw attention to the doer ... One combatant can perform many of them, without having to turn to collaborators or having to make a detailed plan beforehand ... Our sacred cause needs to have more men and women to join its ranks in order to perform these sabotage tasks.'

The tasks begin with a kind of go-slow or work-to-rule, combined with minor sabotage, that is familiar in cases of pure industrial or trades union conflict:

Don't do maintenance work on vehicles and machines.
Hide and damage tools, throw tools into sewers.
Come late to work – delay in completing tasks.
Call in sick so as not to work.
Leave lights on – leave water taps on.

141

Plant flowers on State farms.
Hoard and steal food from the Government.
Leave open the corral gates on State farms.
Spread rumours.
Telephone to make false hotel reservations, etc.
Spill liquids – drop typewriters – damage books.
Steal, hide key documents.
Threaten the boss by telephone.
Telephone giving false alarms of fires and crimes.
Break light bulbs and windows.
Cut telephone and alarm cables.
Put sponges into toilets and drains to cause blockages.
Paint anti-Sandinista slogans.

At a more dangerous level, the manual suggests a variety of ways of sabotaging vehicles.

> Put nails on roads, and next to the tires of parked vehicles – put dirt or water into gasoline tanks – cut the upholstery – break windshield wipers and headlights – cut and perforate the tires – put dirt, or pieces of candle in the oil tank and the distributor – break the distributor coil – steal the rotor cap – pierce the radiator or gasoline tank, cut battery cables, put nails in battery cells.

The most serious level of sabotage illustrated in the manual comprises pulling down telephone lines ('never electrical cable'); starting fires by making a small incendiary device out of cigarettes and matches; making Molotov cocktails, and using them to set light to a vehicle which has had its petrol tank pierced.

The original version of the manual had recommended kidnapping and 'neutralising' Nicaraguan government officials – a deliberately ambiguous suggestion which could mean very different things to different people. It suggested hiring criminals to kill fellow rebels to produce 'martyrs for the cause', and blackmailing citizens to force them to join the rebel cause. Although the manual offers little practical advice that a self-respecting Contra fighter, or an anti-Sandinista radical, would not already be aware of, the fact that it originated from the CIA (and was based on a US Special Forces primer on psychological warfare used in the 1960s) caused widespread public and political protests and an internal CIA investigation. Senator Daniel P. Moynihan said that the original primer had been 'an attempt to summarise the tactics of various communist insurgencies of the previous decades', and added: 'Here is the CIA so much devoted to the task of opposing communism in the world, seemingly incapable of recognising a Marxist-Leninist manual' which its own employees had prepared.

With Congressional disapproval of all aid to anti-Nicaraguan forces, a CIA misadventure and growing evidence of Contra terrorism, the Reagan Administration pursued a new line in 1985, proposing a new law which would remove from Contra forces anyone involved in human rights violations, and provide $27 million in 'humanitarian aid'. President Reagan, who had hoped for new funds for military aid, stated that humanitarian assistance was vital to maintaining the Contras' ability to pressure Nicaragua into halting its alleged support of leftist guerillas in El Salvador. In 1981 the President had alleged that Nicaragua was providing 'a flood of arms' to the Salvador guerillas, and was their main source of weapons. From 1981 to 1984 the Salvador armed forces and their US military trainers had used every technique at their command – sophisticated radar, infra-red equipped aircraft, patrol boats, and even frogmen to intercept some of the traffic. But in that time not a single smuggler or weapon was captured to confirm the allegation – even though it is quite widely accepted that at least some arms must have been supplied by Nicaraguans. Some Administration officials were forced to acknowledge privately that the claims had been exaggerated. 'Don't ask us about any flood of arms,' said one State Department source. 'That comes from some White House speechwriter, not from us.'

The humanitarian aid programme went ahead, and on 30 August 1985, President Reagan announced the creation of a State Department office to administer the $27 million. Referring to the Contras as 'the democratic resistance' rather than repeating earlier comparisons with the heroes of the American Revolutionary War, Reagan asserted: 'This Administration is determined to pursue political, not military, solutions in Central America. Our policy is and has been to support the democratic center against extremes of right and left and to secure democracy and lasting peace through internal reconciliation and regional negotiations ... As Americans who believe in freedom we cannot turn our backs on people who desire nothing more than the freedom we take for granted.'

Even before the office was open for business, however, the myth of 'humanitarian aid' was shot through with holes – ironically by one of its likeliest recipients. In a press conference on 24 June 1985, Alfonso Robelo, a commander of the EFE Contras group, told an interviewer: 'With this "humanitarian assistance", to be very honest, other funds are freed that will be used to buy weapons from the black market. That is the truth. The money that has been approved, $27 million for the next nine months, is sufficient to rebuild the morale of the combatants and equip them with modern armaments.'

Despite the rhetoric of 'freedom fighters' and 'humanitarian aid', then, there is little doubt that the Contras are at least sometimes guilty of acts of terrorism, and that those acts are the once-removed responsibility of the American government – the 'state sponsor'. As the Soviet intelligence defector said of the Soviet responsibility for Palestinian terrorism, 'If they don't like it they can stop it immediately.' The US-Nicaraguan evidence is certainly the more damaging for its public openness, and no less convincing than what is offered to prove the Soviet responsibility for the terrorism of the Palestinians and their clients.

For all the American government's attempts to dismiss this reality by emphasising the ends rather than the means, it has real consequences in terms of the US response to state-sponsored terrorism. For instance, there is one sanction against a 'terrorist state' which the US has not attempted to invoke: that of bringing a lawsuit in the World Court, formally known as the International Court of Justice, in the Hague. It is the highest international court, designed to resolve international conflict and disagreements between states at the

144

highest level. In 1979 the United States sued Iran in the World Court for the release of the American diplomats held hostage in the American Embassy in Teheran. But five years later, instead of the role of plaintiff, the United States faced the prospect in April 1984 of being the defendant in an action brought against her by the government of Nicaragua. Nicaragua alleged that:

> The United States of America is using military force against Nicaragua and intervening in Nicaragua's internal affairs, in violation of Nicaragua's sovereignty, territorial integrity and political independence, and of the most fundamental and universally accepted principles of international law. The United States has created an 'army' . . . [and] has acknowledged spending more than $70,000,000 on these illegal activities since December 1981.

In Nicaragua's contention, the 'covert war' violates

> The Charter of the United Nations, which prohibits 'the threat or use of force against the territorial integrity or political independence of any state';
> The Charter of the Organization of American States, which prohibits intervention in the affairs of another state, through armed force or other means (Article 18), or the violation of a state's territory, directly or indirectly, on any grounds whatever (Article 20);
> Other multilateral treaties, as well as customary and general principles or international law, as reflected, for example, in numerous resolutions of the UN General Assembly.

On the eve of Nicaragua's case being filed, on 6 April 1984, the US State Department announced that it was withdrawing US acceptance of the 'compulsory jurisdiction' of the court for matters relating to any Central American country for two years, with immediate effect. However, the 1946 US declaration accepting the Court's jurisdiction required the US government to give six months' advance notice before terminating the declaration.The SenateForeign Relations Committee report noted then: 'The provision for six months' notice of termination . . . has the effect of a renunciation of any intention to withdraw our obligation (to accept the Court's jurisdiction)

145

in the face of a threatened legal proceeding.' Nonetheless, the American decision to end recognition of the World Court's ruling was later justified on the grounds that the Court was being 'abused for political purposes'. In the light of America's intermittent commitment to the court's value, many critics in the USA and beyond argued that the most flagrant abuse lay at the door of the US government itself.

The legal and moral inconsistencies that underlie the American position on state terrorism are to a large extent concealed by the strength of rhetoric it bears against its foes: in particular, under the Reagan Administration, a rhetoric of retaliation. However, just as former President Carter differed with his successor over the 'international conspiracy' of state terrorism, so he has also argued that 'terrorism can be dealt with quietly and effectively, rather than with threats addressed to the world audience ... That's a mistake for the leader of a great nation like ours.' There are forceful moral arguments why a powerful state like the USA should not retaliate in a general or indiscriminate way against states which are suspected of involvement in individual, specific acts of terrorism: but there is also a powerful pragmatic argument. In simple terms, it is the fear, not so much of escalation, as of still more negative repercussions at a strategic level.

Thus, one of the few good things about the regime of Ayatollah Khomeini – in the eyes of the United States – is that it is equally offensive and dangerous to the Soviet Union. The strongest single objection to retaliation against Iran for acts of 'state-sponsored terrorism' is that the USA might drive Iran and the USSR into some kind of uneasy tactical alliance, the consequences of which would be far worse than occasional acts of terrorism, no matter how unpleasant the latter might be.

Ultimately the same issue arises with Libya. At a pragmatic level it is less unacceptable for the West to suffer the occasional bouts of Libyan-sponsored terrorism, than by the exercise of crude military retribution to make Colonel Gadaffi a martyr or rallying-point for the whole Arab world.

There is, too, another factor which generally inhibits

America's allies from taking part in specific action: self-interest. Thus, in early 1986, while the US Navy played at traditional and provocative gunboat diplomacy in the Gulf of Sidra – international waters which Libya claims as exclusively Libyan – the US government also instituted a set of economic sanctions against Libya. Its impact, however, was considerably diminished by the reluctance of America's West European allies to join in. Britain, Italy, and West Germany – all much more concretely victims of Libyan terrorist activity on their own soil – all declined to be involved in sanctions against Libya, pleading 'ineffectiveness' and 'dialogue' as excuse and alternative. The real reason, of course, lies in self-interest – in the first six months of 1985 Italy and West Germany were Libya's two largest customers for oil sales. Italy imported 6.3 million metric tonnes, and West Germany 5.1 million, at a price of around £900 million and £750 million, respectively. In 1984, Libya was a worthwhile trading partner for Britain, with a balance of payments benefit to Britain of £91.2 million. Despite the rhetoric of the British government in the aftermath of the extraordinary shooting of a British woman police officer in St James's Square, Libyan trade has an apparently higher price than the necessity (otherwise much discussed) of effectively uniting democratic nations against those who cynically espouse terrorist methods.

Terrorism presents no essentially different problems from those in other political spheres: governments can only act within the limits of feasibility, and often of opportunity. This is one explanation for the rise of 'state-sponsored terrorism', in that the sophistication of modern conventional warfare means that state leaders can rarely afford to consider hostilities without crippling or destroying their economies, or their power base, or both. Even the limited campaign in the Falkland Islands was a disaster for the Argentinian regime which embarked on the campaign but lost the war. An American consultant on terrorism – to both business and government – has likened modern terrorism to the Colt 45 pistol in the Old West: it was the 'equalizer' which put every man on the same basis. For states, terrorism can do the same thing – it can even up the odds between a major power and a small one, when neither will go to war, but the weaker wishes to provoke or destabilise. Intelligence services have since their creation carried out illegitimate and illegal activities which their sponsoring states would do everything possible to deny. The modern difference is that terrorist-surrogates are now available, who in some cases can be sent into action without even knowing that they are acting not only for themselves, but also in some wider plan of a state agency.

One must also, however, consider the reverse proposition: the fact that there are terrorists in existence all over the world whom states may sometimes sponsor and deploy. Would they evaporate if the state support were withdrawn? The answer must be that they would not: while the emphasis of new investigation and disapproval in the mid-1980s is on state involvement, the essence of terrorism remains the neglected cause, the uncorrected injustice, the historical anomaly or revolutionary obsession. Terrorists are created by their causes, rather than the other way round, and only when the causes or grievances are addressed, or the political fervour is given some outlet, can the terrorism be diminished; and of course there will be many cases in which no acceptable options exist. While Colonel Gadaffi may support a branch of Palestinian terrorism, no one would suggest that the absence of his support would eliminate such terrorism: indeed, he and successive US governments would agree that the only progress can come from a resolution of the Palestinian quest for national identity – and half of Israel would agree, too. Terrorists regrettably thrive with state support – or without it.

What, then, is state-sponsored terrorism? If the terrorism and the terrorists already exist, the identity of its new sponsor does not amount to a new problem; and if the terrorism is a mere extension of an already unacceptable domestic state terror, one is addressing an existing problem in a new but limited arena. In effect, real 'state-sponsored terrorism' is perhaps a relatively limited problem, perhaps more deserving of attention for its corruption of the international *modus vivendi* than for the numerical incidence of its attacks. It is somewhat predictable, yet just as unacceptable as every other manifestation of terrorism; nevertheless, it still has the capacity to surprise. While Western opinion may not be altogether astonished when the repressive and erratic Libyan regime begins eliminating its opponents on the streets of Western Europe and the United States, it is undoubtedly bewildered when the democratic government of France – committed by its Constitution to guarantee freedom of political dissent – mines the flagship of a legal environmental pressure group in a foreign country, and in the process commits manslaughter upon one of its members.

The French Secret Service attack on Greenpeace's *Rainbow Warrior* is a reminder that even nations which count themselves civilised can slip down the political continuum towards terrorism. It illustrates, also, what is perhaps the greatest problem posed by state-sponsored terrorism: the problem of state response, at whose heart is the ultimate moral core of all political conflict: 'I act properly because I know I am right; you act wrongly because, although you think you are right, I know you are wrong.

The familiar case has been argued by Oliver 'Buck' Revell, Assistant Director of the FBI: 'It is perhaps clearer now than ever before that governments, particularly those that are looked to for constructive international leadership, have a responsibility to counteract the terrorists' attempts at what is essentially extortion.' But when those governments stand equally to be implicated in terrorism by their actions or reactions, they risk a greater fall from grace as they embark on the cycle of threat, exaggeration, and retaliation which characterises international relations at the crudest level. America now argues that if American citizens fall victim to acts of terrorism, the US government is entitled to respond not only against the terrorists, but also against those who provide material or other support. What is required is a calmer and more purposeful response, for retaliation, particularly in anger, is a dangerous weapon which needs to be used with good judgement if it is not to backfire – or perhaps to shoot justice in the foot.

5 DEFENCE OF
THE REALMS

Some terrorism arises, almost spontaneously, from the extremism of a handful of political fanatics. Some arises from the historical traditions of a country, though the present possessors of state power may be quite unrelated to the despotism and injustice of the past. The majority of terrorist action, however, confronts the current political policy, domestic or foreign, diplomatic or commercial, of the state target; and it demands a response. But statecraft combines moral, political, and financial considerations in a complicated game of compromise; and the operations of compromise allow terrorists to feel they have a chance of creating change through their armed propaganda and violent persuasion. Terrorism is an extra ingredient in the mix of a nation's colonial history, international trade and military alliances that together conspire to undermine any absolute moral or strategic positions.

Inevitably, the rhetorical condemnation of terrorism is easier to deliver than the considered measures that will reduce the problem. Inter-state co-operation, new legal treaties on extradition, greater sharing of intelligence through agencies like Interpol and the International Association of Chiefs of Police, are all repeatedly advocated, frequently discussed, and only occasionally implemented. Despite the best intentions, sincerely held by states which are entitled to believe in their reputation for 'constructive international leadership', action against terrorism is substantially hampered by every state's own network of political alliances – or by the simple fact that one country's internal terrorist problem is another's external problem, and they will take sharply different and very political views of the proper or tactically advantageous way to proceed.

One further consequence of the frequent failure of loudly advertised international co-operation is that it offers an unwelcome propaganda coup to the terrorists it is supposed to defeat. Thus, the January 1985 murder of West Germany's Defence Ministry official Ernst Zimmerman – which bore the hallmarks of the Action Directe/Red Army Faction alliance – prompted an 'instant summit meeting' between Chancellor Kohl of West Germany and President Mitterrand of France, while both were in Rome. They promised closer co-operation against terrorists: but by taking up the gauntlet (not for the first time) so publicly, and by making apparently hollow threats of retaliation and the inexorable pursuit of terrorists to bring them to justice, they highlighted the terrorism itself.

Within a nation's borders, the response to terrorism poses a different set of problems; principally, the challenge to any democracy is to find effective measures without an unacceptable diminution of civil liberty. No terrorist, whether a diplomat in disguise or a jargon-spouting communard, can fail to recognise that it is the freedoms of democracy which afford the opportunity to engage in terrorism. The traditional distinction between liberty and licence is as apt in this case as in any. For the tactical component parts of terrorism to work, terrorists need freedom of movement and association, freedom of employment or of none, freedom of expression and free print and electronic media. As Margaret Thatcher said in a speech to the American Bar Association's 1985 annual conference in London: 'Nor is terrorism confined to countries where lawlessness and anarchy prevail. Its followers abuse the very freedom of open societies to do their evil work ... The more open our society, the more we must be on our guard.' In the same forum the then Home Secretary Leon Brittan pointed out that 'In Northern Ireland since 1969 terrorism has killed nearly 2,500 people and left over 27,000 maimed and injured ... It is easy to be tempted into over-reaction by such bloody deeds – and that, of course, along with publicity, is

151

what the terrorists want. Democratic governments, in safe-guarding democracy, must be scrupulously careful about the scale and nature of their reaction.'

This is a classic dilemma, and one whose tensions are highlighted by comparison with a country where the ideo-logical commitment to individual liberty above state control is not so evident: the Soviet Union. There, where the ordinary freedoms – which in Western democracies pass for the simple mechanics of everyday life – do not exist, terrorism cannot thrive; but the terrible price of such policing and 'state security' is paid by all. Soviet intelligence sources suggest that there have been numerous hijackings and attempted hijackings within the Soviet Union, perpetrated mostly by people trying to get out, though very few of these have ever come to light. There was an attempted assassination upon President Brezhnev by a discontented military officer; and a bomb in the Moscow subway which killed several people. But one domestic incident in particular – the hijacking of an airliner in Tbilisi, the capital of Georgia – powerfully illuminates the difference between Western and Soviet responses to such events.

The Tbilisi hijackers in 1983 were a group of intellectuals from prominent families who wanted to escape to asylum in Turkey. The Soviet government's attitude, however, does not even contemplate the process of negotiation, or the prime responsibility of protecting innocent life: to this purpose (and indicating the existence of a wider problem) aircrews are armed and under orders not to co-operate with any hijacker.

As soon as the hijackers identified themselves, a shoot-out in the Aeroflot cockpit left one hijacker and one crew member dead. Behind a locked door the pilot landed the plane back at Tbilisi, at which point a second hijacker committed suicide; and the others were killed and captured when a military squad stormed the plane, killing other passengers in the effort. The only negotiation was to offer the hijackers the choice between unconditional surrender or being taken by force; and there was no reporting of the incident until it was over. Ultimately two passengers had died, three crew members were killed, three hijackers dead and three others (and a fellow-conspirator priest) sentenced to death. Furthermore, their relatives were dismissed from their employment and expelled from the Party. By neat contrast, the man who took charge of the operation was Georgia Party boss Eduard Shevardnadze, the new Soviet Foreign Minister promoted by President Gorbachev to succeed Andrei Gromyko.

It is hard, by contrast, to imagine such an uncompromising response to a hijacking or hostage-taking in the West, particularly when such events take place in the full light of media attention. As long as hostages are alive in the hands of their captors, state authorities are restricted in their choice of tactical response. Much is made of the firepower of highly trained military counter-terrorist strike forces like the British SAS, the German GSG9 (*Grenzschutzgruppe 9*), the French GIGN (*Groupe d'Intervention de la Gendarmerie Nationale*) and the American Delta Force and Hostage Rescue Team (both officially non-existent); but these, and many others, have been distinguished by the extreme infrequency with which they have been deployed.

Despite their infrequent action, such units usually bring fatal consequences upon the terrorists, with severe risks to the hostages – what in American military language are called 'collateral losses'. No state has yet openly declared its sole consideration in ending a hijacking or hostage incident is the killing or capture of the terrorists. The proposition is stated in this way to demonstrate the problem with the alternative assumption – that the lives of the hostages are paramount. If that were the position of those who organise the response to a terrorist incident, then they would concede to the terrorists' demands upon them.

Limited concessions, contrary to the absolute political assertions, are made in every terrorist incident, not least in order to prevent the situation from worsening. The first thing the terrorist hijacker or hostage-taker wants is to communicate – and no police chief will refuse to do that. Commander George Churchill-Coleman, the head of CI3 at Scotland Yard, readily admits that the security forces are bound to make concessions: 'In a terrorist siege with hostages, you have to make some concessions in order to buy time, to see what are the options. If you can't save life, you've got to give in.' But that ultimate possibility may never arise, for the deployment of the military option is almost certainly seen as a life-saving exercise, even though not every life may be saved. It is clear that terrorists will sometimes have to kill in order to convince their opponent that concessions have to be made: and the primacy of hostages' lives is not absolute, being part of an unaviodable trade-off against the feasibility of a military assault upon the hostage-holders.

The Soviet Union, too, has been shown to recognise the inevitability of concessions when dealing with hostage-taking incidents on foreign territory, where its domestic policy of forceful retribution cannot extend. In Beirut, until the autumn of 1985, Soviet vulnerability to the Lebanese epidemic of assassination and kidnap, and the related hijackings and hostage holding, seemed to be nil. Unexpectedly, three Soviet diplomats and an embassy doctor were kidnapped in two separate incidents in West Beirut. Second Secretary Valeri Kornev, Commerce Attaché Oleg Spirin, Cultural Attaché Arkady Katkov, and Dr Nicolai Versky were seized in what appeared to be a kidnapping inspired by rivalries among Moslem militias and factions in Beirut and Tripoli, where Sunni militias were pinned down by pro-Syrian Lebanese and Syrian armed units. The kidnapping was swiftly followed by a telephone call to news agencies from a man claiming to speak for Islamic Jihad, who said that all the hostages would be killed unless Moscow forced her local ally Syria to lift the siege in Tripoli. Within less than twenty-four hours, the body of Arkady Katkov was found riddled with bullets from a burst of automatic rifle fire, lying face down on a West Beirut rubbish tip. Though there were no reports of any negotiations to provide evidence of the process in action, it seems clear that the Soviet Union made concessions, and pushed Syria away from the militia war. An alternative interpretation is that Syria herself, with very extensive contacts throughout the network of Moslem militias, secured the release of the Russians with her own promises – which would be a useful favour to her Soviet patron. The incident was short and simple by comparison with the many cases of kidnapping of Americans in Beirut, and few, if any, such incidents end in a magnanimous gesture of freeing hostages for the sake of goodwill.

Within three months of the Beirut kidnaps, the Soviet Union demonstrated an unprecedented flexibility in agreeing to a UN Security Council resolution denouncing terrorism, when all such previous initiatives had foundered at the starting-point of definitions. The apparent readiness of the Soviet Union to give ground to individual terrorists, while joining an international chorus of condemnation, may prove to represent the familiar set of double standards which could bring an increase of terrorist attacks upon the USSR in future.

The gap between rhetoric and practice is endemic to governments' reactions to the phenomenon of terrorism, despite all attempts to narrow or conceal it. Firm declarations of resolve may be rapidly discredited by a lack of action confirming their meaning, or worse, by being confronted with a situation which actively contradicts the firm stand. However, this by no means diminishes the commitment to rhetorical absolutes. Both Mrs Thatcher and Mr Brittan, for instance, forcefully asserted British policy on terrorists and terrorism to the American Bar Association. Mr Brittan pledged the efforts of the government 'to ensure that there must be no substantive concessions in the face of terrorism'. ('Substantive' differentiates from what might be called 'tactical' concessions during a barricaded hostage or hijack scene – offering food and drink, or access to talk with intermediaries, in exchange for the release of some hostages, and above all to play for time.) Mrs Thatcher expanded on the British position: 'We in Britain will not accede to the terrorists' demands. The law *will* be applied to them as to all other criminals. Prisoners will *not* be released. Statements in support of the terrorists' cause will *not* be made. If hijacked aircraft land here, they will *not* be allowed to take off.'

The obvious danger of such absolute policies emerges at the moment of their implementation. It is hard to picture a hijacked plane on the tarmac at Heathrow Airport, surrounded by the discarded corpses of shot hostages, while a resolute government plays out the no-concessions, stalemate policy to its logical conclusion. Nevertheless the British government, specifically the Conservative government of Margaret Thatcher, has since 1979 shown unparalleled determination to resist the armed blackmail of terrorism, in two particularly notable cases.

In 1980, the siege at the Iranian Embassy was ended by the deployment of the SAS, who killed five of the six terrorists holding hostages inside the embassy building. The Democratic Revolutionary Front for the Liberation of Arabistan had a short, bloody and fatal moment in the spotlight before the SAS ended their adventure in the most effective way, and the use of the military option to end the siege is widely credited with a sudden acute drop in the incidence of Middle Eastern terrorism in London. From that point on, Paris rapidly inherited the role as principal battleground for internecine Middle Eastern terrorist conflicts.

The second demonstration of government resolve, in far more complex and trying circumstances, came with the hunger strike campaign of IRA and INLA prisoners in Northern Ireland's Maze prison as a protest against the refusal of the British government to allow 'political status' to terrorist prisoners. An absolute unwillingness to compromise on such a matter of principle rebounded greatly to the Prime Minister's credit in the eyes of many, despite some sense of unease at the emotive propaganda value of the eleven duly-created martyrs.

For all its very firm stand of principle against the IRA hunger strikes, however, British governments have not succeeded in eliminating the pre-eminent domestic terrorist problem in Northern Ireland. There, Britain faces the terrorist equivalent of a long-term war of attrition, which as in the Basque country is widely enough supported by a part of the community to frustrate most initiatives to quell it.

The terrorism of Northern Ireland and of the Iranian Embassy demonstrates the essential difference between the threat from within and the threat from outside. For the Irish terrorist, Britain is the enemy; to the British government the IRA terrorist is an enemy within, working against the state from inside the state. To the terrorists of Arabistan, Britain is a stage upon which to perform their drama – a focus of world media attention, but essentially irrelevant to their political purpose; while to the British government they are foreign criminals who break the laws of the state but do not attempt to question or undermine the legality of the state itself. The co-operation between states is always easier when it concerns 'other people's terrorism'.

At the heart of the struggle between democratic government and terrorism there is a moral distinction. While Marighella claims that the urban guerrilla is sustained by his 'moral superiority' over the enemy, the vast majority of citizens hold the opposite view. In consequence, government reaction to terrorism needs to maintain both a sense of justice in general, and a sense of justification for the specific actions taken to oppose terrorism. The problem that remains is that attempts to destroy terrorism by democracy do not succeed by moral superiority alone. For every state that suffers terrorist activity there is a varying mixture of police, military and political resources ranged against the terrorists. According to existing and long-standing relationships between different services, there may be problems of co-ordination, or even of competition. In the United States, the Federal/State legislative distinction produces some difficulties: but the sheer number of agencies in the USA which involve themselves in investigating terrorism led one foreign colleague to describe it as 'a zoo of people'. As the Director of the FBI, Judge William Webster, himself acknowledged in February 1985, the example of the arrest of five terrorist suspects in Ohio demonstrated 'close and effective co-operation between the FBI, the New York City Police Department, the Massachusetts State Police, the New Jersey State Police, the Cleveland Police Department and many other state and local law enforcement agencies.' He continued, 'Anti-terrorist operations ... may reach across the nation and require the utmost co-operation and mutual confidence among law enforcement officials.' It is no simple matter.

Police work is the first line of defence, and of counter-attack against terrorism. It is a specialised kind of police work, however, both in its prescribed duties and its methods. Most states have increased and sophisticated their intelligence-gathering and data-collection capacities in an attempt to create a net of (usually computerised) information in which they can catch a terrorist on the basis of the smallest titbit of forensic evidence. The most elaborate example is that of the West German BundesKriminalAmt (Federal Crime Office), whose computerised information database in Wiesbaden is justly famous. As described by West German police official Reinhard Rupprecht, the database is in two essential parts:

'The PIOS system, a file for non-evaluated information about persons, institutions, objects and addresses in connection with terrorist suspicions. As a fifth category of this system, *events* will be added. The speciality of the system is the possible automatic connections among the five categories. Secondly, a data file of persons who are under suspicion, but not wanted for arrest. Being recorded in this file, they are to be registered whenever their papers are checked by police, especially crossing the border. The police agency which put the data of a potential terrorist in the system gets notice about when, where, in which car and with which persons the suspect person has been controlled. Thus, contacts and movements of this person can form a mosaic picture on a long-term basis.'

Such methods are nevertheless essentially reactive to terrorism; though the legends of BKA officials attentively removing everything down to the threadbare carpet from discovered terrorist safe houses may all be true, their work is a response to the terrorist act. Increasingly, police officials are attempting to find pro-active methods, ways of pre-empting terrorist action. One successful instance (though itself relating partly to completed acts), which also throws some light onto operational techniques, emerges in the description given by FBI Director Webster of an operation against the Puerto Rican independence terrorist group, the FALN: 'We began by developing profiles to identify suspected terrorists. Then we used extensive physical surveillance to help us locate the safe houses. As many as 100 law enforcement officers were used simultaneously during these investigations. During the course of this investigation we watched on closed-circuit television as the terrorists collected ammunition and prepared explosive devices for future activities ... When we obtained evidence of an imminent bombing on the Fourth of July, we moved in and made the arrests.'

John Harley, the Chief of the FBI's Terrorist Research and Analytical Center (TRAC), which has been in existence since 1981, describes his department's function as hybrid – 'We are basically an action agency, but we are part of the intelligence community. Most intelligence people are in the business of collecting intelligence, analysing it, passing it around. Our job is to catch the people causing the problem, build a prosecutable case and put them in jail.' (Later, he added, 'and throw away the key.') By contrast with the German approach, the FBI's TRAC team places less emphasis on data collection, and more on intelligence and analysis. According to John Harley, 'Back in the 1960s we collected roomsful of files on people – students, anti-Vietnam War campaigners, etcetera – we had information on everybody but nobody was going to jail. We were buried in data.' The extra emphasis on intelligence clearly implies a political insight into what issues and griev-ances over US domestic or foreign policy may provoke terrorist action.

Police forces have to be extremely powerful, or very lucky, to prevent acts of terrorism, as most terrorists are unknown to them until and unless they act. In a quite different context, Jean-Pierre Bourdier of the FASP, the largest French police union, makes the same case for pro-active steps against terrorism: 'It's not by putting a guard in front of the door that you're going to stop the bomber from letting off his bomb. The thing is to infiltrate the terrorist networks and to stop the terrorist from putting his bomb down.' For that purpose, Bourdier pointed to the creation by the end of 1985 of a new French anti-terrorist Intelligence Brigade.

Infiltration of the closed, committed terrorist group is an impossibility: terrorists are far too security-conscious to permit any new face into the action group. In this context, infiltration means *electronic infiltration*. John Harley observes: 'Our success has been through infiltrating the groups, not through informers – to try to get someone into a group doesn't work, they have known each other for years and won't trust new people. The group would test a newcomer by getting him to commit a violent act.' In the United States, the FBI must show 'probable cause' that the individuals are guilty of committing criminal acts *before* they can get court-ordered wiretaps on telephone lines or permission to instal concealed microphones in a safe house.

Wiretaps are an essential tool for investigating people who have to communicate with each other but are too wary to meet either openly or in secret. In the United States they are authorised and regulated under Title III of the Omnibus Safe Streets and Crime Act of 1968, and every instance of their use is authorised by a Federal Judge. (Title III wiretaps are distinct in US law from 'consensual wiretaps', where an informant has agreed to the recording of a conversation with another party.) There is separate legal supervision of electronic monitoring of the conversations of *international* terrorists, which must be approved by the Foreign Intelligence Surveillance Court (composed of seven Federal District Judges), created by the Foreign Intelligence Surveillance Act of 1978. There is, however, an obvious catch in the requirement upon agents to identify the probable terrorists and compile evidence of 'probable cause' before implementing the electronic surveillance that should give them a cast-iron case. And in court they must reveal the techniques that produced the evidence – so they are constantly changing their tactics.

The only area of terrorist activity in which 'human' infiltration works is when terrorists – usually from outside the country in question – come looking for weapons, training, or expertise where they think it may be available. As Judge Webster explains, 'Many of these groups seek to make contact with persons who are "hit" men or who can provide parliamentary training. Our undercover agents have been inserted into the plot with great effectiveness ... Conspirators offered our agent $300,000 to assassinate Honduran President Roberto Suazo ... Two Libyans who wanted to purchase weapons and silencers to assassinate opponents of the Libyan regime living in the United States ... Sikh terrorists who wanted to pay someone to train them in guerilla tactics so they could conduct operations against the Indian government.'

Infiltration, then, can operate in the specialised area of 'mercenary services' and also, according to the testimony of former Israeli Ambassador Shaul Rosolio, in the case of terrorist action being a part of a wider, but fragmented, political movement – among the Palestinians: 'I do not know the exact number of all the organisations that claim to have attacked Israel, or imperialists, or Zionists, or Jews. One thing is a fact: their numbers, competition, mutual rivalries, hatreds, and infighting were invaluable in the process of successful intelligence infiltration – which was achieved and which was material in foiling most of their attacks.'

Policing practice and methods are part of the state's response to the individual terrorist incident; but the state is also obliged to respond to the *phenomenon* of terrorism, which involves an examination of the political culture in which terrorism arises, and of the legislative structure that exists to control it. The terrorist bombing, as an incident, is essentially political vandalism, and state policing methods to catch those responsible are not very much affected by the nature of the crime – though they are coloured by the ruthlessness of the perpetrators. However, in tackling the phenomenon of terrorism most states have seen the need for new legislation, not so much to make terrorist activities legal offences (since they are almost invariably common crimes, and crimes of conspiracy, already), but in order to change the rules of procedure for arresting, holding and charging terrorists, and enabling testimony, often from confessed fellow-terrorists, to be given against them.

The United States has in the last few years passed several

new laws which intensify the powers of the state to pursue terrorists. Under the Comprehensive Crime Control Act of 1984, in a chapter entitled 'Terrorism', the US Federal law covering kidnapping has been expanded to include a new statute called 'Hostage Taking'. The statute gives US courts jurisdiction over terrorist crimes committed not only at home, but anywhere in the world if American interests are put at risk. It provides for any term up to life imprisonment for anyone who, 'whether inside or outside the United States, seizes or detains and threatens to kill, to injure or to continue to detain another person in order to compel a third person or a governmental organization to do or abstain from doing any act as an explicit or implicit condition for the release of the person detained,' provided that: '(a) the offender or the person seized or detained is a national of the United States; (b) the offender is found in the United States; (c) the governmental organization sought to be compelled is the Government of the United States.'

Under the Comprehensive Crime Control Act, there are further statutes brought in, largely to eliminate loopholes in Federal-State legal disparity. Until 1984, 'murder for hire' was not a Federal offence; nor was the 'possession of, with intention to use, false identity papers, credit cards, or drivers' licenses'. Both loopholes have since been closed (US Code 1952A headed 'Use of interstate commerce facilities in the commission of murder-for-hire' and 18 US Code 1028 headed 'Fraud and related activity in connection with identification documents'), and the US Department of Justice points to the happy coincidence of recent arrests of some American domestic terrorists 'in possession of literally thousands of false ID materials, drivers' licenses, social security cards, and passports – all genuine, but fraudulently obtained.'

One further legal development in the USA is the 'reward statute', which offers financial inducements to anyone who can provide real information on terrorist activity or plans. The Attorney-General, in the case of domestic terrorism, and the Secretary of State in the case of foreign terrorism, can offer rewards of up to $500,000 for information that leads to the prevention of terrorism, apprehension of terrorists, or information relating to any aspect of terrorism.

The need for legislation to cope with the peculiar threat of terrorism is finely balanced, however, against the risk it poses to civil liberties. The FBI's William Webster recognises the risks that all governments face in the development of special laws: 'The government that reacts ... by repressive measures that suspend individual liberties plays into the terrorist's hands. Such a reaction undermines popular confidence in the government and ultimately could bring it down.' Equating law with physical security measures, he observes further that 'It is important that the precautions we take do not signal that our nation is under siege. This is a message we never want to communicate to terrorists. It tells them, in effect, that they are succeeding.'

Similarly, a Defense Nuclear Agency symposium on 'Outthinking the Terrorist' in 1985 heard the potential conflict outlined by Assistant US Attorney E. Lawrence Barcella, who has been involved in the investigation and prosecution of most major terrorist cases in the USA in recent years. Despite the difficulties of pursuing some of the cases, he reminded his audience of the dangers of invoking new laws: 'As the Roman sage Terence observed 2,000 years ago, "Extreme law is often extreme injustice".... the laws we make to control the worst of us equally affect the rest of us.' Pointing to 'legislative overreaction' to terrorism, Mr Barcella referred to South Africa, where 'in situations dealing with what is broadly described as terrorism, the presumption of innocence is removed, the burden of proof is shifted, double jeopardy is diluted, the warrant requirement is removed, and the reasonable doubt standard is rolled on its ear in that the defendant must prove his innocence beyond a reasonable doubt.'

Mr Barcella also pointed to the United Kingdom's 'Prevention of Terrorism Act' which 'specifically outlaws the IRA and makes support for that group illegal'. The fact that the Act and its special provisions must be renewed by order of Parliament every six months may be seen to reflect well upon the state's sensitivity to the civil liberty question. On the other hand, as Barcella argues, 'The British are clearly uncomfortable with the law in that they mandate its renewal at least every two years [*sic*]. Thus, not only has the law not been terribly effective as a deterrent, but it has not been psychologically effective either.'

Another speaker at the same conference, H.H.A. Cooper, the Staff Director of the United States' National Advisory Committee Task Force on Disorders and Terrorism, pointed to 'the tragic example of Argentina ... it is sad that a nation that produced so many illustrious jurists should have felt the need to depart so far from the rule of law.' Moving to the wider issue of states' putting their own legitimacy at risk in the tactics they use in order to quell terrorist activity, Cooper made his position absolutely clear: 'There is no room here for duplicity or double standard. Either we must combat the terrorist by our own rules, holding fast to those principles that are dear to us, or we may descend to the level of the terrorist and slug it out in the slime – but if we do, there may be no hot bath awaiting us when we emerge. Eight years ago, the National Advisory Committee Task Force on Disorders and Terrorism accepted that "Our response should be practical and effective, but it must always be a civilized reply to an uncivilized act." We ought not,' said Mr Cooper, 'lightly to consider departing from that well-mediated advice.'

States afflicted by terrorism have introduced new laws (for example, Italy's *Reale* laws which greatly enlarge the concept of conspiracy and 'moral complicity'), to howls of protest from interested minorities and qualified approval from the majority who are more worried about terrorism than they are about technical aspects of civil liberties. There is a constant suspicion in mostly-peaceful democracies that those most vocal in the defence of civil liberties are those who will most likely wish to abuse them. But when the balance tilts the other way, as in the case of Sweden, laws which have been brought in to deal with a very limited problem of terrorism have been overturned in favour of reinforcing existing general statutes. Some countries have been deliberately slow to take legislative measures – Belgium is regarded as the prime example – in the belief that defences against terrorism only make its incidence more likely. But the opposite reaction also has its dangers. At its worst, legislation passed to enable states to lock up more terrorists more quickly can unleash state terror upon more than terrorists. Argentina's 'Dirty War' upon urban guerillas and terrorists, with the wholesale repression of all political dissent from the military junta's regime, has been well documented.

For all the claims of 'extreme libertarians', however, there are few cases of nations which have allowed terrorism to destroy, indirectly, their democratic legislative systems. Despite the justifiable horror which acts of terrorism provoke, the terrorists never have the firepower to present a threat to the integrity of a state, unless that state allows them to take the initiative, in which some of the civil libertarians will support them. Pragmatism is essential – but only up to a point. As William Webster rightly claims, 'We've become more effective in investigating terrorist groups without creating the Orwellian police state that civil libertarians have warned about.' Webster illustrates this by reference to a case in which the fine balance in American law (based not least upon First Amendment rights to political dissent) was neatly demonstrated. 'In our investigation in Chicago of the FALN,' the FBI Director recalls, 'we used closed-circuit television cameras to effectively gather information on the terrorists' bomb-making. We watched them assemble their weapons and make their bombs.'

During the pre-trial phase of the case, the District Court ruled out the use of the videotaped evidence 'on the grounds that there was not statutory or other basis for the judge authorizing the Title III [wiretap] surveillance to grant an order for the use of closed-circuit TV cameras.' Ultimately the Court of Appeals reversed that verdict, when Judge Richard Posner summed up the limitations of the case for civil liberty in the context of terrorism in one sharp sentence: 'There is no right to be let alone while assembling bombs in safe houses.'

Another legislative response to terrorism – and one equally dogged by the potential conflict between justice and abuse –

has been the passage of laws in several countries which seek to contain terrorism by effectively re-integrating terrorists into the legitimate spheres of political activity. Policies of re-integration are made necessary by the existence of a terrorist threat which stands within the state's territory, and usually represents a radical element within a far larger minority group, whether separatist, religious, or linguistic. The issue of re-integration is defined in the question 'What happens to the soldiers after the war is over?' or, more appropriately, 'What happens when the terrorists come out of the jails?' It is therefore also closely related to the legal matters involved in getting the terrorists into jail in the first place, and in getting terrorist recruits to 'exit' from their group before committing violent acts.

When Italy faced an epidemic of terrorism throughout the 1970s, simply tightening up police procedures was an insufficient answer. The state had to try to enable terrorists to retreat from the commitment they had made. Two different laws were enacted in Italy (*Legge Cossiga* and *Legge sui pentiti*) which implied a substantial reduction of sentence if terrorists collaborated with the authorities, providing information on their own activities and those of their comrades; or a smaller reduction of the sentence if they simply 'dissociated' themselves from the group. The laws were a major element of the relatively successful formula which reduced terrorism in Italy quite sharply by the early 1980s. It is estimated that about forty per cent of the official figure of two thousand jailed terrorists are either *pentiti* or *dissociati* (repented or dissociated).

Oddly enough, the measures – known universally as the *pentiti* Laws – do not mention the word itself, and merely list the options of collaboration, denouncing comrades, becoming a state witness, dissociation from former activities, and the consequences for the individual. The idea of repentance is moral, while the laws are essentially political, intended to make the potential for terrorism manageable within the state. It is widely accepted in government and among security experts that the most damaging concession the state can make to terrorists is to treat them at their own valuation – as an enemy and equal of the state.

Possibly more effective as a demonstration of the state maintaining its authority in the face of terrorism, and re-integrating terrorists within the body of the state, is the similar treatment of *arrepetidos* in Spain. These 'repented' terrorists are offered a conditional amnesty: if they will submit to Spanish legal process, confess to their own past activities and plead guilty to charges in court, the sentence passed upon them will be automatically suspended until and unless they are caught engaging in the same activities again. The Spanish government does not require the *arrepetidos* to provide information about comrades, and in the context of militant Basque nationalism, it seems most unlikely that such a con-dition would work. Indeed, the scheme is sufficiently lenient that it provides a convenient way for a terrorist simply to retire when he or she chooses, without necessarily compro-mising the ongoing struggle.

By analogy with the case of Italy, where *pentiti* have enabled a substantial round-up, in Britain the 'supergrasses' (or 'converted terrorists' in government language) have in-stigated a number of large-scale terrorist trials in the courts of Northern Ireland. As elsewhere, formal legal process is seen as a necessary step to maintain the political integrity of the state, and ultimately to enable the re-integration of the political movement that gives rise to terrorism. The major problem in Northern Ireland, however, is the difficulty of getting volun-tary witnesses to come forward to give evidence against terrorists, or of getting men and women to serve on juries, due to the very real danger of intimidation and violent revenge. In the words of a Foreign Office/Northern Ireland Office document on the subject, 'Those suspected of giving in-formation, or of being prepared to, may be maimed or killed. Consequently, many who are willing to give information to the police will not necessarily risk giving evidence in open court ... The intimidation of juries in Northern Ireland – and in the Republic of Ireland – by terrorists sometimes makes the conduct of trial by jury impossible, and in both jurisdictions courts sit without juries in trials for "scheduled" offences, a category which includes all cases involving terrorism.'

Some 'supergrasses' are apparently disenchanted with the terrorist life, having enrolled at a young age; some appear to be unconvinced of the need for extreme violence; others want to give evidence in order to get the relocation, protection and financial arrangements that will ensure they can make a clean break from terrorism. The British government points to the United States 'Federal Witness Protection Program' as a notable precedent for the kind of deal a 'converted terrorist' can expect in exchange for his possibly-uncorroborated testimony, arguing that other nations have accepted such evidence and protected the witnesses 'in certain types of prosecution, for example those involving terrorism and organised crime, where other potential witnesses might be deterred from coming forward.'

A 'converted terrorist' may be prosecuted, convicted and sentenced before he or she gives testimony against former accomplices – this in order to eliminate the suggestion that the process of conversion has diminished the severity of the court's judgement. In practice, however, the 'supergrass' will rarely give evidence except on the proviso that he is 'freed from the possibility of prosecution', in the language of the Attorney-General. Furthermore, he may well be able to claim the additional protection of being provided with a new identity and the money to move his home to the other side of the world.

Official sources accept the legal risks of these procedures: 'The question for the courts is not whether such evidence can be used – it can and always has been – but how far it is safe to rely upon it in a particular case ... The grant of immunity is normally unconditional and irrevocable ... The court should consciously have regard to the danger of relying on such evidence unless it is corroborated, and direct itself to this effect. Provided this is done, it is open to the court to decide that, even in the absence of corroboration, it is satisfied that the evidence of the accomplice is true and sufficient.'

The Attorney-General summed up the criteria for

granting immunity to an accomplice in November 1981:

(i) whether in the interests of justice it is of more value to have a suspected person as a witness for the Crown than as a possible defendant;

(ii) whether in the interests of public safety and security the obtaining of information about the extent and nature of criminal activities is of greater importance than the possible conviction of an individual;

(iii) whether it is very unlikely that any information could be obtained without an offer of immunity and whether it is also unlikely that the prosecution could be launched against the person to whom the immunity is offered.

The record of such trials is mixed: some have produced outright guilty pleas from defendants, while others have ended in all charges being dismissed by the judge on the grounds of the complete unreliability of the 'converted' witness. Terrorist organisations, however, have recognised the power of the tactic, and have responded by stepping up intimidation; by apparently winning back some 'converts' who subsequently withdraw their testimony; and by resorting to kidnapping relatives of 'supergrasses' and threatening to kill them unless the intended evidence is withdrawn.

Despite the inevitable unanswered questions about the methods whereby justice is being done, the British government clearly takes the same view as others facing terrorist activity: that provided justice is being *seen* to be done in one way or another, such a spectacle is a strengthening force for the political unity of the state, and increases the possibility of re-integration of political fragments, rather than the risk of further explosions – in any sense.

The legislative responses to terrorism that a democratic state commands are all affected by the same necessity to find a middle way between the preservation of order and the imposition of unacceptably repressive laws. This imponderable area of tension and compromise is nowhere more acutely reflected than in the debate over how far the press should be free in its reporting of terrorism.

The print and electronic media are an asset to terrorism, and a part of the tools of their trade, though generally they can exercise no direct control. Latin American terrorists, however, have carried the search for publicity to its logical limits, by seizing TV and radio stations to transmit their propaganda. Black September developed a plan to gain control of the Munich television transmission tower in order to broadcast their demands in 1972 or 1973. In Uruguay, the Tupamaros had a mobile transmitter for their propaganda, making impromptu political broadcasts in the hope of mobilising new supporters. They also specialised in seizing meeting halls and factory canteens with literally 'captive audiences' for their instant political education programme.

Terrorists, as is observed repeatedly, both need and seek publicity – as do politicians, salesmen, ideologues, even religious leaders. The fact that terrorists get what they want – in that respect if in no other – does not mean that the reporters, editors, producers and directors are doing wrong; it means that with valued freedoms come certain imperfections. But with every case, the behaviour of journalists and news teams is examined with new concern; and it is inevitable that states beleagured by terrorism will discuss different methods of shooting the messenger, in the form of 'the media'.

In July 1983 Margaret Thatcher described 'the search for publicity – the food without which these creatures cannot live' as constant, something which imposes 'very special responsibilities on the media'. She continued: 'The border-line between informing the public and serving the interests of terrorists is a narrow one. The way the facts are reported is crucial. Gangs of assassins must not be dignified with the word "armies". Terrorists should not be called "freedom fighters". Brutal murders must not be cloaked with that legal-sounding word "execution".'

Government leaders have proposed a wide variety of voluntary restraints for the media: in June 1985 Prime Minister Felipe Gonzalez of Spain proposed to seek a 'voluntary agreement' with the Spanish press and TV which would reduce the publicity given to terrorist acts. His initiative followed ETA's assassination of four people, including an army colonel, in Madrid on the day that Spain signed its treaty of accession to the EEC. In Britain, in the aftermath of the Shi'ite terrorists' hijacking of TWA Flight 847 to Beirut in June 1985, Margaret Thatcher enlarged on her 1983 metaphor of publicity as the 'food' of terrorists, by inquiring whether terrorists could not be denied 'the oxygen of publicity'.

A month later, her Cabinet Secretary, Sir Robert Armstrong, addressing an International Press Institute seminar in London, argued that the terrorist is 'reasonably confident that when he hijacks an aircraft full of innocent passengers he is also hijacking the television screens, the radio waves, and the headlines.' He portrayed the interests of the authorities in a terrorist incident like a hijacking as threefold: 'To bring the incident to a peaceful conclusion as quickly as possible without loss of life, and with minimum use of force; if possible – terrorism being a crime – to apprehend and bring to justice the perpetrator; and to demonstrate that terrorism does not pay. These are all objectives to which I suggest the media can subscribe.' And, he went on to ask, 'Should it not be possible for the media to agree that they should in principle be willing to accept constraints on their freedom to report on at least some aspects of such incidents while they are in progress?'

Armstrong and others have pointed to the very responsible co-operation by editors and reporters with police authorities in cases of criminal kidnapping, where requests for restraint or complete silence about such a crime are almost invariably obeyed. Such crimes, however, are essentially different from acts of terrorism, despite some superficial similarities. They are not directed at the state or its citizens, but at a chosen individual, usually wealthy or connected to wealth. They do not have a political content such as to require the attention, where it exists, of a free and independent press and broadcasting system. Kidnappings are often kept quiet precisely because the sole solution is to make the concessions and pay the ransom, while acts of terrorism need to be reported not least so that the government's firmness and refusal to give ground to terrorists can be fully publicised. But no free press will accept that it may report the government line and nothing else. Journalists and broadcasters would 'subscribe' to most of Sir Robert Armstrong's arguments, but in democratic nations with free media they will never agree that their role is the same as the government's in demonstrating 'that terrorism did not pay'. It is self-evident that elected governments should have that objective; and equally obvious that the journalist's proper concern should be (though he and she often fail) to report fully and neutrally what terrorists do, say and demand, without providing a political commentary.

The word 'terrorvision' has been widely used to reflect the allegedly sophisticated manipulation of TV and press coverage of terror incidents by the terrorists themselves, and in particular the manner in which the American TV networks allowed themselves to be 'manipulated' by the Shi'ites of Amal in June 1985. *The Times'* leader on 24 July 1985 asserted that 'The behaviour of American television crews and companies during the Beirut hijacking was a disgrace. They revealed all that potentially unsatisfactory side to contemporary news gathering which characterises the medium as being half way between journalism and show business, without fully identifying itself with either ... perhaps worst of all, there is the fact that the very presence of cameras at an event conditions and distorts that event so that the details lose their objective reality and become a media event instead.'

Terrorism is and always has been 'a media event', within the context of whatever channels of news and communications exist to disseminate information. While terrorism thrives in the age of the Global Village and instant worldwide communications, it is inconceivable that any terrorist could be motivated by the existence of the media alone to bomb, shoot, hijack and hold hostages. The real motivation of the terrorists – which governments perhaps inevitably prefer to dismiss – is the true message, and in the most modern context possible, states still employ the oldest option in times of outrage, of blaming those who report it.

It has been suggested that the Lebanese terrorists have even begun to display a TV-orientated dress sense, to make themselves a more appealing subject. The sad truth is the reverse: that warlike dress and behaviour are presented as an admirable norm in the other, far more culpable sector of 'the media' – the TV-movie and the largely American feature films in which gratuitous violence is described, even by its critics, as 'a new spirit of American patriotism'.

The American news networks, engaged in a permanent competitive battle, have become entirely accustomed to news events being staged, and stage-managed, in order to attract cameras and coverage – that is the lifeblood of the American political system. Their venturing beyond the bounds of good taste and judgement is tolerated in other areas of American life, but terrorism is where the line is drawn – after the event. In the coverage of the Shi'ite hijacking of TWA 847, the least acceptable pictures and interviews were those stage-managed by reporters and camera crews in which the American relatives of hostages were filmed in the worst moments of their stress and grief. They were unacceptable because they were not real events, but set up for the cameras: genuinely, therefore, 'media events'. But in Beirut, however much sophistication the terrorists may have used in manipulating the crews and reporters, the events from hour to hour were all too real. The guns that were fired at the cameras at Beirut Airport were real, and the crews had no weapons with which to defend themselves; the 'press conferences' were real events, however contrived and distasteful; and, whatever was said by the hostages, their ordeal was real and impossible to misrepresent. The terrorists held all the cards to make things happen, and the press had the job of recording it.

One of the most powerful and authoritative figures in the American press and broadcasting world, the Chairman of the Board of the *Washington Post* Company, Mrs Katharine Graham, offered a timely defence of the freedom of the press to report terrorist incidents when she became the first woman to deliver the annual Churchill Lecture at the Guildhall in London on 6 December 1985. She declared herself 'in favour of as full and complete media coverage as possible', and argued that terrorist events are 'too big to hide' from the public. There was no evidence to suggest that terrorism would stop if there were no publicity, and there was the additional fear that terrorists might 'turn up the volume' of killings in response. Government actions needed to be known and understood by the public. Mrs Graham naturally and rightly accepted that terrorism put journalists' sense and good judgement to an acute test, and prescribed that in terrorism, as in the (more common American) experience of urban riots, press and television journalists should minimise their role as participant or intermediary, and maximise their role as neutral reporter.

In the case of the Beirut 'press conferences', painful though they were, one must consider what might have been the consequences had TV crews and journalists either voluntarily boycotted the events, or had they been instructed, because of government pressure, to do so. In the first case, one might assume that hostages would have suffered severely until the cameras arrived again; in the second case, as the press corps was overwhelmingly American, it is easy to imagine their becoming a second wave of hostages, found guilty of following the orders of the 'enemy' US Government.

Thus media representatives should strive not to be manipulated, particularly (as occurred regularly in the Beirut instance) not in competing for 'exclusive' interviews with terrorists, entirely on their terms. Nor should journalists be seen to be putting pressure on government for an answer to terrorists' demands, in which case they become the terrorists' proxies: with government equally they have the right and duty to inquire about policy decisions and report them. Such detailed reporting, however, makes life all the more difficult for the politicians whose unfortunate lot it is to bring such events, if possible, to a peaceful conclusion. As Margaret Thatcher told the American Bar Association, the terrorists 'see how that coverage creates a natural wave of sympathy for the victims, and pressure to end their plight no matter what the consequence. And the terrorists exploit it.'

An act of terrorism, however, is so dangerous, so life-

174

threatening, and so directly aimed at destabilising the equilibrium of the state, that it is the last context in which there should be any doubt as to the neutrality of journalists. To argue that the public needs to be protected from the neutral reporting of terrorist acts, even in circumstances as intense and explosive as those of Beirut in June 1985, suggests that governments believe their citizens will accept the statements and claims of terrorists uncritically, and that revulsion at terrorist violence will not give them pause. In the words of former Israeli Ambassador Shaul Rosolio, 'A major element within the whole structure of counter-terrorism activities is psychological indoctrination – otherwise called public relations.' It works for governments, inevitably and self-evidently, more than for the terrorist criminals whose violence or threatened violence brings them to the attention of the public. But such qualms and uncertainty reveal the insecurity of governments when dealing with terrorism, which suggests that press freedom is particularly required at such times. The hard-won freedom of the press represents a protection from the dangers which may befall any nation; whether from the acute but marginal risks of terrorism, or from the insidious potential corruption of power in government.

The debate on media coverage of terrorism gets nowhere, not because of the lethargy or irresponsibility of practitioners, nor by virtue of government weakness, but because of a collective, passive recognition that the free press – despite the faults which can be highlighted, and to which attention should be paid, when covering terrorism – has too much value for a democracy to justify tampering with it. More widely, the restriction or abolition of civil liberties in general, which could severely limit terrorism, would limit the very freedom that is the antithesis of the terrorists' unrepresentative, unelectable claim to power.

Publicity is the most provocative instance of the truism that terrorists use and abuse the freedoms and facilities of ordinary democratic life to their own corrupt purposes. They need publicity, but they also need to be able to travel by air, road, and rail; to work, rent accommodation, and identify themselves with formal documents. The vast majority of the components of terrorist activity can be controlled and monitored, almost to the point of elimination: the perfect vehicle for eliminating terrorism is the police state, in which freedom can be eliminated for all in order to limit the extreme anti-social behaviour of a few. The police state has the ultimate advantage of a controlled press, so that if terrorists should somehow slip through the net and perpetuate their act, all formal news of it can be suppressed. Yet in spite of all such control, violent protest will never be finally quelled so long as there are extremists, of whatever political complexion, with access to petrol, matches, and the inner resources to engulf themselves in flames.

The extremism of terrorism invites, and intends to provoke, extreme reaction – particularly from a democratic nation that would resort to extremism only reluctantly. In spreading fear and insecurity, its purpose is to undermine public confidence in the institutions of government. A more sophisticated extension of this argument holds that terrorists regard state reaction in the form of severe repression as a tactical victory. The theory is that the citizenry will rise up in spontaneous revolt at the imposition of 'police state' interference with civil liberties, out of proportion to the real threat of terrorism. But even those who have cherished this vision, and survived their participation in terrorist campaigns, accept that it rarely happens. Most anti-terrorist legislation in democratic countries, caught in the gap between civil liberty and repressive control, falls on the side of liberty; and it is important that it should do so. For by retaining faith in its own democratic institutions, even at the cost of failing to extinguish terrorism altogether, the state reinforces public confidence in its system of government and publicly asserts the moral and practical superiority of its own methods to those who 'slug it out in the slime' of political violence.

6 DEALING WITH TERRORISM

Armed with legislative tools to confront terrorism, states also naturally protect their most prominent citizens, their public occasions, their international sports events and their national monuments. Of all the possible targets of terrorism, however, one of the most tempting categories must be the growing number of international conferences and symposia at which academics, police and military officers, newspaper columnists and other assorted consultants review aspects of the modern terrorist phenomenon. Under the auspices of the Georgetown University Institute, the US Defense Department, the Israeli Jonathan Institute and many others, the experts constantly reiterate their views to one another, read papers which are published and re-published in the books and journals they themselves edit, and advise the world's governments on anti-terrorist methods. Few of them are asked to play a role in the task itself. While they prescribe the legislative means and military firepower to defeat terrorism, they ignore the real – but less theoretically satisfying – options which governments have no choice but to implement, often as a matter of last resort:

Many states act in ways that their citizens might prefer not to hear about, and they may often be justified in so doing when they face the potentially fatal proposition of the terrorist incident. In the battle against terrorism, states cannot always restrict themselves to policing and legislative initiatives. Other options are available when these alone fail; and these other lines of defence reflect in turn both the nature of the terrorist threat faced by each state, and the political complexion of the government which uses them. In the simplest terms, we can distinguish three responses: negotiation, compromise and retaliation.

Negotiation is the policy of states which openly recognise (what most acknowledge behind closed doors) that terrorism is a form of politics, and optimistically believe that any political problem can be solved by negotiation; a policy infinitely easier to execute when the negotiating state is not the principal enemy and target of the terrorists, though that has not been an absolute obstacle.

Compromise is meant in its negative sense: a policy of inadvertent pragmatism, whereby states are unsure of their power to confront terrorism in the delicate balance of political, diplomatic and economic interests, and consequently get tough with one terrorist only to act weakly towards another; or worse, to threaten all kinds of retribution and severity while failing to deliver action.

Retaliation is the chosen policy of embattled or isolated states with a terrorist enemy which either lies outside the borders of the state, or if within has no meaningful political support, or such support that the state cannot afford to recognise.

When the overwhelming majority of states take the firm stand of 'We will not negotiate with terrorists', it may seem unlikely that negotiation can be described as a major political response to the problem of terrorism. But states *are* required to negotiate the effects of terrorism, whether overtly or not, in pursuing new political initiatives and mounting propaganda strategies; and sometimes they *do* resort to negotiating with the terrorists directly. France is the most conspicuous example.

France, as a nation whose modern existence is founded upon the revolution of 1789, has a constitutional commitment to offer asylum to political refugees – a concept which covers a multitude of sinners. The preamble to the National Constitution asserts that 'Anyone persecuted because of his activities in the cause of freedom shall be entitled to all the right of asylum within ... the Republic.' The phrase which describes France as a land of asylum (*une terre d'asile*) represents a fine revolutionary notion which in the 1970s and 1980s has led to France only half-reluctantly harbouring a large number of terrorists who are either ignored or treated a great deal more leniently than would be the case in any similar nation. There are more than 140,000 exiles registered in France as 'political refugees', and many more aliens are resident on other forms of permit which require less rigorous evidence of real or likely persecution.

In 1981 François Mitterrand was elected as France's first Socialist President. As a candidate, he had pledged himself to restore the traditional rights of political asylum in France, which had been somewhat neglected by his predecessor Giscard d'Estaing. On taking office, he issued an amnesty to some two thousand convicted criminals in French jails, including the two leaders of Action Directe, Jean-Marc Rouillan and Nathalie Menigon. Partly because of an apparent exodus of Middle Eastern terrorists from Britain, but largely because of France's extreme laxity towards a grand assortment of political extremists, Paris became the international crossroads of terrorism. Most notably, several hundred Italians – fleeing from arrest or sentence for terrorist crimes in Italy – set up in Paris, where the Italian government regarded them as 'the external column of the Red Brigades'. In 1982 a series of anti-Semitic attacks, culminating in the slaughter of six people in Goldenberg's restaurant in the Jewish Marais district of Paris, forced Mitterrand to act. He appointed a Minister for Public Security, Joseph Franceschi, made Action Directe illegal, and pledged a new tough approach to terrorism.

The real departure of the Mitterrand government was to take the political Constitution of 1789, and the contemporary political problem, and seek political solutions – by negotiation. There was outcry when leaks from police and intelligence circles revealed the French government was involved in detailed negotiations with every kind of domestic and foreign terrorist outfit, from renegade Middle Eastern states, to Corsican separatists, to domestic revolutionaries.

Government advisers, including one of President Mitterrand's closest political associates François de Grossouvres, were reported to have been assigned to exploratory talks with potential exponents of terrorism.

Appointees talked to the Syrian state security apparatus, headed by the sometime French resident Rifat Assad, brother of the Syrian President. The Syrians had long been suspected of waging unofficial war on dissidents and opponents based in Paris, and the French Foreign Ministry threw out a Syrian diplomat who, it was claimed, had been implicated in a car-bomb explosion outside the much-bombed office of the Arabic magazine *Al-Watan Al-Arabi*. Retired French intelligence officials met the PLO in Morocco, allegedly to discuss matters of mutual interest – such as keeping Palestinian violence off French soil. The PLO certainly owed the French government a favour: legend had it that a high-flying French diplomat in the private office of Foreign Minister Cheysson at the Quai d'Orsay, had personally saved one of Yasser Arafat's senior aides from falling into the hands of the Israeli invasion force in 1982, by driving him across Beirut in the boot of his car.

Ministerial aides were dispatched to conciliate Corsican groups who exploded more than one bomb per day throughout 1984 on the island; they assassinated one of the Paris intermediaries sent to deal with them, however. Sympathetic pro-Armenian statements were made even by the President himself, in the hope of limiting the threatened action of ASALA, the Armenian terror gang whose European stronghold was France. No less than three senior government ministers had significant Armenian minorities in their constituency towns, and some observers took the view that domestic politics, as much as an effort to limit terrorism, lay behind the efforts to conciliate the Armenians in France.

Most extraordinary of all was the effort by the French government, through the head of the GIGN anti-terrorist force, Captain Paul Barril, to make contact and negotiate with the most notorious of France's domestic terrorists, Jean-Marc Rouillan. Barril, writing by hand on Elysée Palace notepaper headed *Présidence de la République*, issued a remarkable invitation on 22 January 1983:

> Monsieur Rouillan,
>
> I should like to meet you personally, where and when you wish, in order to open a dialogue which could permit the regularisation of your position. I am authorised by the Presidency to deal directly with you.
>
> A bientôt j'éspère, Paul Barril.

Barril's signature was overstamped with the insignia of the GIGN. On another card he added, 'You can contact me by telephone early in the mornings (7–9 a.m.) or in the evening at my home,' and enclosed his private telephone number.

In an earlier attempt to open negotiations with Europe's most dangerous terrorist, Barril had written, in October 1982, on GIGN headed paper: 'I, Captain Paul Barril, commander of the GIGN, commit myself to ensure the physical protection of Jean-Marc Rouillan, and to present him directly to a magistrate. I further commit myself to give evidence in his favour of the fact of his voluntary appearance before the legal authorities.' This letter was accompanied by another, from Barril's superior officer Commandant Christian Prouteau, the chief of Elysée security and co-ordinator of anti-terrorist forces.

Perhaps not surprisingly, Rouillan did not rise to the bait. But both Barril and Prouteau have had notable careers on the periphery of terrorist activity. Barril, at about the time that he was awaiting Rouillan's call, had drawn up a plan to sink a houseboat on the Seine which investigations had established was occupied by Action Directe militants. His plan was turned down, but bore remarkable similarities to the successful execution of the bombing of Greenpeace's *Rainbow Warrior* in Auckland Harbour, by another branch of the French secret services. The man who turned it down was Prouteau, who was briefly involved in controversy during President Mitterrand's state visit to Britain in 1985, for having staged an eccentric 'security-test' in the grounds of the French Embassy, involving weapons and explosives.

Despite the controversial leaks about the negotiation policy, it has a substantial basis in logic. Although police officials are among the most outspoken critics of such tactics, some nevertheless accept that political terrorism can be susceptible to political solutions. Jean-Pierre Bourdier of the FASP (*Federation Autonome des Syndicats Policiers*) illustrates the point with a British example: 'In the United Kingdom you will continue to have terrorist attacks by the IRA until a political solution to the Irish problem is found. In France we have problems with the Basques, with the Corsicans ... and these will not cease until political solutions are reached.'

The central objection to attempting negotiations with terrorists, however, is that they place themselves beyond the rule of law, to which governments must be seen to adhere. The consequences of the relationship formed by French officials with representatives of the Armenian terrorist group ASALA demonstrate the possibility of disaster. In summary, the French government reached an understanding with ASALA that the group would not launch any attacks on Turkish or French interests, in exchange for which the government would publicly state its sympathy for the cause of Armenian independence, and argue for public, international recognition of the massacres suffered in 1915. Whether they were also motivated by domestic politics or not, such statements were made by President Mitterrand and certain of his ministers. The deal was, however, complicated by two factors: on 24 September 1981, four ASALA terrorists (calling themselves the 'Suicide Commando of Yeghia Kechichian' (a dead comrade) and naming their attack 'Operation Van' after the lake in the Armenian region of Eastern Turkey) seized the Turkish Consulate in central Paris, killing a Turkish security guard, seriously injuring the Vice-Consul, and wounding a French police guard and three other hostages. The leader of the terrorists, Vasken Sicilian, was wounded in the takeover, and about an hour later he was carried out of the building on a stretcher, shouting, 'I demand political refugee status!' After deadlines, threats and telephone negotiations with police, the terrorists surrendered to police.

182

Two days later, in Beirut, the alleged leader of ASALA held a press conference. Hagop Hagopian (a *nom de guerre* equivalent to John Smith) announced that two more ASALA suicide commandos were ready to take action 'to continue to strike at the Turkish establishment'. Hagopian, wearing a black hood with ASALA's insignia on the forehead, spoke in Armenian to a hastily assembled group of Western pressmen in an apartment building in West Beirut, with an English translation supplied by Alec Yenicomechian – blind, and missing his left hand, but by now released from the Geneva prison where he had been held. Hagopian claimed that the Paris commando had surrendered to authorities because their leader had been promised that all four would receive political asylum. They were apparently pushing too hard, for on the same day the French government denied any such suggestion, though it qualified the remarks with a most unusual degree of apparent tolerance for the 'cause' that the terrorists espoused: 'However sorrowful the historical events that the perpetrators of this act invoked,' the French statement read, the attack 'was an inadmissable assault on elementary human rights and becomes even more intolerable because once again Turkish diplomats assigned to France have been attacked.'

Private contacts between the French government and the representatives of ASALA continued, however: the French press widely reported that a 'Technical Counsellor' in the Prime Minister's office was in charge of contacts not only with Armenians, but with Italian terrorists of *Prima Linea*. According to press reports, Louis Joinet, a forty-nine year old magistrate, was appointed by Prime Minister Pierre Mauroy as Counsellor for 'Justice, public liberty, human rights and re-patriated persons'. (In another context, during the IRA Maze Prison hunger strikes campaign, it fell to Joinet to meet the mother of hunger-striker Kieran Doherty on 18 July 1981, to hear the IRA's anti-British propaganda in the emotional tones of an about-to-be-bereaved mother.)

However, the understanding with Armenian terrorists that had minimised their actions in France and against French interests, was put under severe pressures with the arrest in Paris of one 'Dimitriu Giorgiu', an Armenian carrying a false Cypriot passport of the same numerical series as the passport carried by 'Alexander Panadryu', an alias for a man wanted in connection with the anti-Semitic bombing of the rue Copernic synagogue in Paris in October 1980, in which four people died. 'Panadryu's' passport had been used to buy the motor-cycle on which the bomber had arrived at the synagogue, and was used as identification by the man who set off the bomb.

French Air police arrested Giorgiu for carrying a false passport, and were particularly interested in him as the possible suspect in the attempted assassination of a Turkish diplomat in Rome a few weeks earlier. The gunman had fled with a wound in his shoulder after the diplomat drew his own weapon and fired back; Giorgiu had a poorly-healed shoulder wound. Giorgiu was held for questioning, and while he was in police custody a woman telephoned French news agencies warning that unless he were released immediately, French targets would suffer attacks by Armenian terrorists. The same night, an Air France office and a French cultural centre in Beirut were heavily damaged by bombs: after forty-eight hours, Giorgiu was released. A police investigator said that although Giorgiu had made no secret of his affiliation to the Armenian terrorist group, 'We can't hold a man forever for having a fake passport'.

Within twenty-four hours, however, Giorgiu was re-arrested as he again attempted to board a plane to Beirut: in his possession were the false passport, 10,000 Swiss francs, papers linking him to ASALA, and a sheaf of press cuttings relating to the 24 September Consulate attack. Although Giorgiu was shortly released again, and put on a plane to Beirut, the next few months saw French interests in Lebanon, where they were most vulnerable to Armenian attack, suffering repeated bombings. French banks and Air France offices came under repeated attack.

In January 1982, a statement issued by ASALA in Beirut said that it would suspend all terrorist operations against France because the French authorities had promised a fair trial, and political prisoner status, for the four Armenians awaiting trial for the Consulate attack. (When the case duly came to trial on 23 January 1984, the Court President Guy Floch, putting into judicial effect the attitude of tolerance present in French political thinking on terrorism, outlawed the use of the words 'terrorism' and 'terrorist'. He told the court: 'I don't like the word "terrorists". If you will agree, we will use other words in the course of this trial ... Anyone might be considered as a terrorist by some other individual.' The four Armenians were convicted and sentenced by the judge to jail terms of seven years – which might be considered as lenient by some other individuals.)

Later in 1982 the circumstances were repeated, with the arrest by French police of an Armenian named Vicken Tcharkoutian. An engineer employed by the Fluor Corporation of California, Tcharkoutian was wanted by American police in connection with a minor bombing in Los Angeles. While police in Paris interviewed their latest Armenian suspect, ASALA in Beirut issued a statement, charging that the French government was breaking an agreement not to interfere with Armenian militants in France, as long as they were not acting against French targets. They threatened immediate retaliation, and did not wait to fulfil their threat, as one bomb exploded on the Boulevard St Michel within a day, and another was found and defused. Within a day or two Tcharkoutian was out of custody, and placed on a plane bound for the Middle East.

The final demonstration that both negotiations and deals had broken down came in July 1983. Because of continuing arrests of Armenian militants – though by no means the degree of stringent control of their activities that many would have liked to see – ASALA once again alleged publicly from Beirut that the French government had 'broken its word' in an unspecified manner. ASALA's response was a suitcase-bomb at Orly airport, which killed seven people. French police officials, already astonished by the policy, were horrified by the outcome. Police union leaders of the right alleged that the Socialist government placed more faith in terrorists than in the French police services; and that it discussed ways of diminishing terrorism first with the terrorists, and only subsequently with the police.

Because the terrorist always holds the initiative, deciding when, where, whom and how he will attack, states' policies are always vulnerable to being irrelevant to the dramatic possibilities of the event in hand. The greater the ruthlessness or recklessness of the terrorists, the less likely it is that government and security agency contingency plans can be made to work properly, at a tactical level. The same is true, however, of the politics of state reaction to terrorism. States can say, and certainly mean, that there will be no compromise with terrorism, but as with so many of the clearest political objectives, reality produces fumbling compromise, and performance falls far short of promise. One can point to almost any country to find an example of the workings of inadvertent compromise: but they are perhaps most striking when they arise to contrast dramatically with the forceful attitudes of those states which are looked to for 'constructive international leadership'.

Britain provides an immediate example. In April 1984 the notion of 'state-sponsored terrorism' came into the sharpest focus when a gunman inside the Libyan People's Bureau in St James's Square, London, opened fire on a crowd of anti-Gadaffi demonstrators, wounding a number of them, and killing a young British policewoman who was on patrol alongside the demonstrators. National and international opinion was outraged; and armed police settled in to lay siege to the occupants of the building. Ultimately, however, despite the near-certainty that a murderer was among the Libyan 'diplomats' still inside the building, all the occupants were escorted by the police to Heathrow Airport and allowed to leave the country. The People's Bureau was inevitably closed, and so was the British Embassy in Tripoli, where the British diplomatic staff had become counter-hostages to the Libyan authorities.

Later that year, in the wake of the affair, Mrs Thatcher specifically cited it in a typically forceful denunciation of terrorists: 'Whether he pursues his callous trade in Brighton or in Beirut, in Belfast or in St James's Square,' she promised, 'he must be brought to understand that his savagery will only strengthen our resolution.'

Resolution, however, is easier to deliver than action. Libya, for all the eccentricity and dangerous behaviour of Colonel Gadaffi, is a major trading market for Britain, in particular for substantial engineering projects, for which the contracts run into billions of pounds and are largely reserved for European countries. Her oil and oil wealth make her a nation that countries which depend for their livelihood on international trade cannot, perhaps, afford to alienate entirely. Whatever the explanation, the performance of Britain did not live up to either the expectations or the rhetoric, as the Director of the Office of Counterterrorism and Emergency Planning of the US State Department, Robert Oakley, made clear in his testimony to the Senate Committees on Foreign Relations and on the Judiciary: 'In London, following the shooting of the British policewoman from a window of the Libyan Embassy, there was a cry of outrage against Libyan terrorism ... A few months later, when we tried to talk with the British about stronger actions against the Libyans ... *the normal bureaucratic reasons for inaction again dominated the dialogue.*'

An earlier instance of compromise, again involving Libya, illustrates how the reasons for 'bureaucratic inaction' may lie in the extreme difficulty faced by democratic countries in weighing up the relative advantages of 'law and order' on the one hand, and 'foreign relations' on the other – particularly when foreign relations involve a trading partner. The immediate cause in this instance was the murder in 1982, as part of Gadaffi's 'stray-dogs' campaign, of Aziz Laderi, who was shot dead in the forecourt of Milan's railway terminus. As events developed, the case rapidly became the focus of a triangular international blackmail.

Laderi was a Libyan businessman, trading in farm machinery. According to Italian police, two Libyans accompanied him by train from Switzerland to Milan, apparently in the vain attempt to persuade him to return to Libya. When their persuasion failed, they gunned him down. A Milanese judge issued an Interpol warrant for the arrest of two Libyan citizens, and several months afterwards one of them was arrested in Paris. Rashid Said Muhammad Abdullah had arrived in Paris by air from Africa, and was arrested a few hours later in the expensive Hotel Nikko, a Japanese-owned and -operated hotel in the shadow of the Eiffel Tower. To the grave embarrassment of all concerned, the other person in Rashid's room at the hotel was the head of the Libyan People's Bureau in Paris.

Although extradition papers were prepared in Milan and despatched to Paris, Libyan pressure overtook judicial developments. Firstly, Colonel Gadaffi ordered an Air France jet with twenty-seven French citizens on board to be prevented from taking off from Tripoli Airport, and for the French nationals to be held. Next, he made serious threats to deny various Italian banks the repayments due on loans worth an estimated $1.5 billion. At the time it was suggested that several minor Italian banks could collapse if the threat was carried out. Furthermore Libya's state holding company for foreign investments, LAFICO, has since 1976 - when Libya was rich in petro-dollars and looking for secure longterm investments - held substantial shareholdings in a number of Italy's most important industrial and energy concerns, including Italy's largest multinational, FIAT (where LAFICO holds thirteen per cent of the shares). Two Libyans are FIAT board members, and one of them, Muhammad Siala, is a member of the five-man FIAT 'inner cabinet' or Executive Committee under the chairmanship of the multimillionaire Giovanni Agnelli. That, and other investments including a substantial Libyan property portfolio in Sicily, make the Italian government extremely nervous of giving unnecessary offence to the Libyan regime. Finally, both France and Italy enjoy very high levels of trade with Libya, Italy in particular having a substantial share of the country's massive infrastructure contracts.

As the twenty days' period for delivery of extradition papers to the French Ministry of Justice passed, political motives rather than merely judicial ones were given thorough consideration. Overall, would it be worthwhile for Italy to destabilise a difficult, but valuable relationship by prosecuting an individual terrorist for a matter of internal Libyan politics? Was it worthwhile to France to extradite a suspect in another nation's domestic politics – one whose arrest had provoked a very unpleasant reaction?

Maître Roland Dumas, then President Mitterrand's personal lawyer, was despatched as a special Presidential envoy to Tripoli. After talks lasting little more than twenty-four hours, the Air France jet was released with the French passengers and M. Dumas on board. Within days, the arrested terrorist suspect, Said Rachid, was released by the French authorities and escorted to a private Libyan plane which awaited him at Orly Airport. Nothing more was heard of the incident. And Rachid resumed his duties in the Libyan 'Department of External Security'.

The French government, pressed to explain Rachid's surprising release, argued that they had no choice but to release him, as Italian extradition papers had not arrived within the time limit of twenty days. Italian government sources insist that the French simply gave a promise to Libya, conditional upon the release of the French hostages in Tripoli, that they would release Rachid and ignore extradition procedures. French government sources, however, insist that it was the Italians who lost their nerve to prosecute.

An ability to handle such diplomatic complexities is a clear asset to any government which seeks to maintain its international political and commercial alliances, and to retain credibility in the international forum of nations committed to 'giving a lead' in the combat of terrorism. In this instance, M. Dumas' conduct of the affair was rewarded handsomely; first with a seat in President Mitterrand's Cabinet as Minister for European Affairs, within weeks of his involvement as a private emissary to Libya, and subsequently with elevation to Minister for Foreign Affairs, a post in which he succeeded the respected Claude Cheysson.

(An historical footnote suggests that Roland Dumas was an appropriate choice for the role of delicately unravelling the knot of politics, statecraft and terrorism involved in the Laderi-Rashid-Gadaffi case. Exactly nine years earlier, on 20 September 1974, Dumas had appeared in court in Jerusalem to represent Roman Catholic Archbishop Hilarion Capucci in a PLO gun-running case. The Archbishop, charged with carriage and possession of illegal weapons and contact with foreign agents, was alleged to have carried weapons into Israel from Lebanon, and to have supplied them to PLO fighters for attacks inside Israel and the Occupied Territories. His defence team, of Roland Dumas and the veteran Palestinian lawyer Aziz Shehadeh (murdered in a local Palestinian dispute in Ramallah in December 1985), failed to avert a guilty verdict, and Capucci was sentenced to serve concurrent sentences of ten and twelve years in the high security prison at Ramla, where most of Israel's imprisoned terrorists are incarcerated. Among other individuals, Capucci was one of those whose freedom was demanded by Black September terrorists in the hijack which ended at Entebbe Airport, Uganda, at the hands of Israeli troops.)

Expedient self-interest of one kind or another is behind every political compromise with terrorism. Even Israel, the state whose commitment to unequivocal retaliation has been consistently demonstrated, has recognised the occasional necessity of arranging trade-offs with its sworn enemies. Thus its tough national policy of immediate retribution for acts of terrorism was abruptly qualified by the decision in 1985 to release over a thousand Palestinian detainees, many of them convicted terrorists from the Occupied Territories of the West Bank and Gaza Strip, in exchange for three Israeli military prisoners of war held in Lebanon. Among those released were Kozo Okamoto, the deranged survivor of the Japanese Red Army group which carried out the 1972 Lod Airport massacre, and responsible for more Israeli deaths in a single incident than any other terrorist. Another man freed was Abu Einan, who was arrested in the United States and extradited to Israel in 1983 for his involvement in a 1979 bombing in Israel. Such mass releases sparked a vigorous debate in Israel: while some said that the release of prisoners undermined the 'No concessions' policy for which the state was renowned, and was tantamount to negotiating with terrorists, others argued that the consequence of such a concession should be the speedy release from prison of the fifteen Israeli West Bank settlers convicted of a series of terrorist actions, including the attempted assassination (and actual maiming) of two Palestinian mayors, and an attempt to blow up the Dome of the Rock in Jerusalem. The Israeli government argued that saving Israeli lives – or rescuing prisoners-of-war – was their first priority at any price, and was therefore not inconsistent with a strict policy of 'No concessions'. In truth, Israel is *not* exempt from the occasional pressing need for compromise or expediency – in this case, at least, in circumstances of her own choosing.

Under more immediate pressure, the Swiss government – not by any means a major target of terrorism – took the option that other states believe weakens the collective international stand against terrorists. A plot to bomb the US Embassy in Rome was uncovered by Swiss and Italian police, both forces arresting Moslem extremists in possession of weapons, explosives and documents indicating their target. The attempt was pre-empted, but the US government was keenly interested in seeing the testimony of the arrested suspects and ensuring they were locked up. Next, a Swiss diplomat, Erich Wehrli, was promptly abducted in Beirut, and his kidnappers demanded the release of a man arrested carrying explosives through Zurich Airport. To the disgust of the US State Department, the Swiss released him instantly. In the words of Robert Oakley, Director of the State Department's Office to Combat Terrorism, 'It certainly was not with US approval . . . It's something that we discussed with the Swiss government . . . indicating our – if you will – dissatisfaction. Everyone was convinced that this man is a terrorist, but there was nothing to link him to a specific violent act. Therefore, the Swiss courts gave him a certain benefit of the doubt and he was allowed to return to Lebanon. We think this is a mistake because we think that it invites more terrorist activity.'

Such concessions guarantee the confidence of terrorists that states will cave in to the kind of pressure presented by kidnapping and hijacking. Robert Oakley gives the Swiss government the benefit of the doubt with some diplomatic soft-soap; their decision to release the arrested suspect can only be regarded as a simple compliance with the demand of the Beirut kidnappers. It is hard to believe that carrying explosives through Zurich International Airport is not covered by the Swiss criminal code, or that someone doing so cannot be tried and ultimately sentenced to a meaningful term in jail.

It is perhaps natural that the disgust to be expected of American policy-makers at such an apparently feeble response should be played down: for American policy in a number of international arenas demonstrates the simple and genuine advantages of operating a system of double standards. Its effect is undoubtedly diminished by public revelation, however, though such exposure tends to come only when the advantages have come to an end. In the case of Palestinian nationalism, the United States faces a classic dilemma, which illustrates the vicious circle in which the adherents to a 'just cause' become trapped. Acts of terrorism provoked the world, and the United States in particular, to pay attention to Palestinian nationalism (though the Palestinian quest for national independence has been, and remains, far more than a terrorist campaign). The United States, naturally enough, condemns terrorism and all those tainted with it. The Palestinians, who got nowhere without terrorism, can get nowhere with it; and while the majority remain frustrated but passive, a minority pursues the option of violence in the hope that something, ultimately, will give.

Leaving aside for the time being the nature of America's Middle Eastern strategic interests, and equally ignoring domestic political lobbies, the United States had to have a functioning diplomatic presence in the Middle East during the 1970s – after the immense upheavals of the 1973 'Yom Kippur' war between Israel and Egypt. In the Lebanon, where a substantial number of Palestinian refugees had led a meagre United Nations-sustained existence since 1948, the PLO began to build a substantial strategic presence, not least because in 1970 King Hussein had finally decided that the PLO was becoming too powerful a force in Jordan, where half the population was Palestinian. He simply deployed the Royal Jordanian Army to drive the irregular Palestinian forces to retreat, in what the victims of the purge called 'Black September'. Lebanon was their natural refuge – an artificial state composed of warring religious and tribal factions, with the military advantage of lying adjacent to Israel, and offering a tactical second front for Palestinian attacks, in addition to their underground terrorism in the occupied West Bank.

The United States National Cemetery at Arlington, Virginia – across the classical Memorial Bridge, spanning the Potomac River, with elegant Washington on the other side – contains the grave (Section 5, Site 134) of an American diplomat whose death at the hands of PLO Black September terrorists can be seen to have initiated a secret US-PLO pact. Ambassador Cleo Noel was shot dead in a Khartoum Embassy siege in 1973, when Black September terrorists stormed into a diplomatic cocktail party at the Belgian Embassy; they held the Belgian and American ambassadors hostage, offering their freedom in exchange for three Black Septembrists jailed in Europe.

The American response was confused, according to a former member of the State Department Office for the Combat of Terrorism: 'President Nixon made a public statement, saying "No negotiations" when an Assistant Secretary of State was on the plane to Khartoum to try to negotiate.' (Still more extraordinarily, as long after the incident as January 1986, American politicians began lobbying the US Justice Department to issue a warrant for the arrest of Yasser Arafat for Noel's murder, on the unconfirmed claim that a tape-recording existed of a telephone call in which Arafat personally ordered the Black September gunmen to kill their ambassadorial hostages. Those pressing for the charge overlooked the fact that the US government's recent extension of jurisdiction was not retrospective.)

In his memoirs, *Years of Upheaval*, the former Secretary of

State Henry Kissinger refers to contacts in July 1973 and a secret session on 3 November 1973, conducted by CIA Deputy Director Vernon Walters with a senior PLO official. A secret non-aggression pact between the US and Fatah was the result and, as Kissinger wrote, 'attacks on Americans – at least by Arafat's faction of the PLO – ceased.' Kissinger himself was the first beneficiary: in December of that year, during a visit to Lebanon, the Secretary of State received 'a report that there was ... a plan to shoot down my plane', which was quickly diverted to a Lebanese airbase in the Bekaa Valley. The primary purpose of the pact was to protect Americans and American interests in West Beirut, the site of the American Embassy, and increasingly under Palestinian dominance as Lebanon grew ever more unstable and moved towards civil war.

The Palestinian liaison man for the pact was Ali Hassan Salameh, the chief of Fatah security, and widely believed – in places other than Israel – to have been a chief planner of most Black September terrorist activities, including the Munich Olympics attack in 1972. Such notoriety gave him the power to deliver the PLO's side of the bargain, allegedly mobilising a 6,000 man security force for Kissinger's visit to Beirut. It also made him the most obvious target for a terror-reprisal attack by Israel. On 22 January 1979, he died in a car-bomb explosion that is generally credited to Israel's counter-terror 'hit team'.

Very few American officials are prepared to discuss the effect of the pact that Salameh conducted for six years, or indeed its existence. One, the former ambassador to both Egypt and Saudi Arabia, Hermann Eilts, was quoted (in the *Wall Street Journal*'s investigation of Salameh's activities) as saying of him: 'Over the years I was in government, I learned a good deal about his activities. I know that on a good many occasions, in a nonpublic fashion, he was extraordinarily helpful – as was Fatah – in assisting in security for American citizens and officials. I regard his assassination as a loss.'

Other documented instances of PLO protection include the escorted evacuation of 263 Westerners from West Beirut, at the height of the Civil War in June 1976, by uniformed

Palestinian forces; a warning of an assassination attempt against Ambassador Eilts himself; and a no-assassination guarantee for the new US Ambassador Dean Brown in the spring of 1976; besides constant security and protection services which, as the *Wall Street Journal* commented, gave rise to a civil war joke that 'it was wise to live in the same building as American diplomats because the Fatah security was so tight'.

According to a former White House official, the gain to the USA was the obvious one of being enabled to operate securely in an area of PLO domination: 'I don't know of any incident after [the pact was agreed] when they attacked an official US target' – that is, until Operation Peace for Galilee. He goes on to say, 'We were in an area which was PLO territory, but Americans were not bothered. What the PLO got out of it was harder to say. I suppose they thought that they might gain by getting a political relationship out of it.'

In fact, looking at the relationship from the PLO's point of view – people who desperately need support for their cause from outside the Arab world, and above all need to drive a political wedge between Israel and the USA – it was something of great value. As a high-level Washington source described the pact's workings, 'It functioned. It's clear that there was a degree of contact that was consistent with keeping things cool and dealing with security problems: but it went beyond that as well. We got a lot of information through that channel – a lot of it was fed, and a lot of it was disinformation – but it did mean that messages could get through in both directions and that was of value to Arafat when he didn't want to rely on Arab intermediaries.'

While it may be less surprising that the unofficial US-PLO relationship was sustained through the years of the Carter Presidency – which was distinguished by its concern for human rights, and for the Camp David peace process in the Middle East, from which Palestinian interests were inevitably absent – it was in fact formed by a Republican Administration, under Presidents Nixon and Ford, and ultimately maintained, though without enthusiasm, by another under President

Reagan. In the words of a Washington source, 'The Reagan Administration was less keen on keeping it alive, but something continued until the PLO's expulsion from Beirut (in August 1982).' Most remarkable of all, the channels of communication were kept open at the highest level until the last days when, as the PLO evacuated Beirut from under the muzzles of Israeli invasion forces, President Reagan was preparing his new Peace initiative – publicly unveiled in his speech of 1 September 1982.

For any American initiative, the most important elements are that there must be something to involve Jordan in the 'peace process'; something to make the Palestinians feel that their grievance will be addressed; and enough to placate Israel and US domestic fears that the Israelis are not being sold out. Secret diplomatic contacts ensured that King Hussein was given notice of the plan a few days ahead of its publication, 'so that he would respond positively', in the words of an insider. Israeli government leaders were 'furious that they were given no warning', being left to learn of the plan only when it became public. According to a knowledgeable Washington source, 'The only other person informed was Arafat – someone went into West Beirut to brief Arafat in the hope that the PLO response would not be entirely negative.' The PLO chairman left Beirut on 31 August 1982, indicating that he was briefed at least two days before the Reagan Plan became public; despite the mechanics of the relationship, however, the PLO response was very negative.

The PLO's departure from Beirut can be seen to have had extremely poor consequences for the United States and her interests. While there can be no certainty about the matter, there is a clear case for observing that US casualties in Lebanon since 1982 specifically relate to the PLO's absence from the region and the loss of their protection. After September 1982, American interests became vulnerable to the attacks of the PLO's successors as power-brokers in West Beirut, the Shi'ite Moslems – a sector of the Lebanese population whose connections to Iranian Moslem fundamentalism and the Ayatollah Khomeini made them both incomprehensible and untouchable to American policy-makers. The true facts of the US-PLO relationship may never be established, and partly because of a Shi'ite suicide bomb attack. The first such major attack, which half-demolished the American Embassy in West Beirut, almost certainly killed the American intelligence official who was responsible for liaison with Ali Hassan Salameh of the PLO, along with the whole of the high-ranking Middle Eastern CIA team which was meeting in the Embassy at the time. (There have been repeated suggestions that the timing of the suicide attack is attributable to this meeting; with a wide variety of explanations being offered as to the source of the knowledge that it was taking place, and the identity of those responsible for authorising the attack – even including the idea that Israel could have done so, in order to make the USA more dependent on Israeli intelligence-gathering.)

The era when such a pact was possible, has passed, at least in terms of United States policy. The American blood shed in Lebanon, and splits within the Palestinian ranks which have led to more terrorism by fewer and less representative people, have hardened American attitudes and led the Palestinian cause back into the vicious circle. Kenneth W. Dam, as Acting Secretary of State, said on 1 October 1984, in a speech where the words 'PLO' and 'terrorist' had apparently become synonymous: 'Anyone who thinks we can stop these suicide bombings by cozying up to the PLO, or by walking away from Israel, is dead wrong. Terrorists feed on instability; they are the scavengers of strife and conflict. No moderate state is safe from them. No change in policy will appease them. Only an implacable desire for peace can stop them.' Mr Dam, however, went on to reiterate the proposals of the Reagan Peace Plan, describing it as 'balanced and fair ... designed to bring about a just and lasting peace that will both recognize the legitimate rights of the Palestinian people and, at the same time, assure the security of Israel, our commitment to which remains "ironclad".'

Such a policy actually has an inbuilt tendency to promote terrorism: while the Palestinian element of the peace process has been recognised as impossible to ignore, the USA attempts to marginalise the PLO. But to deny the PLO participation in political channels merely confirms the influential minority who believe such methods will always fail, and that violence alone will bring results. Successive American Administrations have tried to identify and cultivate moderate, acceptable Palestinians to speak for their people, respectable academics and newspaper editors. Yet such spokesmen are certain, whatever the small print of their allegiances, to deliver whatever deal can be struck into the hands of the unacceptable PLO – the sole meaningful representative of the Palestinian people, rich, armed and organised. The PLO will not have been forced by negotiation in the meantime to abandon all acts of terrorism, or in effect to make themselves an acceptable negotiating partner to the United States, Western Europe, or above all Israel.

Beyond legislation, negotiation and compromise, lies retaliation: a policy of response at once simpler in its action and more beset by problems than any of the others. The state which most conspicuously, consistently and dramatically pursues this course is Israel. Not least because of Israel's almost uniquely vulnerable position in relation to its neighbours and its region, the nation is highly militarised and highly motivated to identify and eliminate threats to its security, which are openly and repeatedly made. Acts of terrorism against Israel, perpetrated by a variety of Palestinian factions, themselves sometimes hostile to each other and enjoying the backing of different states, are regarded very simply as attacks on the integrity of the state, and Israel treats them, in effect, as *casus belli* – the justification for going to war, or at least employing substantial military force in reply. Conversely, all enemies of Israel have become 'terrorists' in the eyes and language of the government, and all actions against Israel, even in her role of occupying power, are assailed as 'terrorism' – even when in only slightly different circumstances they might be regarded, for example in Washington, as acts of legitimate resistance by courageous patriots.

No Israeli government has been able yet to contemplate

dealing with Palestinian terrorism in any less dramatic way, despite the considerable unease which Israeli military retaliation causes even among her allies. Other nations share her attitude, however, and many would like to: South African troops have engaged in 'hot pursuit' of terrorists across borders into the territory of neighbouring sovereign states, and British security forces would dearly love the freedom to cross the ragged border from Northern Ireland to the Republic in pursuit of IRA terrorists who shelter behind it.

What distinguishes Israel's retaliation is the extension of the definition of an 'attack on Israel' to include any attack, on any Israeli interest, anywhere. By this very exacting interpretation of the Israeli national interest are created the awkward anomalies which somewhat undermine Israel's extreme insistence on her right to defend herself from her enemies. The most conspicuous such instance arose when, after some months of relative peace in Northern Galilee (where shelling by Palestinians from Southern Lebanon had been commonplace), the Israeli invasion of Lebanon was launched under the guise of 'Operation Peace for Galilee'. In an apparent search for justification, the Israeli government proposed in all seriousness that the invasion was a response to the near-fatal shooting of their Ambassador to the United Kingdom, Shlomo Argov, by a team of terrorists who claimed allegiance to the Palestinian renegade Abu Nidal – based alternately in Baghdad and Damascus.

The full-scale invasion of Lebanon, and its continuing occupation for three years, are so extreme an example of the retaliation policy as to be almost absurd – and clearly Israel had far more at stake in trying to sort out the Lebanese chaos in her favour than a mere recess in terrorist activity. Not least of the objectives of the exercise was in Israel acting as a proxy for the United States in attempting to restore order in Lebanon, where Israeli and American interests were parallel. Few in Washington would deny that the invasion went ahead only after General Alexander Haig – at that time Secretary of State in the Reagan White House – had given the tacit approval of the Administration.

199

The essential questions to be asked of the retaliation policy as executed by Israel, however, are whether it works, and whether it can be justified. On the first point, the answer is bound to be negative. It is probably a minority of Palestinians that espouses or justifies terrorism in pursuit of the cause, but it is a substantial minority – far greater than could ever be distracted or dissuaded from their belief that nothing but direct action will win them a homeland, a flag, and national identity.

In the nature of Israel's retaliation, it might be possible to argue that one form of it has greater dissuasive powers than another. After the Black September terrorist attack on Israeli athletes' quarters at the 1972 Munich Olympic Games – which was not only a slaughter, but also brought immense attention and publicity, albeit negative to the Palestinian cause – Israel launched a counter-terrorist campaign. One might regard the campaign as a traditional intelligence exercise, in that Israeli intelligence services painstakingly tracked down, and then killed, as many of the planners and perpetrators of the Munich attack as they could find: in Beirut, Rome, Paris and everywhere. Using boobytraps and car-bombs, they seemed to use terrorism to eliminate terrorists. At such a level of intelligence and state determination, it may be that the methods employed are irrelevant: clearly the Israeli government of the time was convinced that if the terrorists were to be found 'in the slime' then that is where they should be tackled. Few would claim that those responsible for the Black September Munich action deserved anything better. Revenge, however, is far from being the same thing as retaliation; while there may have been a sense of 'justice done' in killing the killers, there is little likelihood that no one came forward from the ranks of the Palestinian terrorist organisations to take their place.

Israel's other retaliatory method, however, fails to be effective, and is indeed almost certainly counter-productive in the long term, precisely because it is so hard to justify. It is now an entirely familiar sequence for an act of terrorism against Israel to be swiftly followed by an air raid on the alleged 'terrorist bases' of the Palestinians. Israel regards her

Palestinian aggressors as being the responsibility of whichever territory gives them shelter, and thus simply refuses to recognise the existence of international boundaries which lie between Israel and her target. Equally, if the Palestinians have been so ruthless as to base their terrorists within civilian refugee camps in Lebanon, the Israeli retaliation will take no account of the risks to the innocent of a strike against a heavily populated refugee community. The responsibility emphatically lies with the perpetrators of the original act, in Israeli government eyes.

Thus within six days of the Palestinian attack in Larnaca, Cyprus, in which three elderly Israeli citizens were shot dead, Israeli Air Force planes were flying across the Mediterranean to bomb the Tunis headquarters of the Palestine Liberation Organisation, killing up to sixty people, including many Tunisians. (In an apparent diversionary air-strike four days earlier, Israeli planes had launched a night-bombing raid on a Palestinian base near the village of Majdaloun, outside Baalbek in the Lebanese Bekaa Valley, which did little damage and caused only one minor casualty.) The raid entirely destroyed the PLO's buildings at Hammamet Plage, including one which may have housed the PLO's apparent successor to Black September, 'Force 17' – alleged by Israel to have been responsible for the Larnaca murders. In killing Tunisian citizens uninvolved in Palestinian affairs, or in killing Palestinian refugees in Lebanon whose involvement in Palestinian violence may be entirely involuntary, the Israeli government embraces the most extreme form of political response to terrorist activity. Yet its policy is absolutely open and consists of a constant public warning that acts of violence against Israel will be repaid in kind. Within hours of the Tunis raid, the Israeli Defence Minister reiterated his government's position: 'The PLO have to understand that they have no immunity and that the long arm of the Israeli forces will seek them out wherever they are. Israel wants peace as soon as possible, but it reserves the right to fight terror with terror.'

The response of most democratic states to terrorist acts is, first, a call for perpetrators to be brought to justice, and secondly, an appeal for vigilance and international co-operation to ensure that general standards of justice prevail. Under no known definition of justice does the retaliatory killing of people who may be associated with actual criminals, or who happen to inhabit the same town, village or refugee camp, find acceptability. So when terrorists deliberately conceal themselves among civilians – as the Palestinians do in Middle Eastern refugee camps – is it enough for the Israeli government merely to say that civilian casualties in their air raids are the responsibility of the PLO? Or does retaliation simply mean that states sink to the moral level of terrorists? Clearly, the issue of retaliation and pre-emption is hung about with moral questions: as a former CIA Director Stansfield Turner (who served under President Carter from 1977 to 1981) expressed it: 'What we may think of as justifiable counter-terrorism is someone else's terrorism.'

Unlike Israel – which retaliates massively against acts of terrorism, but confines its response to those acts which specifically attack the State of Israel itself – the United States appoints itself to a wider role. It claims a role as the leader of the free world, and sees any assault on freedom, or on a democratic society, as an implicit attack upon itself. If an American life is taken or endangered – even in somewhat random circumstances – the full weight of state response is unveiled.

With the very public decision to mount a substantial air-strike against Libyan targets on 14 April 1986, the United States followed Israel's example in retaliation, in meeting terror with terror. It sought to overcome the problem of justification by trying to convince every other Western government that US intelligence agencies had conclusive evidence of the involvement of the Libyan People's Bureau of East Berlin in the bombing of a West Berlin discothèque, the 'La Belle', when it was full of American servicemen. Nevertheless, the decision not to publish what evidence there was tended to reinforce the lack of confidence that such evidence could, for example, satisfy an international court of law. (No

proceedings against Libya have been started in the World
Court – perhaps because the US has been forced to withdraw
recognition of it in the light of Nicaragua's suit against the
United States herself.) But there was no moral justification for
the consequences of the action. It is all too obvious that when a
single US air-raid kills more Libyans (the accepted figure was
about 100) than could possibly be attributed to acts of Libyan-
sponsored terrorism, and they are all 'innocent civilians' just
like the victims of terrorism, then that state action must be seen
as at least morally dubious, if not far worse.

This was not an issue, however, designed to trouble the
American government. As Secretary of State George Shultz
had remarked some time before the action, 'We may never
have the kind of evidence that can stand up in an American
court of law. But we cannot allow ourselves to become the
Hamlet of nations, worrying endlessly over whether and how
to respond. A great nation with global responsibilities cannot
afford to be hamstrung by confusion and indecisiveness.'

But Shultz's refusal to quibble over the morality of retaliation does not eliminate the question of how effective such
action is. For if it does not work as a deterrent it must be seen
simply as vengefully punitive and superfluous violence –
increasing the polarisation of minorities and simply adding to
the sum of violence as a whole, while solving nothing.

American policy may yet follow Israel's course. If it makes
political sense to bomb Libyan targets (inaccurately), which
will not eliminate the root causes of the terrorism which Libya
partly sponsors, then it may be regarded as acceptable in
Washington to sponsor a Libyan patriotic coup, or indeed to
invade Libya and depose Colonel Gadaffi. Failing such
action, it is hard to see how the United States could possibly
claim to have acted meaningfully to quell terrorism; therefore
US government actions may continue to demonstrate a logical
progression, but an abject lack of political understanding.

Indeed, the example of Israel should offer American policy-
makers a salutary example of how retaliation is too often a
mask for escalation. Israel's policy of automatic military
response to terrorist attacks upon Israel or her representatives

simply failed to eliminate the violence from Palestinians based in Lebanon. The only logical (if neither sensible nor success-ful) consequence was to do what Israel did – to enter Lebanon, driving the Palestinians first away from the border, beyond the range of their weapons, and then driving them from the country altogether. What Israel did not do, all too obviously, was to pursue political solutions to Palestinian dissatisfaction, to eliminate the root cause of the violence. Within a year of the final Israeli withdrawal from Lebanon, Southern Lebanon is once again heavily populated with Palestinian fighters ready and willing to act.

The three essential problems with a policy of retaliation have all been played out in the recent history of American involvement in the Middle East, and more particularly in Lebanon. The American retaliation which kills innocent Lebanese villagers; the redoubled energy of the terrorists in response to such actions; and the moral/tactical debate on whether states can ever legitimately use terror against terror-ists: all these issues have been amplified in the context of Lebanon's extraordinary political stew.

Until October 1983 the American Embassy in West Beirut stood on a dominant corner, with a broad boulevard between it and the waterfront. Almost a year later, the ruins had become a monument to terrorism. It was possible to stroll straight into the rubble, still forming a deep crater at the base of the arc-shaped shell which was all that remained of the building. Massive chunks of concrete hung as if by threads from high above ground, though the threads were half-inch steel reinforcing rods, and poked out from the fabric of the building at every conceivable angle. From behind recognis-able office doorways on the fifth floor, there waved in the breeze what seemed to be ribbons or unseasonal party decora-tions. The ribbons were roll after roll of 35 mm microfiche film, unravelling and waving in the breeze as the elements penetrated the wrecked Embassy. Those that had fallen all the way to the ground were microfilm copies of the *New York Times, Wall Street Journal, Washington Post, USA Today* and more – page after miniaturised page of yesterday's news, rendered meaningless by the most spectacular incident of terrorism against a superpower so far, and infinitely more important than anything in the files.

The wreck of the US Embassy provides a salutary reminder of the physical meaning of terrorism: it bears witness to the awful power of a massive bomb, ripping walls and bodies apart with equal ease. The close-up actuality of the violence makes the witness question whether any ends justify such methods – whether employed by a minority which feels excluded from all political dialogue, or used by states in which democratic trust is placed.

Lebanon, a country that has crumbled to anarchy under various native religious factions and several ill-motivated neighbour states and groupings, represents a baffling mix of Islamic fundamentalism, secular strategy, and apparently Westernised society. It also provides the USA with one of its most perplexing foreign policy problems.

'Operation Peace for Galilee' brought Israeli troops to the outskirts of Beirut. The Palestinians, skilful propagandists at all times, left in a mood of triumph and celebration that made their departure seem like a victory; indeed, Israel was left bogged down in Lebanon, fighting futile rearguard actions against new terrorist attacks, for almost three years. After the massacres of Palestinians in the Beirut refugee camps of Sabra and Shatila – for which the Israeli government's Kahane Commission found Defence Minister Ariel Sharon to bear a heavy responsibility – troops of three NATO countries (Britain, Italy and the USA) and France arrived to keep the peace. With Lebanese irony, the US Marines soon became the principal target of the violence they had hoped to quell.

The Marines did very little peacekeeping – and were constantly on the defensive from attacks by both Druze and Shi'ite militias. According to one well-informed Washington source, US policy-makers completely missed the opportunity for a useful alliance with the Lebanese Shi'ites, by dealing exclusively with the Christian President Amin Gemayel: 'There was a mistake when the Shia saw the opportunity to regain a position after centuries of subjugation; a lot of the Shia were not particularly anti-Israel, and they were glad to see the PLO out. Their demands were for representation and reform, but not revolutionary stuff. But we did not use our influence: we dealt with Amin Gemayel as if we could see all our interests protected through him.' Inevitably, in the nature of Lebanese conflict, the fact that the US neither assisted the Shia, nor complied with the Druze militia's idea of what America should do, meant that the Marines became a target for the shelling of both groups, from Druze and Shi'ite villages in the hills above Beirut.

In response, the USS *New Jersey* was summoned to the waters off Beirut and began the thunderous and far from accurate bombardment of the hills above the capital. 'When we started bombing with the *New Jersey*, we were bombing Shia villagers,' says a former State Department official. 'Three years later, after the TWA hijack, one of the hostages said she couldn't understand why the hijackers were so angry at her country. That was the reason.' But there was a far more immediate response to this American retaliation: the suicide bombing of the US Marine barracks at Beirut Airport. On the night of 23 October 1983, a truck loaded with explosives was driven headlong into the compound of the American Marines, killing 241 servicemen, and the driver, a suicide volunteer.

Internal military investigations indicated that American security had been poor and lacking in common sense about the risks involved in a military presence. In Lebanon, the distinction between conventional warfare and the irregular warfare of terrorism is invisible, but US intelligence sources soon let it be known where they placed the blame: with Lebanon's radical Shi'ite Moslems who were closely linked with the fundamentalist leader in Iran, Ayatollah Khomeini.

After the suicide attacks on the American and French Marine compounds, terrorists identifying themselves as Islamic Jihad (or Holy War) claimed responsibility. Their campaign has been maintained ever since with kidnaps and murders of Americans and other Westerners in Beirut and elsewhere. The United States soon arrived at a firm view of where ultimate responsibility lay for these attacks. In August 1984 Ambassador Robert Sayre, as Director of the Office for Counterterrorism and Emergency Planning, reported that ' the weight of the evidence is that Syria and Iran were directly involved in the three major bombing incidents in the Middle East in 1983 – the destruction of the American Embassies in Beirut and Kuwait on April 18 and December 12 and the bombing of the Marine Barracks in Beirut on October 23.'

The high-profile response of the US military was further naval shelling of the hills above Beirut, where many innocent people died alongside perhaps a few of the guilty. The undercover response came in March 1985, when American intelligence sources began to leak the names of the people they held responsible for the suicide bombers. One was Hussein Moussavi, the Islamic Amal chief; a second, Hassan Hamiz, a Lebanese with 'high-level Iranian contacts' who allegedly financed the explosives for the attacks, and was personally paid $50,000 for his role; and another Sheikh Muhammad Hussein Fadhlallah, the Islamic mullah whose leadership of the pro-Iranian *Hezbollah*, or Party of God, makes him Ayatollah Khomeini's Lebanese lieutenant. Richard Helms, the Director of the CIA from 1966 to 1973 and US Ambassador to Iran from 1973 to 1976, simply refers to Fadhlallah as 'Khomeini's spiritual man in Lebanon'.

American intelligence reported that Fadhlallah had travelled in and out of Iran and held secret meetings with Moussavi in his flat, before the suicide attacks. They further claimed that he had personally blessed the suicide commandos, assuring them of an instant place in heaven. Fadhlallah simply deflects all questions relating to such accusations: 'We don't see ourselves as terrorists, because we don't believe in terrorism,' he says. 'We see ourselves as *mujahideen* who try to fight a Holy War for the people ... You will find the real terrorists in the United States.'

On 8 March 1985, a week after he had returned from a long visit to Iran where he and other Shi'ite clerics had been granted an audience with Khomeini, Sheikh Fadhlallah miraculously escaped a massive car-bomb blast in Bir Abed, which lends some weight to his counter-accusation. The area around his apartment was devastated, sixty-two people were killed and more than 200 injured, when a car packed with explosives blew up outside the building with the apparent intention of destroying Fadhlallah's headquarters, and certainly of killing him. Lebanese Radio reported that the force of the explosion indicated that up to 2,000 pounds of explosive had been used, though another estimate put the figure between 100 and 375 pounds (the variation may be attributable to the fact that fire broke out when gas drums in a neighbouring bakery exploded). The holy man himself escaped injury, though several of his staff were killed.

The first public accusation of responsibility was made by Lebanese Minister of Education Selim Al Hoss, who said he had 'no doubt that Israel was behind this ugly crime'. But rumours quickly followed that the CIA was behind the attack; that it was finally acting on the promise to respond forcefully to eliminate the terrorist threat by whatever means necessary. It was suggested that a Lebanese unit (probably from the Phalangist forces) armed and trained by the CIA had attacked a target identified by the USA's foreign policy priorities and problems. On 21 May 1985 George Shultz was asked to comment on the rumours. He declined to deny CIA involvement, or to refute the proposition that the US government was somehow connected to the murders. Finally, he replied: 'There is a time when actions must speak louder than words.'

Although Shultz had neither confirmed nor denied the accusation, the idea arose that the United States was at least indirectly responsible – an idea that many people tried hard to disbelieve. Could it be the case that more than sixty people, having avoided the endless dangers of civil war in West Beirut, had died in the fearful violence of a superpower bent on revenge? The answer appears to be indirect, but affirmative. Michael Kraft, Counsellor for Public and Congressional Affairs in the State Department Office for Counterterrorism, spoke obscurely about the attack in August 1985. He agreed that there was 'a distant connection' between the CIA and the perpetrators of the Bir Abed bombing. In his words, 'It was done by a group which had had some discussions about receiving training and assistance from the CIA. But there were many fights about control and reliability. These guys then went off and did this and hired someone else to carry out the attack itself. It was a very distant kind of thing.'

That there should be any contact with people capable of such plans may be unnerving to those who take American government claims of moral superiority at all seriously. As one Washington source asserts, 'The CIA's technical denial is correct. They didn't order it, I'm quite sure of that. The people who carried it out were not on the US payroll. They hired other people, and they knew the kind of targets that the US would like to have attacked. The US made it clear that if there were opportunities it would be no bad thing to see them killed.' Of course, there are no documents which confirm arrangements of this kind – 'It's expressed in "ifs" and "how about's."'

The testimony of two former Directors of the CIA seems to confirm not only the general principles behind such clandestine deals, but also provides at least hints that the employment of surrogates was the precise explanation of the bombing in Bir Abed. As Richard Helms observes, 'If the blow-and-burn stuff is done by surrogates whom you've trained in the black arts and given a suitable cover ... they may be very hard to control. You may think you've called the operation off and wake up one morning and find out they've gone and done it anyway.' And Admiral Stansfield Turner argues: 'We don't want to be seen as a Wild West country that takes the law into its own hands ... What assurance do we have that our proxies won't take out eighty innocent people? When you hire assassins, you're not dealing with the cream of humanity ... I'm not sure that retaliatory assassination, even when it might be justified and much as it helps vent our frustration, really solves the problem of terror. It can make things worse. It can invite brother Shi'ites to engage in more martyrdom.'

The next wave of retaliatory action came not in martyrdom

but in the well-planned and ruthless hijacking of TWA Flight 847 from Athens to Rome, on the morning of Friday 14 June 1985. The crisis that unfolded over the next seventeen days demonstrated the irrelevance of neat and rhetorical solutions.

The hijacking of Flight 847 was the first time an American aeroplane had been taken over in the Middle East since 1970. But there was nothing about the choice that was fortuitous: the target had to be an American plane, in turn likely to be filled with American passengers whom the terrorists intended shortly to become American hostages. A large number of hostages gives the terrorists immense bargaining power, provided they have the motivation to make their threats convincing. This they very clearly demonstrated, at the expense of the life of Robert Dean Stethem, a twenty-three-year-old navy diver who was shot on board the TWA jet on the tarmac at Beirut Airport and dumped out of the plane in the darkness. No one saw him fall to the ground, but airport officials heard the thump as his corpse hit the ground. It is a good image for the obscure cruelty involved in terrorism – so rarely does the individual identity of the victim matter, and so rarely is there a known enemy who can be identified and pursued; yet so concrete and fearful are the hostile acts he perpetrates. Despite all the promises that terrorists would be brought to justice, both before and during the TWA crisis, the most powerful government in the world was once again made to seem powerless.

Governments inevitably find it easier to react to the last threat than to protect against the next: terrorism has a tantalising capacity to make every incident seem like an exception to the rules that ought to apply. In this respect, the TWA hijack was typically unpredictable. The hijacking apparently began with the simplest breach of security at Athens Airport, the kind which governments think they have made impossible. The hijackers kept the plane moving, from Athens to Beirut, Beirut to Algiers, Algiers back to Beirut, Algiers again, and finally Beirut once more. They abruptly murdered Bobby Stethem for the simple, chilling reason that he was an American military man whose death would confirm their own ruthlessness.

In Lebanon, an airport with no security and a government with no authority made negotiations a farce, as hijackers received reinforcements, changed shifts, led political rallies and conducted interviews at gunpoint. It is an indication of the total breakdown of Lebanese state order that intelligence services leaked – and gave considerable credence to – the rumour that the two original hijackers were Ali and Hassan Ezzedine, respectively the bodyguard of Nabih Berri, the Lebanese Minister of Education (and, far more importantly, the representative in government of the long-oppressed Lebanese Shi'ite minority), and the head of 'security' at Beirut International Airport. For the first time since Entebbe (where a handful of hostages were taken off the plane) the passengers' ordeal did not end with their leaving the aircraft: for almost two weeks thirty-seven American men were hidden somewhere in the sprawling barrios of West Beirut, out of reach of any rescue mission – except for one which would have killed at least as many hostages as it could have saved.

The paraphernalia of operational response to a terrorist hijack is impressive: the State Department had assembled its Task Force and opened up a twenty-four-hour Operations Room within four hours of the hijack of the TWA 847, by about 8 a.m. (US time) on 14 June 1985. The Operations Room itself, forty feet long and dominated by a large oval table – like a newspaper City desk, according to one participant – is equipped with banks of telephones, maps of world time zones, and cable and telex machines. A communications link to the Federal Aviation Administration is always open, in this case providing contact and consultation with TWA. Side rooms with secure telephones and Wang desktop computers are available for the Task Force Co-Directors to make secret communications: during the TWA 847 incident, the calls were being made to the American Ambassador Reginald Bartholomew in Beirut, and Ambassador Newlands in Algiers.

Algeria had two levels of involvement: the plane shuttled

twice to Algiers from Beirut and back again, letting twenty-one hostages go free on the first stopover; and there was the hope that, as in the case of the Iranian hostages, Algeria might be able to play a role as mediator to resolve the problem. But despite the quick-response capability of the State Department, the instant net of communications, and the involvement of the highest political levels, up to and including the President himself, the TWA 847 episode demonstrated yet again – as President Reagan himself was forced to acknowledge – that the terrorists 'hold all the cards'.

No terrorists, except the Islamic Guards in Teheran from October 1979 to January 1981, can ever have had a stronger bargaining position. However good US intelligence might have been in Beirut, it is inconceivable that any US forces or covert operatives could have located all the hostages once they had left the aircraft. (To attack the aircraft on the ground at Beirut would have required not intelligence but insanity. The pilot, Captain John Testrake, told an interviewer from the cockpit, with a gun at his head, that if anyone mounted an assault they would all be 'dead men'.) The southern suburbs of West Beirut where the hostages were held, separated into small groups, is a warren of tumbledown concrete shanties; refugee camps end and private houses begin without noticeable divisions; substantial apartment buildings have gaping holes and scorch-marks from repeated shelling attacks; few roads are more than tracks between the random building-plots; armed militiamen, rarely in any recognisable uniform, stand menacingly at every corner. These conditions provided the blank answer to the sort of pledge President Reagan made on 18 June: 'We tell the assassins in Beirut and their accomplices that America will never make concessions to terrorists.'

The United States had no choice but to make concessions, and while they may have been 'non-substantive' in some people's opinion, they must be regarded as real nevertheless. These terrorists were staging armed theatre – they made only one simple, clear, but apparently impossible demand, for the release of 'our Arab brothers jailed in Israel'. Despite the diplomatic niceties which demonstrated that the

US government had no power to order Israel to comply, and despite public statements that it would not request such a thing, there can be no doubt that in fact the State Department and White House took an extremely close interest in Israel's existing plans to release Shi'ite prisoners. It cannot be claimed with certainty that the process was speeded up, or that more prisoners were ultimately released by Israel than had been intended. But certainly no one can have been surprised when the Israeli government duly released the prisoners, in batches, neatly track-suited and shod in training shoes, protesting that it had all been planned months earlier as part of the overall plan for withdrawal from Lebanon. Equally certainly, it cannot have been an appeal to a sense of justice and fair play alone that encouraged the mediator, Mr Nabih Berri, to bring about the freeing of the American hostages from their informal imprisonment in the Beirut suburbs.

The extraordinary role of Berri himself – the only man whom the American government was able to enlist as mediator – is summed up by his own remark early in 1985, when he said: 'If everyone who fights against the Israeli invasion is a terrorist ... maybe I am the biggest one. Let's speak very frankly.' (On the other hand, because of the long-running feud between Lebanese Shias and Colonel Gadaffi, whom they believe to be responsible for the murder of their religious leader the Imam Moussa Sadr in Tripoli in 1978, Berri is dismissed by Gadaffi as 'an agent of Zionism'.) It was from secure phones in the State Department's twenty-four-hour Operations Room that National Security Adviser Robert McFarlane telephoned Berri 'at stages when he wanted to throw in some extra chips', in the words of one State Department man. When the US government is forced to negotiate for the freedom of hostages through a man who is a minister of a foreign government, but to whom at the same time the terrorist hijackers appear to owe allegiance, it is clear that all the rhetoric in the world cannot replace relevant action. But relevant action is precluded, time after time, by the regional pressures or local peculiarities of the individual incident – creating the overwhelming impression that even

America has almost no power to act against terrorism except in ways which make the United States government seem as ruthless and careless of innocent life as the terrorists themselves.

No one could have argued, however, as the incident came to an end, that either legislation or military hardware had provided any sort of answer to the problem that a handful of terrorists had posed to the superpower. It demonstrated the disproportionate potency of terrorism all too clearly, and underlined how governments need to employ every available method of political statecraft against it.

7 TERRORISM AND AMERICA

The problems which terrorism presents to a state power are seen most acutely in the case of a superpower and most clearly in the case of the United States, where even in the face of serious and damaging terrorist attacks, a public openness distinguishes the conduct of defensive policy. Where other states may conceal both their uncertainty and their compromises, the recent American experience of terrorism has plainly revealed the inability of political leaders to find simple solutions, and brought about at least a partial recognition of the constraints under which they are bound to operate. Such conclusions have emerged only indirectly, and principally because almost all important political events in the United States occur in public. Consequently the gap between stated policy and actual conduct is open for all to see, as is the endless wait for action on promises and threats made in haste. A more restrained political climate offers more protection for the pragmatic policy-maker, with less pressure to deliver the impossible promise.

For this reason, the emphatic assertions of the nature of American policy on international terrorism seem transparently to be wishful thinking. While President Reagan may insist that 'America will never make concessions to terrorists', the record of the American experience in the Middle East alone presents contradictory evidence. The 1979 seizure of the US Embassy in Teheran (which the US government has always regarded as the action of terrorists, though it could be argued that it was truly the action of the state) contributed largely to President Jimmy Carter's failure to be re-elected – a historic failure which bears ample testimony to the impact of terrorism on the American political culture. In 1983, the suicide bombings of the US Embassy and Marines compound led directly to the withdrawal of US troops from Lebanon, where they had come to keep the peace, but left behind a far greater instability and violent chaos. A third example, perhaps more significant than any other, is represented by the TWA hijacking in June 1985, when it is no exaggeration to suggest that America was in a state of national crisis because of a single terrorist act in an area where US policy had practically evaporated.

The level of violence directed at American interests is high and continuous. As US State Department figures show, the annual number of terrorist attacks on American interests worldwide has varied between 133 and 215 since 1970; the lowest incidence was in 1984 when, after the massive bombs and casualties in Lebanon of 1983, security procedures were immensely intensified. The first four months of 1985, however, with 94 attacks, suggested that a new record would be reached that year. In the thirteen months from 1 January 1984 to 1 February 1985, there were sixty-three attacks on American diplomatic and military facilities – which bear the brunt of the terrorists' violence. Three persons were kidnapped, eighty-five wounded, and forty-two killed; the deaths were distributed between West Germany (11), El Salvador (8), Lebanon (7), Colombia (5), Spain (5), and Italy (4). Besides the actual violence, hostility to the American presence is expressed in the form of threats, and at a remarkable level: on the anniversary of the Beirut Marine Barracks bomb (23 October 1984), American installations were receiving more than one hundred threats from terrorist groups around the world every week.

US State Department statistics show that the US is the prime target for international terrorism. Over forty per cent of all terrorist actions in 1983 were directed against it (205 attacks), and numerically more, though a lower percentage, in

1984. More acts of terrorism are perpetrated in Western Europe than any other region of the world: in 1983, almost twice as many as in the Middle East; in 1984, about ten per cent more. But of the 191 Western European incidents in 1983, 95 were attacks upon US interests; of the 231 in 1984, 49 were attacks on US interests. In 1983 in Latin America, 58 of 125 attacks were upon American interests, and in 1984, 45 out of 81. By contrast with this high incidence of attacks abroad, there were in 1983 just eight acts of international terrorism on American soil, and in 1984, only five. Another demonstration of the United States' external experience of terrorism is provided by the figures for 'explicit threats against US citizens and property' in 1983, when out of 171 explicit threats, only seven were made in North America.

Terrorist attacks upon the USA occur for the most part on foreign soil, by citizens of other countries. The most economically vigorous nation on earth is attacked at its extremities, where its diplomats are cultivating US interests, where its businessmen are grabbing opportunities, where its tourists are exploring, where its political and military advisers are ensuring that allies are preserved and enemies fail. American citizens – perhaps unique in the fact that an immigrant nation consists of people who have chosen their national flag – face the problem of being universally identified with their high-profile nation, while suffering the absence of America's protective embrace. In the 1980s, the American passport – which has for so long represented a doorway to freedom for the refugee and the oppressed of the world – has become a ticket to danger for any hostage confronted by terrorism.

Such terrorism is the price to be paid for power – or superpower – and its effects on America are both the consequence of, and complicated by, its perceived position in the world. The ideology that underlies this position was expressed in simple terms in the immediate postwar period when, despite the fact that they had been recent allies in the defeat of totalitarianism, America and the Soviet Union set themselves in contention for global domination. In the words of President Harry S Truman, speaking on 12 March 1947, the 'Truman

Doctrine' established the future role of the United States as 'the world's policeman':

> At the present moment in world history nearly every nation must choose between alternative ways of life ... One way of life is based upon the will of the majority, and is distinguished by free institutions, representative government, free elections, guarantees of individual liberty, freedom of speech and religion, and freedom from political oppression. The second way of life is based upon the will of a minority forcibly imposed upon the majority. It relies upon terror and oppression, a controlled press and radio, fixed elections, and the suppression of personal freedoms. I believe that it must be the policy of the United States to support free peoples who are resisting attempted subjugation by armed minorities or by outside pressures.

In a speech nearly forty years later, in October 1984, George Shultz effectively confirmed the moral and political currency of Truman's vision, reminding his audience that

> the United States ... are morally committed to certain ideals and to a humane vision of the future. Nor is our vision limited to within our borders ... The terrorists who assault Israel – and indeed the Marxist Provincial IRA in Northern Ireland – are ideological enemies of the United States. We know the difference between terrorists and freedom fighters, and our policies reflect that distinction. Those who strive for freedom and democracy will always have the sympathy and, when possible, the support of the American people. We will oppose guerrilla wars where they threaten to spread totalitarian rule or deny the rights of national independence and self-determination. But we will oppose terrorists no matter what banner they fly.

The United States pursues its mission in two ways which identify the nation as a superpower. Firstly, by standing as a global judge of the world's behaviour – which is the prerogative of all states in proportion to their power; and secondly, by seeking to mould the world and its affairs more to its own liking and advantage, which is the prerogative in reality only of states with great power. But by extension

218

America has a double problem. Firstly, its ambition to protect and extend the boundaries of democracy in the world make it vulnerable to attacks from those whose jargon assails the USA for seeking world hegemony, control over natural resources, cultural imperialism and economic exploitation of the people concerned. Secondly, America regards any attack on any American citizen as an attack on the nation itself, and on its avowed moral commitments to keep every citizen free.

This conflation of the political and moral vision is fundamental to the American experience of terrorism: as Shultz asserted in 1984, 'We are attacked... because of who we are, and what we believe in.'

In a world so polarised between political systems and power blocs, and where the faint hopes of oppressed or neglected minorities look ever more insignificant as they fall into the long shadows of the superpowers, there is no reason to believe that Shultz's statement will lose its validity in the foreseeable future. The actions of the United States are so resonant in international relations that for every instance in which it believes it is 'doing right' there will at least be groups, if not powerful sovereign states, who believe it is 'doing wrong'.

To take the most current and acute example, that of Islamic fundamentalist sentiment, one can look to the words of Imam Mohammed Asi – a Moslem fundamentalist with allegedly close ties to Ayatollah Khomeini, but who nevertheless is an American citizen. In 1985 the Imam promised that Americans would be driven out of the Middle East, and threatened a continuation of terrorist activity 'if the Americans continue to pursue the same policies that they have been pursuing in the past, policies of a carte blanche identification with the interests of the occupiers of Palestine – if that is the case, then the United States will continue to receive the same attacks and the same terrorist acts, as they are called here. Of course I do not subscribe to that description ... I would call these legitimate strikes by the Moslems as acts of liberation.'

Elsewhere, the positive commitment to preserve other nations' independence and self-determination is interpreted by

America's ideological enemies as self-interest run riot, as for example in the Action Directe document of 1982, *Pour un Projet Communiste*. Despite its garbled argument, the venom and resentment of its sentiments are unmistakable:

> Under the aegis of the United States and the institutions which implement its strategy – the IMF, for example – the international capitalist division of labour puts France in the second rank of imperialists: dominant towards the Third World, but dominated by the European community and American multinationals ... The Americans deliberately organised structural economic disorder ... They systematically financed the world's invasion by their multinationals – and the happiness of hamburger-eaters (McDonalds, of course) ...

And so the indignation goes on and on; against the easy targets of McDonald's imperialism, Cowboy Reagan, Peanuts Carter; presenting NATO as an instrument of oppression rather than of collective defence; identifying all Western economic activity as oppression of the Third World. The woeful rhetoric could be disregarded if it did not go hand-in-hand with acts of terrorism which kill, injure and destroy.

Less intemperate opponents of America's 'Globalism' point with concern to the immense scale of American military assistance and military sales around the world, and to the hostilities that seem necessary to consume such a volume of arms. In 1983, the United States provided military assistance to her allies around the world valued at $179.3 million, according to Defense Department figures. But US military sales to her allies amounted to a fraction under $11 billion worth of weapons, ammunition and associated services. In 1982, the USA accounted for twenty-four per cent of total worldwide military expenditure, or $196.3 billion (out of a NATO figure of $308.4 billion). In the same year, the Soviet Union individually spent $257 billion, out of Warsaw Pact expenditure of $300 billion – very slightly less than NATO. In respect of both superpowers, the scale of expenditure, and thus the scale of political commitment to spheres of influence, is massive.

Michael Kraft, spokesman at the US State Department's

Office of Counterterrorism, has a ready answer to the super-ficial critics of 'McDonald's imperialism': 'They don't have to drink Coke or wear tight American blue jeans,' he counters. In serious political terms, he recognized that terrorists, particu-larly in Europe and the Middle East, have a view that does relate to strategic realities: 'There's an element of political motivation – the Red Army faction and others feel that the US and NATO reflect the imperialist West. Also there's a feeling that we might be able to pressure other countries: the TWA 847 hijack was to put pressure through the US on Israel to release prisoners; and the hijack which ended in Teheran was to put pressure through the US on Kuwait to release their prisoners.'

Kraft acknowledges that terrorism provides an attractive opportunity to some: 'People dissatisfied with the world can lash out – terrorism is relatively cheap and risk-free'. The problem for America and Americans is that the nation's global interests and economic power have put American facilities, commercial enterprises, diplomatic representatives and citi-zens in the firing line in almost every place where there are opponents prone to violence. As Kraft puts it, 'The basic problem is we are out there in rather large numbers, so we are a relatively conspicuous target. We are looked at as the major Western country in power, in the way that Great Britain could have previously been ... Somebody comes out as Satan.'

The first line of defence against international terrorists acting on American soil is the accidental fact that American targets are so easy to find elsewhere in the world, where the immense additional risks of entering the USA do not arise. However, American defences against terrorism inside the US have also proved to be relatively successful: according to the FBI's own figures, terrorism inside the borders of the United States has suffered a consistent and encouraging decline since 1977, when there were 111 terrorist incidents in the US. In 1978 there were 69 incidents; in 1979, 52 incidents; in 1980, 29 incidents; in 1981, 42 incidents; in 1982, 51 incidents; in 1983, 31 incidents; and in 1984, 13 incidents. Terrorist actions in

1983 left four dead and four injured, while those in 1984 caused neither death nor injury at all. America's terrorism in 1983 occurred principally in Florida and Washington, D.C., implying that the activity was mostly the result of Cuban internecine warfare, and attacks on government facilities (largely by groups pursuing independence for Puerto Rico); and in 1984 most attacks occurred on the island of Puerto Rico itself, and in the New York area where the targets were major US business interests.

The domestic terrorism in the US is encompassed by four categories: Cuban infighting, largely in Florida; a rising incidence of what can only be called 'backwoods terrorism', which is variously Christian fundamentalist, anti-taxes, anti-government, racist and anti-Semitic, characterised by three groups – 'The Order', the 'Aryan Nations' and 'The Covenant, the Sword, and the Arm of the Lord'; violent Puerto Rican independence groups (as distinct from legitimate political groups pursuing the same goal), of which the principal names are the FALN (Armed Forces of National Liberation), the EPBM (*Ejercito Popular Boricua Macheteros* or, literally, 'machete-users') and the PRAR (Puerto Rican Armed Resistance); and a handful of domestic revolutionary Marxist groups forming a family tree whose roots are in the 'Days of Rage' – anti-Vietnam war campus movements like the Students for a Democratic Society – and whose genealogy loosely links the Weathermen, the Weather Underground, the Prairie Fire Organising Committee, the May 19 Communist Organisation, the Republic of New Africa, the Black Liberation Army, the United Freedom Front, the Revolutionary Fighting Group, Red Guerilla Resistance and Red Guerilla Defense.

According to Judge William Webster, the Director of the FBI, by the half-way point of 1985 'in the United States, with only two actual incidents, we have been successful in avoiding seventeen proposed terrorist actions ... Some were on the drawing board, and some were close to execution.' These figures would appear to represent a triumph for the FBI; the breakthrough, however, must be seen against a suspicion that the US government and its law agencies define terrorism in such a way as to minimise the domestic problem statistically. Thus, the FBI defines terrorism as 'the unlawful use of force or violence against persons or property to intimidate or coerce a government, the civilian population, or any segment thereof, in furtherance of political or social objectives'. However, a briefing paper adds: 'For an incident to be labelled terrorist by the FBI, one of two things must have occurred. First of all, the incident must itself fit the definition of terrorism and secondly, either a terrorist group or individual must have claimed credit for the incident, or investigation by the FBI developed the fact that a terrorist or terrorist group was involved in the commission of the act.' There is scope in this last clause for manoeuvre, and one particular series of violent attacks demonstrates a clear refusal to recognise terrorism as terrorism, for apparently political motives. If the 25 arson and bombing attacks upon abortion and family planning clinics in the United States during 1984 were to be added to the FBI statistics, they would increase the total of incidents by 200 per cent. According to Barbara Radford, the head of the US National Abortion Federation, some 89 bombing, arson and serious vandalism attacks were carried out between 1982 and the end of 1984 against clinics where abortions were performed or abortion-advice offered. A total of 220 separate acts of violence occurred in all, including one case of a physician and his wife kidnapped and held hostage for a week, another of a physician threatened at gunpoint, and a third case where a doctor's home was sprayed with rifle-fire with his wife and child narrowly escaping injury.

The purpose of this campaign of violence, naturally, is to coerce the clinics and doctors to stop performing abortions, a social and political motive which exactly fits the FBI's definition of terrorism. These acts of terrorism, however, are not terrorism, according to the FBI. Its Director, William Webster, has stated that the campaign does not constitute terrorism because it is not the work of an organised group which publicly identifies itself as responsible. But, by the FBI's own guidelines, it could still qualify as terrorism if FBI investigation 'developed the fact that a terrorist or terrorist group was involved in the commission of the act'. So if the FBI asserts that these terrorists are not terrorists, their crimes are not terrorism, the statistics are healthier, and America doesn't have a domestic terrorist problem.

What is the motive for this deceit? The Reagan Administration is very strongly anti-abortion – or 'pro-Life', as the campaign leaders coyly describe themselves. President Reagan campaigned on Republican political programmes in both 1980 and 1984 that pledged to appoint anti-abortion judges to the United States Supreme Court. His first act on his Inauguration Day was to meet officials of the anti-abortion movement, and his Secretary of Health and Human Services, speaking at a 'right-to-life' rally on the same day, promised a 'pro-life Administration'. It is the privilege of elected office to re-organise the political agenda, to re-order political priorities and to promote the goals and campaign promises of the victorious candidate. It is clear that, with the absolute revulsion for terrorism expressed by both political leadership and popular opinion in America, the allies of the public anti-abortion movement (naturally not connected with the violent fanatics) saw that they could not afford to have their cause tarnished by association with terrorism. In keeping the two elements apart they won a disturbing victory that diminishes the credibility of the American position on terrorism in general.

The absence of an officially recognised, sustained political terrorist campaign in the United States, however, has deprived the US government of the opportunity to demonstrate its firm resolve against terrorism on American soil. A decline in the incidence of international terrorism in the United Kingdom, Italy and West Germany can be at least partly attributed to the determined resistance those countries have shown in quelling or attempting to quell domestic terrorism. But the American government has had no such opportunity of demonstrating a clear and tough policy at home which might serve as a deterrent to terrorist assaults against its interests abroad.

Nevertheless, in 1984 four enormous public events – the

224

Los Angeles Olympics, the New Orleans World's Fair, the San Francisco Democratic Convention and the Dallas Republican Convention – posed a theoretical target for terrorism and the need for an immense security strategy. Publicity about the security measures themselves – and the high level of concern that terrorists might strike – served as the greatest individual protection: indeed, the defences were as much a news story as the sports, politics and commerce that were the real concern.

The cost to Federal agencies of protecting the Los Angeles Olympic Games alone was $65 million. This massive budget succeeded in preventing terrorism, and also served to discourage petty crime, violence, vandalism and many other undesirable aspects of major public events. Such expenditure is never recovered specifically; it merely adds to the cost of an event, and is paid ultimately by sponsors, advertisers and thus by the public. Moving from the individual event to the permanent problem at a state level, it becomes apparent that the commitment to protection and security must be open-ended, permanent, and massively expensive. For the United States, which is the country most likely to attract terrorist attacks and the country with the largest diplomatic and commercial representation around the world, such protection represents a global financial drain and a considerable personal strain on those Americans whose work places them in the ever-mobile frontline.

For several years, the State Department has run a seminar 'Coping With Violence Abroad' for all new recruits to the US diplomatic service, for all staff in the process of transfer from one foreign service post to another, and as a refresher course for longterm career officers. According to its co-ordinator, Arnold Campbell, 'It is mandatory for all United States government employees in the State Department, United States Information Agency and the Agency for International Development, and strongly suggested that all of their adult dependents attend, though it is not required.' Other US government employees who travel widely are also brought in

– from agencies like the Internal Revenue Service, Department of Agriculture, Department of Economic Affairs and Department of Commerce. In Campbell's words, the course 'attempts to bring together a number of experts – on security, on counter-terrorist psychology, on fire safety, on personal preparation for evacuation, all things which we feel they need – and there are also experts on the policy of the US government'.

The purpose of the seminar is to cover far wider risks than those of terrorist attack, including an alert to the most popular forms of common crime in individual nations. Nevertheless the clear emphasis of the seminar schedules of 1985 was on terrorism.

Employees are told frankly that as servants of the US government, they are statistically and politically at risk from the threat of terrorist attack, and that sometimes little can be done to protect or even to rescue them. The experts on government policy reiterate that the United States will not negotiate with terrorists on what it describes as 'substantive matters', though it will negotiate on 'non-substantive matters' in order to gain the release of hostages. It is a negative part of the job-description, though it is worth remembering that the employees are far more likely to be murdered on the streets of their American home town that they are to be killed by a terrorist anywhere.

The State Department, meanwhile, has issued an assessment of risks which predicts that 'a broader spectrum of citizens will be the victims of terrorist attacks. Comparing the victims of terrorist attacks in 1984 with those of 1983,' reported Robert Oakley, Director of the State Department Office for Counter-terrorism, 'one can see that diplomats and military personnel are a declining share of the total, while businessmen, journalists, and even clergymen are increasingly the targets of attacks.'

At the human level, awareness and caution are the sole, relatively insubstantial means of protection against terrorism. But at the physical level there is a mass of practical measures – and expenditures – which can make it harder for the terrorist to hit the most obvious targets. In summer 1984, in response to the climbing incidence of terrorist attacks on US interests and diplomatic facilities in general, and to the Beirut attacks of April and October 1983 in particular, the US government passed a measure to allocate an *additional* $360 million for the financial year 1985–86 for enhanced security measures at United States diplomatic posts. The State Department's Security Division was allocated some $80 million, while $275 million went to fund new buildings and building alterations.

The huge sums involved were to provide means to make existing embassies and consulates more terrorist-proof, and to construct new buildings which would be likely to have more the characteristics of a bunker than of a conventional embassy. As Deputy Assistant Secretary of State for Security David Fields suggests, the simple dilemma is striking a balance 'between openness and protecting our people'. The protection consists of every conceivable device: concrete crash barriers, hydraulic steel hurdles, bulletproof glass, metallic 'blast curtains', computerised identity passes, electronic metal-detectors, 'inner rings' of secure rooms with access for escape to the roof. When the bulldozers move in to 'landscape' the surrounding areas to provide defensive earthworks, the twentieth century seems to have reverted to the medieval era. With decorative balconies removed, ornamental ponds drained and footbridges demolished, the purpose of the buildings – to allow the international public face of the United States to meet the international public – may seem to have been lost.

The State Department has also initiated a new departure in protection measures, in forming 'Mobile Training Teams' – described by David Fields as 'a small group of highly-trained security people who will work with Marine guards, locally-recruited security guards, and other staff, on weapons training, defensive driving training, personal protection, and surveillance awareness.' A mobile Crisis Management Team is available to go to anywhere an incident arises. In addition, the State Department has set up emergency or crisis exercises – previously confined to domestic situations – to test responses to plausible risk-scenarios. Using compressed time techniques, a Crisis Simulation tests the capacity of the diplomatic post and its staff to react at a tactical and human level to a synthetic hijacking, kidnap or armed assault and hostage-taking incident.

Government arranges its own defensive measures, but American business has to face the same international vulnerability to terrorism without governmental power or statutory measures available to it. All it can do, in effect, is to spend money on security, protection and intelligence. It is impossible to quantify the scale of US business security budgets specific to terrorism, but anecdotal evidence suggests that the sums of money involved are immense – almost certainly dwarfing even the State Department's 1984 'security supplemental' of $360 million. The gross expenditure for 'protection' in the United States, other than police services, was an estimated $25 billion a year in 1985. With American businessmen and their corporations as much, if not more, in the frontline as government officials and diplomatic facilities, the scale of their protective expenditure can only be guessed at. One indicator, however, is the ever-growing number of private security consultants, almost invariably staffed by former employees of the CIA, State Department or military intelligence areas. For substantial annual subscriptions, these companies offer a constant stream of intelligence and risk-assessment material about any countries of the world in which US businesses are either operating, or considering doing so.

Secretary of State George Shultz spelled out the repercussions of terrorist attacks on business at a Government/Industry Conference on Terrorism: 'I know how important it is that your people abroad have some degree of confidence in their safety. Without that confidence, doing business effectively is practically impossible. And when America's businesses have a hard time doing business abroad, all of America suffers.' In an initiative to strengthen protection for American business against international terrorism, Shultz announced the formmation of the 'Overseas Security Advisory Council' – a joint venture between the State Department and the private sector, which would 'establish a continuing liaison between officials in both the public and private sector in charge of security matters; to provide for regular exchanges of information on developments in the security field; and to recommend plans for greater operational co-ordination between the government and the private sector.'

While the opportunity to participate in such co-ordination exercises as this or to consult the Threat Assessment Group of the State Department Office of Security, is of undoubted value, the essential matter is attitude. For its own protection, what business must do is to accept the risks – and invest time, intellectual energy and resources in first comprehending the problem and then combatting it – just the same approach that governments should exercise. Senior staff in particular, but all staff ultimately, need to be conscious of what makes terrorism happen, as well as the fact that it may happen to them.

An early example of an American citizen falling victim to attack out on the fringes of American foreign policy was a US police adviser, Dan Mitrione, killed in Uruguay by the *Tupamaros* terrorists in about 1970. American policy-makers have considered both their defences against such attacks and more active measures to pre-empt or retaliate against them. An intermediate step is the active promotion of better intelligence and defence measures against terrorism in nations prepared to accept American funds for the purpose. In Central and Latin America, where Americans and American interests fall victim to repeated instances of terrorist attack, the US government took an initiative in 1985 to provide funds for the improvement of 'counter-terrorism capabilities'. An aid request for $53 million was scheduled for Congressional approval, to provide additional military support and police training funds to El Salvador, Honduras, Costa Rica, Guatemala and Panama.

A further example of external action to enhance defence is found in the decision of the United States government to offer rewards of up to $500,000 for information leading to the arrest or conviction of terrorists who act within or against the United States, *wherever* they may be arrested. Under US Code 18, Chapter 204, Paragraphs 3071–3077 (on domestic legislative ground) and US Code 22, Paragraph 2708 (for international legislative application), the rules are defined and the funds authorized (a single fund of $5 million without fiscal year limitation). A reward of $100,000 or more may not be made without the personal approval of the Attorney-General or the President (or in foreign matters, the Secretary of State or the President), 'and no court shall have power or jurisdiction to review it.' Government officials are not eligible, and the recipient of a reward may be entitled to protection of his or her identity.

The 'Reward Statute' and the 'counter-terrorism capabilities' of others came together in an example of anti-American terrorism in El Salvador, which simultaneously illustrated the dangerous temptation of pure retaliation. On 19 June 1985 a Salvadoran rebel group, the Central American Revolutionary Workers' Party, claimed responsibility for the killing of thirteen people at a pavement café in San Salvador. The dead included four off-duty American Marines and two American businessmen. On 22 July 1985 the State Department offered a reward of up to $100,000 for any information leading to the prosecution and/or conviction of the terrorists responsible. On 31 July 1985 the American Defense Secretary Caspar Weinberger announced (with some apparent satisfaction) that the army of El Salvador had raided a 'terrorist' camp, killing some twenty-six people and capturing thirteen responsible for the June killings. The Defense Department promoted the impression, at least, that the terrorists had met instant justice as a result of information received and passed on through intelligence channels. The Salvadoran government, however, discounted the idea that they had eliminated the terrorists – it was a routine military assault on the guerillas against whom they are waging continuous war. It remained uncertain whether the terrorists were alive or dead, but the State Department had created the impression that it applauded a bloody retaliation – and against the wrong people. Defense Secretary Weinberger himself had cautioned – on the occasion of the bombing of the US Embassy in Beirut on 18 April 1983 in which seventeen US citizens, and forty-six others died – 'It's very tempting to unload a bombing on the brute you think *may* have done it.'

The fact that the targets had almost certainly nothing to do with the outrage of 19 June was confirmed when, only a month after the military raid, the Salvadoran President Jose Napoleon Duarte announced that his government had arrested three terrorists believed to have been involved in the murder of the six Americans. For the second time, the US Administration was applauding its ally on an anti-terrorist success: as White House spokesman Larry Speakes said on 28 August: 'We congratulate President Duarte and his government for the speed and efficiency of their work against the terrorists responsible for those brutal murders.' The special investigations commission, under the Salvadoran Attorney-General's office, had received American financial assistance and FBI training in evidence-gathering and forensics, before making the arrests.

The final irony (and evidence of clear dissent on counter-terrorist strategy within the Administration) came in a public statement from National Security Adviser Robert McFarlane, which welcomed the arrests in El Salvador as a demonstration that 'terrorists can be brought to account without widespread reprisals'. In giving publicity and approval to the El Salvador government's earlier killing-raid, the Administration gave the impression of making revenge – or misdirected retaliation – a plank of public policy.

America's peculiar vulnerability to terrorism is only partly the consequence of its worldwide exposure to terrorist actions. It has also to do with the conviction that the American political mission of world leadership is morally authoritative – a conviction which leads the US to regard itself only as a *victim* of terrorism – hence its fudging on the issue of domestic terrorism; for terrorism is an anomaly in a morally just society. But this sense of itself as aggrieved victim sits uneasily with the consciousness of being a great power: for in this sphere, terrorism repeatedly exposes the impotence of the USA to act consistently or effectively against it.

This quandary is all the more acute for a President swept to office with promises of 'swift and effective retribution', after President Carter's inability to resolve the Teheran hostage crisis. Indeed, the dilemma it poses cannot be better illustrated than by quoting the remarks of Ronald Reagan on three separate occasions: the first, as a Presidential candidate in 1980, reflecting on his opponent's handling of the crisis: 'There comes the time when a government has got to be willing to set a date for [the hostages'] release and let [the hostage takers] know privately what the option will be if they are not released ... We should have done it back about the end of the first or second week that they were held.'

In the euphoric aftermath of the hostages' release after an ordeal which had lasted 444 days, the now-President Reagan warned: 'Let terrorists be aware that when the rules of international behaviour are violated our policy will be one of swift and effective retribution.' Such bullish statements guaranteed that any major terrorist incident, and in particular the first hostage crisis of his Presidency, would be carefully observed to see if rhetoric was translated into action. Reagan should probably have been grateful that he had to wait four and a half years for such a test. But when it came, at his first press conference on the TWA hijacking, on 18 June 1985, there was no announcement of dramatic new action. Instead he merely restated the problem that has beset the USA for twenty years, with an admission of the terrorists' real tactical advantage that brought all the high rhetoric back to haunt a President who had won office by the upbeat confidence of his homespun political arguments: 'The United States,' he said, 'is a nation being attacked by international terrorists, who wantonly kill and seize our innocent citizens as their prisoners ... Terrorism is a cowardly crime in that they hold all the cards, once they have these people in their power.'

In effect, the most powerful nation in the world is confronted by the violent actions of tiny handfuls of fanatics, and is unable to find a meaningful response, either during or after the event. With regard to terrorism, the superpower seems curiously flat-footed, stung by a terrorist gnat despite the global arsenal of firepower.

*   *   *

The frustrations of this position are further compounded by the nature of the American political system, and of Presidential politics in particular; and by the way such crises are played out in public day-to-day in the full glare of media attention. The American media have made a lot of money from political advertising. Television is the sole conduit for information about politics circulating beyond a handful of major American cities, and professional politicians have embraced the TV screen as their ticket to power, above all at the level of Presidential office. So if you are elected in the wake of a major hostage crisis, and you defeat your opponent not least by projecting a thoroughly different image, promising tougher action and retaliation, the media which put you there are absolutely entitled to examine every syllable of the public statements, and every nuance of the actions taken.

Some political opponents and other observers therefore took the greatest satisfaction in hearing the President utter some distinctly un-combative and realistic judgements of the passive role in which he and the nation's Administration found themselves. 'I have to wait it out as long as those people are there and threatened and alive and we have a possibility of bringing them home,' he admitted. Pressed on the question of retribution, he reflected openly on the inconvenient moral realities which his earlier promises had plainly ignored: 'The problem is the "who" in perpetrating these deeds, who their accomplices are, where they are located, because retaliation in some people's minds, not just striking a blow in a general retaliation and the result would be a terrorist act in itself and the killing and victimising of innocent people' [sic]. The President subsequently enlarged on the difficulties of retaliation in another interview; he said the problem was that of 'killing somebody ... in revenge without knowing whether they had anything to do with the dastardly deed or not ... You can't just start shooting without having someone in your gunsights.'

At the end of the Beirut hostage crisis, Senate hearings were held to debate the behaviour of the networks in collaborating with the Amal hijackers to stage press conferences, in overstepping the bounds of taste by intruding on the stress and grief of hostages' families, and in their almost continuous coverage of the crisis in its every aspect, no matter how trivial. To the extent that hearings on Capitol Hill debated the actions of the networks *vis-à-vis* the President – who was questioned more intensely, and more damagingly, than ever before – and the political management of the crisis, they were an exercise in hypocrisy.

In June 1984 it was necessary to have three or four sets of accreditation to work in West Beirut alone – from the government, from the PSP (Druze Progressive Socialist Party), from both 'Amal' and 'Islamic Amal' – and more if one wanted to cross the Green Line to East Beirut – from the Phalangists, the Sons of the Cedars and others. The militias' press liaison people would quite freely call journalists to ask them what they were doing and where they had been, or drop in on them at the Commodore Hotel, the centre of Western press activity. Such sophistication tends to baffle the policy-makers and speech-writers in Whitehall or Foggy Bottom who attempt to preserve clear distinctions between terrorists (who are assumed to be crazed and clandestine) and political parties (which are assumed to be civilised, legal and legitimate). Once the initial terrorist act of the hijack of flight TWA 847 had been perpetrated, the manipulation of the camera crews in covering the daily ups and downs of the hostages' status was easily done, and the crews and reporters were in no position to decline to report or shoot what was going on.

Of course, networks don't have to show what their camera crews shoot, and despite the enormous expense of preserving the option, usually they don't. American networks pay their news crews a lot of money to wait for the Lebanese 'bang-bang' to resume: one network cameraman in Beirut in 1984 was paid his regular $7,000 for a month in which he produced forty seconds of aired material. The networks needed to show all of the Beirut hostage crisis, because the hostages were American citizens: but the real editorial decisions were made not in Beirut where the journalists and crews were being shot at from the flight deck of the TWA jet, or in the maelstrom of

234

armed press conferences amid fistfights and pistol whipping, but in editorial offices in New York.

The American electronic and print media – like the nation as a whole – place a high value on 'Americanness', and when its citizens are attacked for no other reason than that they are American, there is a national crisis of indignation. There is a very important judgement of taste to be made as to whether it is appropriate for the network cameras to invade the family homes of hostages or to shoot live pictures of the grief and relief of close relatives. Television networks are under no pressure from terrorists to make such obvious breaches of privacy and good taste, which are a product of their own competitive practices and are otherwise found to be broadly acceptable. But what is far more important is the prevailing national mood – a mixture of politics and nationalistic emotion – in which excesses of taste, and of political judgement, can take place.

No one who witnessed the 1984 Presidential re-election campaign of Ronald Reagan, and in particular the spectacular excess of showbiz politics at the Republican Convention in Dallas in August 1984, could be surprised at the high profile of patriotism in the American culture of the late 1980s. Nationalism tinged with chauvinism dominated a months-long litical event which had almost no political argument in it. America was exhorted 'to feel good about itself again'; America was 'on the way back'; America was urged to 'go for it'. Exhaustively researched artificial locations saw stage-managed appearances of the President – repeating the same speech to crowds whose rehearsed reactions verged on the hysterical. Television was the chosen medium – conspicuously more than ever before – in which the political life and heart of the nation was communicated to the electorate.

In the TWA hijack, circumstances conspired to bring the chickens home to roost as the medium of television demonstrated its ability to communicate real events of genuine concern to the American people far better than the political leadership. Television, normally the creature of Presidents (and in particular of this President), fulfilled its potential as a dangerous force in real events. All the circumstances of the incident ensured the maximum interest of television: a President whose election owed a good deal to rhetorical threats against anyone who dared to attempt terrorism against the USA; a terrorist group whose political thinking and apparent sophistication about journalists and the media was far above the expectations of Washington; and a substantial press corps in the Middle East who had themselves recently been driven out of Lebanon by a rising physical threat, and who knew the issues, the tactics and many of the protagonists inside out.

Every state has found it necessary to criminalise the terrorist, to try to treat terrorist criminals like other murderers of kidnappers or vandals, albeit of a particular sort. To do otherwise permits the terrorists and their wider circle of supporters to claim a special status, a position unequal to the state but standing alongside it, conferred a degree of legitimacy. 'I emphasise the word "crime",' says William Webster. 'As a law enforcement official, my concern is not political or ideological motivations of terrorists. Terrorism is a special kind of crime, and it involves a special kind of criminal.'

But as the TWA 847 hostage incident ended, the US government made a major mistake. Instead of criminalising the incident, they ceremonialised it. In what may be a tribute to American resilience, or evidence of a refusal to face realities, a tragic event which should have prompted serious reflection on America's international political role became little more than an excuse for patriotic self-congratulation. Whatever was needed to resolve the hijacking – whatever concessions were made – were quickly forgotten as the USA breathed a collective sigh of relief that the hostages were safely released – though with one fatal exception, Marine Bobby Stetham, buried with full military honours at Arlington National Cemetery alongside his Marine comrades who had died in the Beirut barracks truck-bombing.

Stethem was about the 320th American to die at the hands of terrorists during the 1980s. But the tragedy and the crime abruptly became an 'event', a state occasion to be considered for its on-screen presentation value. The state embraced the hostages for being victims. These were ordinary civilians, who set out from Athens to Rome on their private business on a TWA civilian plane which was almost certainly hijacked because it was likely to contain a large proportion of American passengers. Once the hostages of all other nationalities had been dismissed, these civilians became unwilling representatives of the United States of America. During their ordeal they had become surrogates for American political leadership, and once it was over the President – whose impotence to respond to an act of terrorism had been publicly displayed, giving the terrorists a huge propaganda victory – was there to welcome them home. It was perhaps inevitable that after the dreadful public-relations impact of his press conference earlier in the crisis, Ronald Reagan would be in the limelight on the day that the good news finally came. But in allowing the President of the United States to be so directly in touch with the incident, answering (or failing to answer) questions on direct operational responses to the hijacking, the Administration's officials gave the terrorists an extra publicity coup. The actions of criminals, terrorists and, in due course, murderers succeeded in putting the leader of the world's most powerful nation into a position of public discomfiture and apparent uncertainty.

For the media, the politicians and their fellow citizens, hostages have a real potency. Richard Clutterbuck has written, 'The public can't identify with the thousands who are killed in a battle but we can and do identify ourselves with the individual hostage ... This very awareness does strengthen the hand of the terrorist and makes his political violence more effective.' It hardly seems credible, considering that the most important response to an act of terrorism is to exclude the potential for repetition, that the American government contributed to the success of the terrorists – in a quite unnecessary fashion – with prime-time television coverage of the homecoming ceremonies. The government seemed to take at face value the two-dimensional view of the terrorists, that every American represents America, and then gave it public confirmation.

American citizens, who got to Beirut by accident in a civil jet airliner, were retrieved from Damascus in a United States Air Force jet. They were given medical check-ups in an army hospital in Wiesbaden, West Germany, where Vice President George Bush had greeted them with a formal speech. The United States Air Force flew them back to Andrews Air Force Base near Washington, to be greeted by President Reagan. The victims of a random incident were greeted as heroes; and they participated in the show themselves. One can only imagine what guidance they were given by State Department escorts on the long flight from Frankfurt to Washington. But by the time they landed, their spokesman Allyn Conwell – a handsome Texan whose clear and calm tones in the frenzied Beirut 'press conferences' had seemed the essence of discretion and reassurance – had been replaced by the TWA Captain John Testrake. Conwell, it emerged, 'wasn't patriotic enough'.

No doubt the return home gained high ratings on the nation's TV screens. No doubt Captain Testrake's impressive faith and dignity impressed viewers more than Mr Conwell's alleged 'sympathy for Amal'. No doubt the President's short speech, paying more attention to the dead Navy diver than the surviving civilians, did him credit, too. But the ceremony – from Damascus to Andrews – had one far more profound implication. It showed that the terrorists were tactically right. They were vindicated in their hope that an attack on Americans – any Americans – would take their cause and their action immediately to the highest levels of government. The greatest concession that the Reagan Administration made to the Shi'ite terrorists was in permitting them to force a national mood of crisis upon America. Making any concession to terrorists tends to increase the price in the next incident. Thus, in Colombia, three successive kidnappings of public figures resulted in the terrorists' demands being met, first for eleven, then thirty, then seventy imprisoned comrades being freed from jail.

The next terrorist group to hijack or kidnap Americans, whether plane passengers or businessmen, can be even more certain that their action will thrust to the heart of the American

238

Administration. The President himself will be grilled by the White House press corps, frustrated by his inability to act forcefully, embarrassed by his ignorance of the terrorist group – whoever they may be – and held hostage by anything he may have said previously about terrorism. Talking tough makes acting cautiously look like weakness: this is a high price indeed to pay for America 'feeling good about itself'.

Times change, and the so-called 'Teflon presidency' seems immune to damage from any foreign policy reverse. First the commitment of US troops in Beirut, then the deaths of 260 Americans in military or foreign service; then the evacuation of those troops, and the impotent shelling of Lebanese villages; and finally a drawn-out hostage incident where the USA could only wait, or give ground, or both – nothing seems to damage the credibility of the Reagan Administration. One possible interpretation is this: that the media campaigning of the Reagan era, employing the slickest of advertising techniques, has produced an electorate who now believes in slogans for their own sake, rather than in the values and objectives that represent the real business of politics. Is it the case that 'America feels good about itself' at the expense of all serious understanding of the difficult, real world of international relations? This may provide the true meaning of the ceremony at Andrews Air Force Base: that the American nation is prepared to go on ignoring the political reality and substance of an international crisis as long as it can ultimately come together amid the bunting and banners and cheering to welcome released hostages – until the next time.

It appears that President Reagan's popularity has experienced three notable high points: when he survived an assassination attempt in 1982; when he came through an operation for incipient cancer in 1985; and when he presided over the secret concessions and agonising wait for the Beirut hostages to be released. But if his Administration's conduct of the episode has truly encouraged and ensured further such incidents, with perhaps larger numbers of casualties, it seems unlikely that America will continue to approve. No one in Washington, or Europe, or the Middle East has any expectation that the United States will become less of a target for international terrorists: indeed, the most conspicuous result of America's reprisal raid on Libya was the marked reluctance of many Americans to travel anywhere near Europe or the Middle East for fear of still worse terrorist retaliation. It is quite arguable that with external terrorist threats, and attacks which take place outside the borders, almost nothing that the target-country does in tactical terms will make much difference. America, the biggest target, pays the highest toll – and to say that it is merely the price of power does little to diminish the pain and anguish of each victim's individual human tragedy.

8 THE *ACHILLE LAURO* EPISODE

In October 1985 the dramatic succession of events which began with the apparent hijacking of the Italian cruise vessel *Achille Lauro* twisted and turned through every facet of the operational, strategic and political factors that are present in every international terrorist incident. For a combination of quite random and separate reasons, all these factors were to be found on the surface of the events rather than hidden beneath as undercurrents and mystery. Thus it is worth examining the course of events in the *Achille Lauro* case in some detail.

The terrorists bought their tickets for the cruise on the strength of a single stolen passport – an Argentinian document, stolen from a church hostel in Rome. A thirty-year-old Arab man bought five tickets for an Eastern Mediterranean cruise, which cost about £1,900. The names he gave were all false: Antonio Alonco, Diamantino Ribeira, Staale Wan, Walter Zarlenga and Istvan Sabo, supposedly a Yugoslav. This last name is so similar to that of the Hungarian film director Istvan Szabo (*Mephisto* is his best-known film) that one is tempted to speculate that the names were simply plucked from the pages of a newspaper – in this case, the Arts pages. But the name was the chosen alias of an Arab arrested in Genoa, where the cruise tickets were bought, in possession of two false passports, at least one of them Moroccan. The man's real name was Kalaf Mohammed Zainib/Zaimab. He had arrived in Genoa from Tunis, where so many of the PLO's leadership and military structure had established themselves

241

after their enforced exile from Beirut; and the Italian authorities had already arrested three other Palestinians carrying false Moroccan passports in September, in connection with bombings of a British Airways office and a smart café on the Via Veneto.

The arrest prompted a minor change of plan for the Palestinians' travel manager – he returned to the Lauro Line ticket office, cancelled Sabo's cruise, and no doubt collected a refund. After all, he or his paymasters were by now becoming valued customers: in preparing for this mission, he had already paid for tickets for small groups of 'friends' on three similar cruises to Egypt and the Holy Land. The important part of the cruise itinerary was the latter country: holy land to both Jews and Moslems, Palestinians and Israelis. The port of Ashdod was intended to be the scene of the latest effort at armed blackmail against Israel as the liner sailed out of Genoa on 1 October with four Palestinian terrorists in the comfort of Cabin 82.

The four young men, aged between nineteen and twenty-three, spent a week aboard the *Achille Lauro*, no doubt uneasily passing themselves off as tourists. Perhaps with a nervous sense of the imminence of their mission at Ashdod, they took out the weapons which they had smuggled on board. Most of the ship was at dinner, but a waiter passing the cabin saw the group cleaning their machine-guns and pistols. These they had probably obtained in Italy where Palestinians have enjoyed considerable freedom to work towards their objectives without much supervision from the authorities as to their methods.

The decision they took to hijack the ship immediately was inevitable: but it may simply have come sooner than they had intended, for their ultimate motives and tactics are not clear. They rushed into the ship's dining-room, firing wildly and injuring two people. They were now effectively in control of the ship, thirty miles off Port Said in international waters, with fewer passenger hostages than might have been expected as many had disembarked at Port Said. Nevertheless, the terrorists who identified themselves as representing the Palestinian Liberation Front had more hostages than any state could

242

possibly countenance losing before it would act, either to make concessions or to retaliate with military assault.

First reports of the seizure of the *Achille Lauro* concentrated on two elements unique to the marine setting: the grave difficulties of mounting a military response against a mobile target at sea; and the even worse problem of expanding security measures, like those now customary on airline travel, to protect passenger shipping from the risks of terrorism. Compared with the relatively familiar problems of airline hijacks, the tactical problems of this seajack were immense. The ship had massive supplies of food, drink and fuel, enough for weeks; it had radar systems which were certainly capable of detecting any other ship coming within miles of it. Indeed, the terrorists warned off an Egyptian naval vessel said to be eight miles away, and threatened the lives of hostages in reply to being shadowed by an Italian helicopter gunship. Military and naval experts began elaborating on the feasibility of a submarine-launched counterstrike by anti-terrorist frogmen.

Setting aside for a moment the question of the hijack itself, it is worth considering the original mission of the four men to attack Israel. Their colleagues at the Tunis headquarters later said they had planned a 'suicide mission'. However, their first demand on taking control of the *Achille Lauro* was the release of fifty Palestinian prisoners in Nahariyya prison in Israel, including the perpetrator of a notorious incident in 1979 when Palestinian gunmen came ashore on the Israeli coast north of Tel Aviv by rubber boat, and killed the first people they came across – an Israeli father and his five-year-old daughter.

There was no element of surprise in the intention to trade hostages for Israel's Palestinian prisoners – though they may have miscalculated the number of passenger hostages. Had they reached Ashdod, however, the terrorists would have had two options: and either of these could have become, very rapidly, a 'suicide mission'. The first option was to leave the ship carrying their machine guns, pistols, and hand grenades. They would have to smuggle themselves through Israel's disembarkation security before staging an almost immediate attack in the vicinity of the ship, and no doubt causing many casualties instantly. The 1970 Japanese Red Army attack at Lod Airport, killing twenty-six people, was similar; and Armenian terrorists have staged the same kind of instant, bloody and suicidal attack both in Ankara's international airport and on a military convoy passing through the old bazaar in Istanbul.

The second option, and objectively the more effective, was to take command of the *Achille Lauro* just before arrival in Ashdod; to issue the customary ultimatum that passenger hostages would be executed after a deadline for the release of imprisoned comrades had passed; and to begin the killing. With the coldblooded execution of the American hostage Leon Klinghoffer, which so incensed the American population, the terrorist group showed that they were certainly capable of fulfilling even the direst threats. But this option was also almost certainly guaranteed to confirm the mission's 'suicide' status.

Unlike the situtation which faced the hijackers of TWA 847– with friendly control of the Beirut airport tarmac, and an enemy (the USA) at arm's length – the situation in Ashdod would have offered the gravest dangers. Israel's prime consideration of rescuing hostages first and counting the damage later, makes the odds less attractive to the hijacker and hostage-taker.

However, there is no doubt that the young Palestinian Liberation Front terrorists could have enjoyed a strong position: with an almost unlimited supply of hostages ('We have enough, thank God', said one of them by radio to Syrian port authorities at Tartous) and a decent number of Americans among them, they might have sat at anchor within binocular range of Ashdod, killing Americans one by one and turfing their bodies and if necessary their wheelchairs overboard, until the US and Israeli governments decided either to attack – at the risk of many more deaths – or to capitulate and hand over Palestinian prisoners. After perhaps five or six Americans had been murdered, one can only speculate on what strains might have developed in American-Israeli relations.

Israel has had to learn to defend itself with both imagination and tactical planning: for the country's size, it has an immensely long Mediterranean coast. Palestinian terrorists are certainly still based in Lebanon, Cyprus and Jordan, besides Tunisia and Algeria. In the years before the hijack of the *Achille Lauro*, several boats had been intercepted by Israel and the passengers removed. None has reached the Israeli coast to mount an attack. And at Israel's other point of coastal vulnerability, Israeli naval vessels have intercepted what was effectively a boat-bomb. A massive quantity of explosives was packed on board a Jordanian fishing-boat and set on course up the Red Sea to the Israeli resort of Eilat, where hotels densely pack the short seafront. The Palestinians tried and convicted for that attempted slaughter can be assumed to have figured on the list of fifty to be freed from Nahariyya jail.

Clearly the use of a cruise liner, bringing much-needed foreign tourist trade and hard currency to Israel (whose massive spending on just these defence measures, and every other kind, has tilted her economy out of all equilibrium) was a useful and apparently innocent way to hitch a ride to within shooting and blackmailing distance of the Israeli enemy. Despite her earlier successes – and this near-miss – it has to be assumed that however exhaustive Israel's disembarkation security procedures are for the cruise passengers, it cannot afford to turn away the cruise trade from its port and its antiquities in the hope of making itself less vulnerable.

In respect of all international alliances except that of the USA and Israel the *Achille Lauro* became a floating diplomatic incident. Egypt, Italy, Syria, Cyprus, Tunisia, the stateless PLO, the enraged United States, and even Yugoslavia – all became embroiled in a rolling crisis which by virtue of its simple mobility became the antithesis of the intractable but static TWA hijack crisis. And wherever the crisis drifted, it caught states acting not with the resolve that characterises multilateral declarations against terrorism, but with the self-interest and fear of local vulnerabilities that every state involved in the Middle East suffers.

Once in command of the ship, the hijackers headed for

Syria: the former member of the élite 'Terrorist Nations' club
as defined by the US State Department, but since the TWA
hijack deleted from the list on the grounds of improving
behaviour. That the terrorists identified themselves as belonging to the Palestine Liberation Front, placed the Syrians in a
quandary: two Palestinian splinter groups sail under that
name, one pro-Syrian, the other pro-Arafat. Both are sub-
groups of the PFLP General Command led by pro-Syrian
Ahmed Jibril, which only confuses the matter further. Syria,
uncertain of the facts, but certain of the dreadful publicity
attendant upon allowing a civilian cruise ship to be com-
mandeered and then docked in its port of Tartous, told the
terrorists to be on their way.

The next obvious port-of-call was Southern Cyprus – the
Greek sector of the divided island, where thousands of
Palestinians have made their homes, temporary or otherwise,
and transferred their fighting and their infighting. Intra-
Palestinian factional murders are common in contemporary
Cyprus, and there is copious evidence to suggest that the
island is a crossroads of weapons supplies and finance for
international terrorism of many complexions. Two weeks
earlier a group of Palestinians had murdered three Israelis on
their yacht in Larnaca marina. The Cyprus government did
not relish a repeat performance with a liner full of innocents,
and refused to allow the ship to dock.

At this point in the drama appeared the character who
would become the focus of the story long after the hijack itself
was over. Mohammed Abbas Zaidan, alias Abu Khaled, alias
Abu Abbas, Secretary-General of the Palestinian Liberation
Front which grudgingly supports Arafat's leadership while
disagreeing violently with his political tactics, made two
almost simultaneous radio broadcasts. The first, by shore-to-
ship radio, probably from Beirut, was to express his outrage
that the planned attack on Israel had failed. There is a report
that the conversation began with one of the terrorists saying:
'Commander, we are happy to hear your voice.'

The second broadcast was an interview which Mohammed
Abbas Zaidan gave to Monte Carlo radio, in which he said he

had ordered the ship to head from Tartous back to Port Said. His ability to issue orders and have them obeyed – for the ship duly headed south – suggested very clearly that his authority was recognised by the four men on the *Achille Lauro*.

By way of confirmation, Israeli intelligence sources also monitored the ship-to-shore radio conversation and later released a recording. The man they claimed was Abu Abbas was heard to say, 'Listen to me well. First of all, the passengers should be treated very well. In addition, you must apologise to them and the ship's crew and to the captain and tell them our objective was not to take control of the ship. Tell them what your main objective is.' Major-General Ehud Barak, the Chief of Israeli military intelligence, argued that this confirmed that the objective of the terrorists had been an attack on Israel, at Ashdod. Abbas's use of the phrase 'our objective' could have left no one in any doubt that he was playing a major planning role in the whole episode.

Italy has an excellent record – from the Palestinian point of view – on Middle Eastern affairs, but the Italian-registered ship, sailing out of Genoa, was legally Italian soil whose jurisdiction clearly fell to Italy. The first action of the Italian government was to contact the PLO and its chairman Arafat in Tunisia, who denied any connection with the incident. They then made contact with the Israeli government, whom – embarrassingly – they had been berating a few days earlier for Israel's vigorous retaliation raid on PLO headquarters near Tunis. Italy also has an élite military anti-terrorist squad of Carabinieri, but it was conventional military forces which were being assembled at the Sigonella air base in Sicily once the hijack became known.

As the ship steamed back to Port Said, it became inevitable that Egypt would play a role in whatever negotiations were to take place. The initiative that the Egyptian government took was to astonish Italy and the United States, because they simply invited Mohammed Abbas Zaidan – the same Abu Abbas whom the hijackers were calling 'Commander' – to help bring the hijacking to an end.

The United States was in official terms a peripheral player in the three days that the ship was in the hands of the hijackers – the ship was Italian; the waters international, Syrian, and Egyptian; the vast majority of the hostages Italian, and only a handful American. But two things made certain that the US would play a role: the Administration of Ronald Reagan has taken the initiative in international concern about terrorism; and the very large American military presence in Mediterranean waters and throughout Europe ensured that American monitoring of any communications traffic with the ship was bound to be comprehensive. More was to come.

In a style that was reminiscent of the sudden and mostly unexpected revelation of Mr Nabih Berri as an international statesman and mediator in the TWA hijack, the process of negotiation in Egypt provided an opportunity for representatives of the PLO to arrive at Port Said and cast themselves, not as the paymasters and planners of an act of terrorism, but as the mediators whose skills would bring it to a peaceful end. Two men arrived in Port Said at the invitation of the Egyptian government: one was Abu Abbas of the Palestine Liberation Front, the other almost certainly Hani el Hassan, a senior aide to Chairman Yasser Arafat and a long term high official of Fatah. (El Hassan has emerged above the parapets on a number of interesting occasions in the PLO's history. In 1981 he wrote an article, 'L'Ingratitude de l'USA', published in an influential French foreign affairs journal, criticising the United States for refusing to recognise the PLO when they had protected American interests for so many years, and throughout the Lebanese Civil War in West Beirut. In 1982, at the height of the Israeli assault on the PLO in Beirut, el Hassan was the senior PLO official almost captured by Israeli troops, but bundled to safety in the boot of the car of a French diplomat.)

On 9 October, the third day of the seajack, the earlier rumours that two passengers had been killed had been succeeded by reassurances that all were safe. It is impossible to be precise as to who was deluding whom: no doubt the terrorists wanted to conceal the fact that they had brutally

murdered a 69-year-old triple-stroke victim in his wheelchair, and then – in an act of utter coldness that added
insult to injury in the most extreme way – had other passengers throw both body and wheelchair into the Mediterranean Sea. Certainly the *Achille Lauro*'s captain, Ferardo de
Rosa, knew that one man was dead, but he was apparently
threatened not to spoil the 'peaceful resolution' of the incident
by revealing this fact.

The four seajackers 'negotiated' their safe passage with their
commander-mediator by radio and by an exchange of notes.
Abu Abbas, known to the hijackers as Abu Khaled, broadcast
to them from the offices of the Suez Canal Authority while a
dramatic meeting was taking place at the Egyptian Foreign
Ministry. The Italian, American and West German ambassadors were discussing with Egyptian Foreign Minister Esmat
Abdul Meguid the terms under which the terrorists would be
offered safe passage out of Egypt. Italy insisted that this was
only acceptable if no act of violence had been committed; but
as the Italian master of the *Achille Lauro* had repeatedly
asserted this to be the case, the ambassador signed an agreement on the authority of Italian Foreign Minister Giulio
Andreotti. The West German ambassador signed the note, but
the American ambassador, Nicholas Veliotes, remained unmoved. American government policy is to make no deals with
terrorists and not to offer safe passage.

Messages were being passed back and forth between the
Achille Lauro hijackers and Egyptian fishing boats. 'The
captain has sent a message with one of the fishing boats,' said a
terrorist who identified himself as Omar. 'I want a special sign
that he [Abu Khaled] is the one sending the letter.' Khaled
replied by radio: 'There is a man on his way to you with a
special sign.' Only five minutes after the Foreign Office
meeting was concluded, and simultaneous with this exchange
of notes, the hijackers surrendered. Shortly afterwards they
entered Port Said on board an Egyptian navy tug.

Egypt's problem with the incident was really only just
beginning. The terrorists were greeted at the dockside by
cheering crowds who chanted, '*Fedayeen, Fedayeen! Allahu*

Akbar! Commandos, Commandos! God is Great!' Egypt, the sole Arab nation to have signed a peace treaty with Israel, enjoys a highly equivocal relationship with the Palestinians in all their manifestations. There is a steadily growing Islamic fundamentalist movement in Egypt, yet her most important foreign alliance since the mass expulsion of Soviet advisers by President Sadat in the early 1970s is with the USA. Sadat's successor, President Mubarak, certainly would not wish to aggravate his national difficulties on the Palestinian issue by getting tough with hijackers who had murdered an American hostage. Fortunately, no one was able to tell him that they had done so, and the deal was to release the hijackers and wipe the slate clean.

There is no great difficulty in understanding why Egypt and Italy, two states demonstrably vulnerable to Palestinian terrorism should have wished to see a quiet end to such a fiercely hostile act against innocent, mostly elderly holiday-makers. What transformed the situation was the revelation of Leon Klinghoffer's cold-blooded execution: the murder of yet another American hostage for the sole, simple reason that he was American.

Public opinion in the United States had reached an apparent apogee of indignation during the course of the TWA hijack two months earlier. But the impotence of the American leadership to act against the hijackers either during the incident or after it was all too clear. This sense prevailed not only among the public and percolated through the American television networks and press: many people in government were just as frustrated. Frustration was therefore the most obviously audible note in the words of US Ambassador Nicholas Veliotes when he got aboard the *Achille Lauro* in dock at Port Said, and confirmed the death of Klinghoffer. Speaking by telephone to his office, some time after midnight, early on Friday 11 October, he gave explicit and angry instructions: 'Leon Klinghoffer is dead. He was murdered by the terrorists off Tartous,' he said. 'I want you to do two things. In my name, I want you to call Meguib [the Egyptian Foreign Minister] ... tell him that in view of this – and presumably they didn't have those facts – we insist that they prosecute those sons-of-bitches. The second thing: I want you to pick up the phone and call Washington and tell them what we've done. And if they want to follow it up, that's fine.' (Six months later, Veliotes was reported to have been 'forced into retirement' after thirty-one years in the US Foreign Service. According to an American diplomatic source, the State Department recalled him from Cairo prematurely to placate the Egyptian government. George Shultz, the Secretary of State, denied reports in Washington of 'a shouted exchange' on Mr Veliotes' departure.)

Washington was doing more than following up. Despite the far-from-convincing vagueness on the part of President Mubarak about the whereabouts of the seajackers ('I think, in Tunis'), independent American intelligence sources were quite sure that they had not left the Al Maza Egyptian military air base, where they had been accompanied by the two Palestinian 'mediators'.

At the very moment that Veliotes confirmed the death of Klinghoffer, President Reagan on board Air Force One gave the executive order to intercept the EgyptAir flight carrying the murder suspects to freedom. Although the Egyptian government has already claimed they were out of the country and thus beyond Egypt's power to prosecute, Veliotes clearly revealed that American intelligence had reason to believe otherwise. But the terrorists and their escorts were by then boarding their plane, and the EgyptAir pilot filed a flightplan, not to Tunis, but to Algiers. United States intelligence sources fed all this information back to Washington, as well as the flight number. The plane was apparently bristling with weapons, but these belonged to Egyptian military guards, rather than the terrorists.

Successful retaliation against terrorists has always been difficult to execute. Terrorists themselves need a set of circumstances which lend themselves to the successful execution of an attack; there is always a softer, less well defended target around the corner, and terrorists won't take unnecessary risks. For any government attempting retaliation, there is the same need for propitious circumstances but none of the control. For once, however, things were going the way of the retaliator. After the ghastly failure of the Delta Force in the Iranian desert, after the frank impossibility of acting to free hidden, dispersed hostages throughout West Beirut after the TWA episode, there was the potential of acting in international airspace against apparently unarmed opponents with the assistance of well-placed allies.

The allies were in two distinct groups: Egypt had effectively provoked the latter stages of the crisis single-handed, and American fury at the prospect of letting cold-blooded murderers go free clearly outweighed the fear of souring US-Egyptian relations. More important in operational terms was the refusal, first of Tunisia and secondly of Greece, to allow the EgyptAir Boeing 737 to land at their airports. This takes some explaining, particularly in the case of Tunisia. The North African country has permitted the PLO to re-establish its leadership and headquarters in and around Tunis, and it is entirely accustomed to seeing Arafat, Abu Iyad, Farouk Kaddoumi and other senior PLO figures travelling in and out of the country. The decision to refuse landing rights bears witness to emphatic US pressure.

Greece, as a recalcitrant NATO ally, can clearly be subjected to US pressure, but the decision to turn away the PLO plane may have been made all the easier by the rash of Middle Eastern terrorism that has broken out in the country in the last two years. Not least damaging have been the activities of the Revolutionary Organisation of Socialist Moslems, whose attacks have included throwing grenades into hotels occupied by English holidaymakers – who represent a major element of Greece's tourism-based economy.

Whatever the pressures and stresses of the present incident, the USA and Egypt are allies. Secretary of Defense Caspar Weinberger argued vigorously that military intervention against the EgyptAir plane would destroy the two countries' relationship, but the decision was taken nevertheless. It must be quite clear that a similar decision could not have been reached so readily, if at all, had the released terrorists been departing the scene of the crime in almost any other Middle Eastern country's aeroplane. The negative repercussions of such action being taken against, for example, Jordan or Syria – in terms of the US government's longterm aims for peace in the region – would almost certainly have outweighed the immediate euphoria of scoring a one-off victory against terrorism.

A third factor in going ahead was the fact that the terrorists had no arms with which to influence their situation once airborne – even though there were at least ten armed Egyptian military personnel travelling as escorts to the Egyptian diplomats making the delivery to Tunis. The terrorists had no capacity to skyjack the plane in which they were travelling, to force it to land at Beirut or anywhere else. Above all, they had no power to face down the F-14 Tomcat fighters which appeared alongside and front-and-back, high above the Mediterranean. The pilot of the Egyptian airliner immediately attempted to contact ground control in Egypt for advice and instructions, but as American intelligence sources pointed out with some satisfaction, an EA-6B Navy Prowler electronic warfare plane was jamming all his radio communication, and he could hear only garbled communications and static. He therefore 'accepted the inevitable', as Caspar Weinberger put it, and complied with the Tomcats' signal to follow them down.

The most emphatic virtue of the American action was the ability to claim in all truth that the intervention brought the terrorists to justice. What would have been far less acceptable, besides all the ramifications of a more violent infringement of an ally's sovereignty, was the instant-justice which armed terrorists might have provoked and brought upon themselves. Had they been armed, the terrorists would realistically have had only two choices: to surrender, or to push the American military commanders to a decision to shoot down an Egyptian civil airliner.

The American catchphrase which promptly made a wide-spread re-appearance was, 'Don't get mad, get even!' But the USA acted with relative restraint and great military precision, aided by highly propitious circumstances. The advocates of 'kick-ass' retaliation – who first appeared in 1979 saying 'Nuke the Ayatollah', and resurfaced in 1985 to greet Rambo as an example for government to follow – may have hailed the successful delivery of four terrorists to the Italian authorities with wild approval. However, the very special circumstances which offered the opportunity for the mission's successful execution are so unlikely to be repeated that this notable achievement may serve as no more than a theoretical precedent.

President Reagan summarised the intended message of the action he had authorised personally. Referring to the Tomcat pilots who guided the EgyptAir plane down to Sicily, he asserted: 'These young Americans sent a message to terrorists everywhere that you can run but you cannot hide.' For once, his threat related to action already taken.

Since the mid-1970s Italy has had a good record on prosecuting and convicting terrorists – but more so with its domestic urban revolutionaries than with the terrorists waging other wars on its soil. For throughout the 1970s the Italian government succeeded in keeping Palestinian-related terrorist incidents out of Italy and away from Italian interests, by making fairly frank political compromises. It was therefore not surprising that the longest-lasting reverberations of the *Achille Lauro* incident concerned the sharply different attitudes of the Italian and American governments about Italy's conduct, once the EgyptAir plane was on Italian soil. Indeed, its arrival was a halting process: air traffic controllers at the Sigonella air base at first refused the plane permission to land, and only agreed when US military pressure forced the pilot to claim he was running short of fuel. At Sigonella, the EgyptAir 737 was accompanied by an American T39 Sabreliner (equipped for highly sophisticated electronic surveillance) and two military transport planes loaded with US Delta Force troops – the special anti-terrorist strike unit. Simultaneously, Italian Carabinieri and American Delta Force troops surrounded the 737 – and at that point it seems clear that the Americans were under orders to seize the terrorists and deliver them to the US justice system. A gun battle among the forces of law and order seemed ready to explode when the Italians fired shots in the air to warn off the Delta Force men from trying to take the plane. Finally, Italian police went on board and arrested the four hijackers.

In transit between Al Maza and Sigonella, Abu Abbas had, at least in the eyes of the Americans, been transformed from 'mediator' to 'terrorist mastermind'. But no such change had occurred in the view of the Italian government. Already deeply embarrassed by the potentially negative consequences of the incident in the light of their highly pro-Palestinian position, they regarded Abu Abbas as the negotiator who had contrived the release of 450 Italian hostages – something the Italian government had directly requested Yasser Arafat and the PLO to do.

Twenty-four hours later, the Italian government was executing an elaborate deception apparently designed to obstruct both the American government and an Italian investigating magistrate. The Egyptian plane flew to Rome's military airport at Ciampino. With the connivance of the Egyptian Ambassador and the Chief of Rome's police, appearances were contrived to suggest that Abu Abbas was then transferred to the Egyptian Fine Arts Academy in Rome. Police reinforcements in bulletproof clothes were posted around the building. The Italian government had already received the US government's formal request for Abbas's extradition on the impressive charges of hostage-taking, piracy and conspiracy.

In fact, far from the cultivated atmosphere of the Egyptian Fine Arts Academy, Abbas had never left the EgyptAir jet. At his request ten armed Egyptian escorts stayed on board to guard him, as he feared some attempt would be made to snatch him from the plane. Meanwhile the results of the interrogation of the hijackers in Sicily led a magistrate there to contact a Roman colleague and request him to interview Abbas. This, for those trying to protect Abbas from awkward questions, was far from desirable, but the magistrate, Franco Ionta, set off for the Academy. First, he was told, there were no Palestinians there. He asked to see the Egyptian plane passengers. The Academy official asked for time. Ionta went back: he was told they had left for the airport.

Ionta arrived at Ciampino to be told that the 737 had taken off for Rome's civil Leonardo da Vinci airport. Despite his high-speed police-escorted dash, he failed to catch up with Abbas, who by then was over the Adriatic in a Yugoslav Airlines aeroplane heading for Belgrade. He had been transferred from the EgyptAir plane to the Yugoslav jet on the tarmac. Although the Italian government officially justified their refusal to extradite Abbas by saying, apparently without irony, that he was 'technically a hijack hostage', they had also managed to appear unwilling under any circumstances at all to put Abu Abbas at risk of prosecution for terrorism. To do so, they would almost certainly have had to resort to force.

Such a move would have been unacceptable against the wider, fragile edifice of Italy's Middle Eastern relations. It is worth remembering that while Britain has faltered in holding a single meeting with two 'non-PLO Palestinian men of peace', diplomatic relations between Italy and the PLO are strong and meaningful. National interest has involved solid relationships with Arab countries for years. Libya is an extremely important market for Italian industry and services, despite the occasional hiatus in Libyan payments, and improving relations with Syria and Iraq have also developed. In deciding what to do with Abu Abbas, the Italian government was faced with a decision which could not please everyone: and while a diplomatic rift with the USA must be regarded as temporary and tolerable, Italian Foreign Minister Andreotti and Prime Minister Bettino Craxi clearly felt the dangers of alienating sectors of the Arab world were more alarming. As Andreotti said as the crisis came to an end, 'Should we ever need to, how could we ever ask the PLO to do us a good turn again?' If confirmation of his fears were needed, the PLO Chairman Yasser Arafat expressed the fear that 'uncontrollable reactions' might arise in the Arab world against Italy. The PLO's spokesman in West Germany and Switzerland, Abdullah Frangi, pursued the point: 'I am afraid that an American or Italian aircraft will be hijacked or that another American will be killed, to force the release of the Palestinians in the Italian jail,' he said. 'Mark my words, this will happen.'

What was not foreseen, or not fully appreciated, was that the Italian government's decision would please least of all its Republican Party coalition partners led by Giovanni Spadolini. Their withdrawal, in protest at the release of Abu Abbas, prompted the (temporary) collapse of Italy's forty-fourth government since 1945. Abbas himself provided an ironic postscript to the events which had such extraordinary and lasting consequences. On his arrival in Belgrade, he gave an interview to the Egyptian Middle East News Agency, confirming that the terrorists' original mission had been an attack on Israel. 'Their mission was not to hijack the ship or threaten the lives of the passengers,' he said. 'Their destination was the Israeli port of Ashdod for the purpose of carrying out a suicide mission inside occupied territory. Pure accident changed the course of events when they were uncovered aboard the ship after it left Alexandria and this forced them to seize it.' When 'pure accident' intervenes in the already tortuous process of acting legitimately and appropriately against terrorism, it adds still more to the relatively obvious and foreseeable difficulties faced by states.

Legitimate states are constantly concerned with the business of deterring terrorism; only time will tell whether the conclusion of the *Achille Lauro* incident will have been a turning-point. In four major respects, there must be grounds for doubt. Firstly, the ultimate fate of the four arrested terrorists will be closely observed. Next, the question arises of whether a policy of deterrence can really work against groups which act so ruthlessly and rashly. Thirdly, the wider implications of the incident on peace plans for the Middle East seem negative. Finally, there is the issue of whether such US actions as the interception of the EgyptAir 737 are pragmatically acceptable when they may bring still more terrorist attacks upon American interests.

The *Achille Lauro* incident technically took place on Italian soil: the ship itself. The hesitation felt within government circles betrayed the certainty that countries which prosecute and convict foreign terrorists only invite further attacks as a bargaining counter for the prisoners' release. This understanding partly explains the decline in numbers of imprisoned terrorists in 'third countries', which have repeatedly preferred to deport rather than prosecute or extradite terrorist suspects – even where the evidence is of a high standard. There is little doubt that if the *Achille Lauro* seajackers are convicted and jailed, they will be unlikely to have to serve their full sentences in jail.

Deterrence is an immeasurable ingredient of anti-terror policy; but there is no doubt that it is over-rated by government spokesmen. Incident after incident shows that the terrorist perpetrators must have reached a state of mind in which death either no longer matters, or matters less than the cause itself. The risks of relatively low-profile attacks like letter-bombs and timed car-bombs are small, at first: but the high-profile methods, particularly in the Middle East, have enormous dangers attached. The fanatical degree of their dedication remains beyond the comprehension of most observers.

The fact remains that there is a fairly truthful inverse equation of risk: the smaller the chances of survival in launching an attack, the greater the probable attention brought to the cause. In making his threat to the terrorists of the Palestinian Liberation Front – and to all terrorists – that 'You can run but you cannot hide', President Reagan probably would not have expected to deter their comrades. The men who were prepared to go to Ashdod in Israel in pursuit of their cause cannot have had great expectations of a long and happy life. The point was proved within a week, when three (probably Shi'ite) Lebanese blew an American-backed Christian evangelical radio station off the air, only a few hundred yards from the Israeli security zone, by running into the building with explosives strapped to their bodies. Defensive fire from the station guards triggered the explosions, and the martyrdom of the attackers.

The *Achille Lauro* incident, and the US government's determination and *opportunity* to do something about it, represent a watershed in the slow Middle East peace process. Alone among the contending interests in the region, the Palestinians have nothing concrete to lose; and as long as that remained the case, there was every reason to expect their different factions to act violently to inject some sense of dynamism into the process. The greatest irony of many in the *Achille Lauro* case, is that the Palestinians exhausted America's patience for putting up with terrorism, after years in which they had scrupulously avoided attacking US interests. It has most recently been the Shi'ites of Lebanon whose attacks have cost American lives, prestige and policy objectives: but with one apparently unintended attack, it was the Palestinians who were presented with the bill.

But still the key factor for the Palestinians in assessing their own future policies, is that terrorism is what has brought them this far – nowhere near their ultimate objective of a free and independent nation, but at least to a central position in the perceptions of all politicians concerned with a resolution of the Middle East conflict. However little point there may be in each individual attack, the events surrounding the *Achille Lauro* will be seen to have guaranteed future waves of Palestinian terrorist action, with all the needless associated death, injury and suffering. (Ironically, one of the first consequences of the incident was the death of a Palestinian-born American in California: Alex Odeh, the regional director of the American Arab Anti-Discrimination Committee, who in two television interviews had defended the PLO and Yasser Arafat. A bomb exploded as he opened the door to his office the next day in Santa Ana, killing him and injuring seven others.)

Whether future attacks are targeted on the United States and her interests plays a large role in the ultimate judgement about the Reagan Administration's actions in 'hijacking the hijackers.' But that will be a pragmatic, *ex post facto* judgement. First reactions applauded the White House for following the advice, 'Don't get mad, get even.' The more important question is whether that is the same advice as 'If you can't beat 'em, join 'em.'

In the immediate euphoria following the successful interception of the EgyptAir plane, international legal experts began to debate whether the interception was itself an act of piracy. Rosalyn Higgins, professor of international law at the London School of Economics, said that it was 'hard to see that the actions of the American government were lawful'. Her technical interpretation was a less popular view, however, than that of Villanova University law professor John Murphy, who argued that violating some technical aviation conventions would be 'overridden by the need to bring the hijackers to justice'. The traditional legal doctrine, 'Badly captured, well detained', has been interpreted at least by American courts to mean that only the fairness of the trial is important, not the means by which the accused are brought into the jurisdiction of the court.

Liberals are concerned that this incident represents a departure into vigilante action. For years the United States has claimed the moral leadership of the fight against terrorism, not least because in the face of attacks it has remained largely passive, effectively above the fray. Slightly bloodied, and certainly unbowed, the United States has told the world's terrorists that they may be able to cause pain, but they will never damage the USA's integrity. The American government's action in concluding the *Achille Lauro* affair with apparently clean and decisive action, has in fact muddied the waters. The 'signal' President Reagan sent had the effect of 'terrorizing the terrorists', and the full-scale military means used to do so were effectively beside the point.

Two things may happen as a result of the *Achille Lauro* case. Either the very special circumstances which permitted the interception exercise will be recognised, leading to renewed caution in any similar circumstances. Or the Administration's 'hawks' will take the military action as just a taste of what can and should be done in future – in circumstances which are almost certain to be less propitious and advantageous. In either case, the USA will continue to face the threat of terrorism, as will the rest of the democratic – and the undemocratic – world. And the terrorists are by definition of their brutal trade one step ahead of any defensive measure except the pre-emptive strike, which brings its own difficulties of surveillance and execution. Just as the *Achille Lauro* story brought a flurry of expert opinion on how to stage a military assault on a ship, there will be new settings for terrorism. Any visitor to Tel Aviv's beachfront hotels – protected by concrete embankments and barbed wire from any assault, the beach patrolled by Israeli troops – will become aware of the justified fear of terrorists hijacking a whole hotel, anywhere in the world.

The US government of Ronald Reagan has cast itself in an impossibly difficult role – that of the defensive spearhead against terrorism. Future American administrations will find it difficult to withdraw from that prominent position, and the policymakers of the White House and State Department will undoubtedly reflect at length on the *Achille Lauro* case. They are people whose job it is to make enormous and sometimes dangerous decisions: risking lives, national and commercial interests, political authority. In reviewing the *Achille Lauro* affair, they see on the credit side a demonstration of just moral outrage and effective visible action against the terrorists whom the world despises. On the debit side, there is a complete, if relatively temporary, halt to the peace process in the Middle East; the likelihood of a net increase in anti-American terrorism; and, of all things, the (temporary) collapse of the government of Italy, a substantial and reliable NATO ally. The bottom line can only be expressed as a question: did the loss of just one American life, however cruel and tragic a loss, justify all those uncertain consequences? Political opinion polls, boosting President Reagan still higher, give one answer: but the future years may offer a sombre alternative.

POSTCRIPT

> 'No matter how high the aims predicated by the
> terrorists ... their activities are always criminal,
> always destructive, throwing humankind back to a
> time of lawlessness and chaos, provoking ... inter-
> nal and international complications, contradicting
> the goals of peace and progress.'
>
> (Andrei Sakharov)

The first Prime Minister of India, Jawaharlal Nehru, wrote in
his autobiography that the appeal of terrorism 'is the call of the
detective story'. But there is almost no evidence of people
indulging in 'terrorism-for-kicks'. Instead, confounding the
simplistic and dismissive judgements on the meaning of terrorism, governments and public must face the uncomfortable fact
that at the heart of every terrorist action there lies a cause, a
political goal, a perceived injustice or denial of liberty that is as
concrete to the activist as any president's or prime minister's
notion of justice and freedom. It seems to be the politicians,
ironically, who pre-eminently fail to understand that terrorism
is a political activity. There are very few terrorists, for very
few men or women have the singleminded devotion to a cause,
no matter how apparently hopeless or irrelevant, to pursue
it to and beyond the logical conclusion. After twenty years
of the modern wave of terrorism, it is clear to extremist
minorities that terror tactics will lead them possibly to death,
probably to jail, and definitely to an outcast's life.

The accidents of history and the grand decisions of map-
makers have nevertheless created enough devotees of lost
causes to exact a significant price. Liberationists are denied by

the boundaries of other nations – so they reject the boundaries of legitimate protest. Revolutionaries are excluded by the political process they abhor – so they attempt to explode the structure entirely. Their objectives are usually comprehensible, but less so, perhaps, the *reductio ad absurdum* of their tactics – to kill in order to give life to a dream of nationhood or social equality. The terrorist is the strongest of all believers that the means justifies the end.

Individuals with a passionate commitment to a cause will go on using terrorism as the most potent means of self-expression. States with a vested interest in instability elsewhere, or a need to act through unconventional tactics when other methods have failed or are too drastic to be justified, will go on enabling terrorism to exist. States with double standards will go on expressing outrage and incomprehension at an activity which repeats as tragedy the farce of governmental hypocrisy. States with active hostility to express will go on learning the advantage of terrorism as a handy weapon. Terrorism, the global equaliser of the 1980s, will continue.

The world is not a tidy place where the White House declares who is for us and who is against us, and the issue ends there. Nevertheless, terrorism attracts condemnation as a matter of routine. Political leaders in the democracies owe their power to wage war and sacrifice lives to elective office. Leaders of totalitarian countries assume absolute power. When unelected, unelectable minorities seize the power of life and death, nations experience a jolt, a tremor which shakes the established order and its apparent security. Yet the indefensible acts of states attract less outrage and less condemnation than the actions of terrorists. The world and its media experience a convulsion of surprise and excitement when terrorists destroy aeroplanes – which they have done five times in the last twenty years. In retaliation for just one hijacking attack – on an El Al plane at Athens on 26 December 1968 – Israeli troops destroyed thirteen Middle East Airlines aeroplanes on the tarmac at Beirut airport. They were unconnected with the terrorists, and substantially US-owned: yet the incident is scarcely remembered.

After twenty years and more of high terrorist activity, a mood of crisis and outrage is wearing thin: it needs to be replaced by a mood of resignation. Resignation need not amount to despair, however, and throughout the world there are issues, conflicts, injustices and iniquities which have not given birth to terrorism, and about which the most potent question is why terrorism has *not* occurred.

The essential complement to a realistic degree of resignation must be a new willingness to take limited political risks with the issues in which terrorism is rooted; to re-direct some of the pressures that explode into terrorist action back into conventional politics, provided that at least some hope of tangible progress can be achieved.

Terrorists want a hearing, and then they want concessions. Every group of terrorists, however, consists of the tiny minority of a wider group who have sympathy for the cause in question. Most Armenians are not terrorists, but Armenian terrorism certainly expresses a grievance which *is* shared by most Armenians. The question for those with any power to bring to bear on the problem, is how to divert the terrorists from their terrorism. The obvious answer is to give their cause the hearing which is their primary demand. The forum for such an audience would be critical: for example, the United Nations is far too compacted with political infighting for any consensus to emerge in support of such an experiment. The simplest and most viable option is for bilateral hearings, at which the American government – or any other – would convene meetings in which representatives of Armenian groups, having once condemned terrorism, would be invited to argue their case.

There would be inevitable political fallout – the Turkish government would be naturally irritated by the development. But for the powerful United States, it is a simple choice between a mere hiccough in diplomatic relations with a country which remains tightly bound to the US, and the alternative irritation of persistent terrorism. (It is of course inevitable that terrorism would continue – the hope would be of a reduced level of activity.) After all, pursuing the

Armenian example, it is anti-Turkish terrorism which the initiative would be designed to reduce. These should not be hearings of the Congress or Senate, as no legislative potential could be assumed. They should be Special Executive Hearings along the same lines as Grand Jury investigations, designed to inform and to propound wider political contexts and solutions to problems of conflict and points of international pressure.

It is certainly more feasible for the most powerful states to grant this 'magnanimous' gesture to the minority groups whose political impotence is in proportion to their angry loyalty to the cause. However, in almost every case the opponent-government is infinitely more stable and powerful than the terrorist cause. Enough has been learned about secret contacts between governments and 'their' terrorists to understand that the process of negotiation, compromise and reconciliation is far from unthinkable, and is in fact a clear objective for most governments dealing with terrorist problems. It is perhaps time to admit publicly that this is a legitimate and justifiable course.

While such a development must be seen as desirable, for all its evident risks, it is a far cry from the current reality. States place themselves at the opposite end of the moral spectrum from terrorists, thereby confirming the assumption of the terrorists that nothing but terrorism will bring them an audience and some form of recognition. In October 1984, Acting US Secretary of State Kenneth W. Dam described US state policy on terrorism in this way: 'Because our positions are balanced, because they are fair, because they can point the way to a just solution, the President is committed to them as they are. They will not be changed. Those who seek a different solution must seek it not through terror but at the negotiating table.' The argument is perfectly circular – to the minority group with a cause to promote, infuriatingly so. It reinforces the terrorists' belief that democratic methods do *not* offer any real hope of change: the United States tells them that its policies are right because they are fair; and will not be changed, because they are right. The negotiating table, in truth, stands behind locked doors.

Terrorism has changed the face of modern international relations and modern daily life – this century will not see the barricades in Washington come down except for improved models: nor will major multinational industries forgo their bevy of security consultants, bullet proof headquarters buildings and kidnap insurance premiums. Diplomatic ranks will suffer more casualties than the military, in peacetime.

The modern air traveller is constantly aware of the risk of the suitcase bomb and the onboard hijack; but he is much more likely to be killed in a car accident on his way to the airport than to die at the hands of terrorists. The international business executive whose company spends tens of thousands of dollars on his bodyguards, bulletproof car and kidnap insurance, is much more likely to succumb to a heart attack than to be killed by any terrorists. The working mother is much more likely to develop a fatal breast cancer than to die in a city centre car bombing.

The modern Western world is already an unsafe, polluted, hectic, alarming environment. Every child's parent knows of the thousands of real and imagined risks that present themselves at any moment of the day. Even with terrorism added to the existing terrors, it remains the same world. The highly marginal risk of falling victim to a terrorist incident is far less worthy of constant anxiety, for instance, than the recent revelation in the United States that the earth exhales radon contamination, invisible but deadly.

The mundane daily risks do not call a halt to daily life, and terrorism must not be permitted to do so. Pragmatism, a sense of proportion and a deliberate objectivity about the meaning of terrorism must by now be demanded of governments, armed forces, security services, reporters and even the public. The simple answers – incomprehension, condemnation and counter-violence – are not answers at all. Panic and fear being the ultimate enemies of freedom, they represent the most unproductive and least intelligent of public reactions for mature democracies and their leaders.

APPENDIX

THE ANATOMY
OF TERRORISM

There are many different areas of practicality, technique and attitude which are essential to the activity of terrorism. This appendix lists in alphabetical order some of the most important ones.

Accommodation
A terrorist group needs long term safe houses in which to hide, live and sleep; short term tactical bases for short term actions; and arms dumps, explosives stores, bomb factories or garages. In the cities, accommodation is usually a nondescript flat, neither too grand and expensive nor too cheap and dirty. Flat-sharing among young people of student age never raises suspicions. The ideal safe house has a minimum of two entrances, to enable some hope of escape. In the country, it should be in an obscure position to make surveillance difficult; a city flat should not be open to view from nearby buildings or other parts of the same building. Cellars or roof-spaces make useful weapon-stores, though terrorists are often careless: police raids on their bases frequently find weapons, explosives, timers and communiqués lying about openly. The safe house will be privately rented or leased. The tenant will be a junior recruit to the terrorist group, who has not yet become connected to terrorism in the police intelligence files.

Garaging is useful both for the cars (usually stolen) and the weapons and explosives.

Terrorists go to great lengths to act out an apparently normal daily schedule. A woman member of Action Directe explained this point in 1981: 'I try to live like everyone else around me. I get up in the morning, I go out, I give the appearance of going to work. I try to have exactly the same life as my neighbour alongside. Which means that during the day I pass the time out of the house, and I go home at a respectable hour ... The organisation takes care of the rent.'

The Provisional IRA used two distinct types of safe house in London in 1979–80. Firstly, there were 'fronts' – flats shared by several people who were ready to open the door to the police, answer questions and justify their answers by presenting evidence of their jobs, wage slips, driving licences and rent books. Secondly, there were 'bomb factories', which were also nondescript rented flats – but were occupied by people with weapons who were ready to defend the unit and shoot their way out if the police should call.

Budget

Most terrorist groups need to commit acts of common crime – theft, extortion, blackmail and burglary – to raise the funds they need. Some are financed by states, but in such cases the group will almost certainly be the 'direct action' arm of a much larger and more developed entity, as in the relationship between Black September and the PLO. *The Times* reported on 19 April 1976 that the Black September Organisation had received a 'budget' of $7 million in order to carry out its notorious attack on Israeli athletes at the Munich Olympic Games. A terrorist campaign does not need to be very expensive.

The price of an effective bomb does not increase according to its fatality: it costs no more to kill than to injure. The IRA bomb attempt on the British Cabinet in 1984 cost very little to set up – probably less than £10,000. While four people died, it was only a matter of chance that no members of the Cabinet were killed – the IRA could have eliminated four Cabinet ministers, even the Prime Minister, for about £2,500 per head. A detailed breakdown of an earlier IRA bombing campaign in Britain shows that sixteen bombs were planted in different English cities, for a total cost of no more than about £25,000. The money allowed for travel in and out of Britain and Ireland, for the rent of flats in London and Essex, for buying second hand cars, and renting others. The cost of the Active Service Unit's weapons and explosives was minimal – no more than a couple of thousand pounds. But the campaign resulted in more than £10 million worth of property damage and nine people injured, though none killed.

Communications

Terrorists are at their most vulnerable when they are communicating with each other: the fronts, false identities and cover stories are all undermined by the practicalities of a planning meeting or a message giving details of a target to be hit. Most terrorist groups operate some form of cell structure, with a leadership that remains out of contact with the separate action units who will actually mount the attack. The distance between parts of the structure may be no more than a few city blocks, or it may be several national frontiers.

Coded communications are essential, and terrorists obey much the same rules as other participants in clandestine activity, like intelligence officers. The telephone is used very rarely, and never to discuss any concrete matters of importance. One terrorist explained that the telephone should be used for absolute emergencies, or completely innocent transactions only.

Terrorists do not use codes in the same way that intelligence officers do; but between co-operating colleagues they do not need to do so. A terrorist group is usually communicating Yes or No decisions about a limited number of options for which a pre-arranged set of coded answers can be agreed. For example, an unmarked newspaper cutting on an agreed specific subject can represent a meaningful message to those receiving it, but nothing at all to an outsider. In European cities where one can buy newspapers of perhaps twenty languages, a cutting in

269

Spanish, together with another in Greek, could be enough to indicate just one of dozens of alternative messages, with no annotation that would risk divulging anything to an interceptor.

For the same reason, battered secondhand typewriters are less useful than modern mass-market electronic machines which leave fewer tell tale marks for the forensic experts to analyse. There is no evidence of terrorists using sophisticated radio equipment – in communications matters, as in most others, terrorism is a resolutely low-technology activity. When messages must be either written or memorised to be passed on to colleagues, personal couriers are employed: and terrorists favour using women in the role.

Discipline and Doubts

Terrorist discipline operates both internally within the group and externally as a kind of alternative policing. All studies of terrorist groups have shown that there is no room for a member with doubts: he or she will either drop out, be forcibly excluded, or physically eliminated in the interests of security. Disputes over tactics and targets result in internal violence, and all the evidence shows that the effective terrorist organisation demands a unanimity of purpose in an environment which excludes and forbids dissent or external considerations. As Robert Clark remarks of the ETA: 'They lived and moved in a sort of hermetically closed compartment where one simply did not raise depressing questions or challenge the ultimate victory of the organisation... They had learned ... the psychological defence of insurgency, as expressed by one of them in this way: "A clandestine organisation is living and dying every day. There are people who quit. Tired people leave. New people join and we train them, and then we do it all over again. You see someone once, and then you never see them again. You don't ask questions, you just do your job."'

All terrorists believe that they are fighting a battle which will bring justice for their cause, their nation or their community after years, decades or centuries of wrongful

270

oppression. Justice and its enforcement is also a strong tactical weapon within the terrorists' home community – in the sense that if the terrorists can enforce justice, or their version of it, they can both gain credit as a moral force, and more importantly adapt delinquent behaviour towards their cause.

Discipline within the group is essential, but has little to do with justice and everything to do with eliminating dissent and dispute about tactics. In Corsica, in the Basque country and in Northern Ireland – the three strongest regional battlegrounds of terrorism – the FLNC, ETA and the Provisional IRA make efforts to impose themselves on the community. Kneecapping – shooting through the kneecaps – and tarring-and-feathering were both invented by the IRA as forms of punishment for dissent or treason. As punishments they are notable for their cruelty and publicity.

The Provos have managed to establish themselves as a sort of alternative police force in the Catholic communities of Northern Ireland, particularly in West Belfast. In the Republican Advice Centres (formerly Service Centres), complaints about anything from housing problems to vandalism can be voiced, and the 'Civil Administration' is the arm of the Provisionals which tackles problems of community discipline and criminality with kangaroo courts, deciding upon punishments in the absence of the offender and carrying them out anonymously but all too effectively.

The level of teenage crime is low: partly through underreporting, but mostly because it is stamped on by the Provo hierarchy. Teenage joyriders – an epidemic crime in Belfast – are encouraged to direct their social dissent towards the institutions of the (British) government, on behalf of the terrorist organisation; and this can serve as the first step in recruiting new blood to the Provos' ranks. Equally, the IRA attempts to police all and any 'collaboration with the enemy'; in August 1985 this 'policing' emerged in the shape of intimidation towards building contractors who accepted contracts to work for the British security forces. The IRA went so far as to issue a formal statement: 'Over the last four months our intelligence personnel have compiled accurate and extensive dossiers on all those involved in such work, or likely to take up these contracts in the future. As a result of this intelligence we are now in a position to take effective action if builders do not henceforth desist from playing an active role in support of the Crown forces.'

The IRA alleged that they had turned down the offer of one businessman of £100,000 in cash in return for a 'non-aggression pact'. Their statement continued: 'Contractors involved are assisting the British in reinforcing their illegal and immoral presence. They are building fortresses and interrogation centres which are being used to oppress our people.' In the case of builders ignoring the warning, the IRA said that 'our volunteers will be directed to take extreme action.'

Explosives

The most common weapon of terrorists is the bomb, whether it be a basic incendiary device for a heightened form of arson-vandalism, or the murderous high-explosive and gas-bottle combination intended to kill and maim. Ease of use for the terrorists contrasts with the enormous complexity of the forensic task for police services in the aftermath, in particular to define and trace the nature of the explosives. In West Germany, according to Reinhard Rupprecht of the Federal Police, arson and bombings represent the vast majority of domestic terrorist crime. He summarises the methods as follows:

1. Explosives. Mostly they use metal tubes or fire extinguishers, screwed on both ends, filled with self-made explosives (a mixture of 'weed-ex' and sugar). Sometimes TNT is used as one of the military explosives, because it can be easily procured.
2. Fuses. Terrorists generally use prepared clocks as delayed action fuses. The tuner is exchanged with the wire of the igniter. Commercial batteries serve as energy. Igniters are often put in a condom filled with a mixture of chlorate and sugar.
3. Incendiaries. Mostly so-called 'Molotov cocktails'

bottles filled with a mixture of gas and oil – are used as incendiaries.

Home-made explosives are surprisingly simple to manufacture, and apparently it is not much harder to steal industrial high explosives. In agricultural areas, the purchase of quite large quantities of farm fertiliser is an unremarkable thing, but it can be processed to produce a powerful explosive. Northern Ireland is the pre-eminent example, but the chemical principle works for any quantity, anywhere. Fertiliser contains ammonium nitrate, which has to be separated from the other ingredients by first creating a watery solution of fertiliser, and then carrying out a chemical filtration process. Fuel oil is then added to the ammonium nitrate, partly to stabilize it, and partly to make the bomb burn when it explodes. The resultant product is known as ANFO, for Ammonium Nitrate–Fuel Oil. However, this procedure may not be possible for much longer – according to Scotland Yard sources, the agri-chemical industry is urgently pursuing ways to eliminate the amateur-explosives potential from fertiliser products.

More dangerous still are the opportunities for terrorists to procure industrial high explosives, either from military sources or from low-security quarrying sites. In one recent and notorious case in the United States, a civilian maintenance employee at the renowned West Point Military Academy was arrested as he tried to sell 100 sticks of dynamite to an undercover agent posing as an IRA representative. In Europe, the wave of bombings perpetrated by Action Directe, CCC and the Red Army Faction was made possible by a single theft of 800 kilos of explosives from a quarry near Brussels in 1984. In Puerto Rico, terrorists belonging to the Macheteros ('machete-wielders') movement stole the huge quantity of 1,500 pounds of Iremite high explosives from a construction site on the island. The same explosives were found to have been used in the terrorist attack on the Puerto Rican Air National Guard, on 10 January 1981, in which $50 million worth of aeroplanes were blown up.

The US Treasury Department's Bureau of Alcohol, Tobacco and Firearms monitors all crimes connected with

273

explosives, whether terrorism or not. The Bureau's statistics on the theft of explosives reveal extraordinarily lax security on explosive materials. In 1984, 71,471 pounds of explosives were stolen in the United States – almost double the figure of the previous year – while only 15,538 pounds were recovered. By the Bureau's own definition, the vast majority stolen is 'high explosive', rather than 'low explosive'. The statistics on 'traces' of stolen firearms in the USA are still more alarming: in 1984, 31,599 weapons were traced. Roughly broken down, there were 20,000 pistols and revolvers, 11,000 rifles and shotguns, and 54 machine guns.

Weapons of mass destruction figure in the nightmarish predictions of some analysts of terrorism who believe terrorists will follow the 'ABC option' – an awkward acronym for 'Atomic, Biological, Chemical' weapons. Though there has been a handful of threats involving anthrax germs and plutonium adulteration of water supplies, there is very little reason to believe that terrorists have any political or tactical advantage to gain from causing mass casualties. Nevertheless, such prospects cause a great deal of concern to security forces and contingency planners. Assistant Commissioner John Dellow described British thinking in these terms: 'In the UK we have given considerable thought to our response, particularly to the placing of improvised nuclear devices. Contingency planning and exercises have taken place, and the issue is joined with ... other criminal threats to water and air supplies by adulteration.' If the idea of 'improvised nuclear devices' seems far-fetched, Retired Admiral Thomas Davies, former Assistant Director of the US Arms Control and Disarmament Agency, argues the opposite: 'A well-organised group of terrorists could obtain enough weapons-grade uranium to make an atomic bomb by raiding a handful of lightly-guarded campus research reactors around the United States.'

The balance of evidence suggests that chilling scenario will not occur: terrorists believe in tactical violence, rather than strategic 'scorched-earth' destruction. They believe they are right, and that they represent the path to justice for their people, so the use of violence is seen more as a trigger to victory than as any victory in itself. Terrorists have a perverse and ironic belief in public opinion; they believe that sooner or later everyone will see that they were right. Weapons of mass slaughter would eliminate their constituency before that realisation would be able to dawn.

Fundraising
From the Action Directe robbery in Condé-sur-l'Escaut, which netted 16 million francs, to a criminal leeching of cash from the Northern Ireland economy which is the largest financial source for the Provisional IRA, money buys terrorism. The methods for raising it are many and various, but probably the most effective is the 'Revolutionary Tax' levied by the ETA on the Basque country.

A member of ETA-Politico/Militar describes the process involved: 'ETA's finances come from bank hold-ups, kidnapping businessmen and the Revolutionary Tax. They send you a letter. It says "ETA demands a tax of x million pesetas." There's always a threat of death that goes with it.' The tax – or the attacks that follow refusal to pay – is accepted as the price of operating in the area at all; in the words of a Spanish diplomat, 'All the major concerns in the region receive Revolutionary Tax demands.' Not all, however, give in to them. The Bank of Vizcaya has consistently refused to pay up, and in consequence had suffered by 1983 seventy bomb attacks, each causing between $6,000 and $11,000 worth of damage. The grand total far exceeds the amount actually demanded by the ETA.

Big business is also susceptible to the kidnapping of owners or directors: for example, in January 1981 Jose Lipperheide, a German-born Spanish industrialist, was kidnapped and held hostage until a $1.6 million ransom was paid. But small businesses and affluent individuals – usually less wealthy than the terrorists' tax demands imply – often leave the area when this Informal Revenue Service gets in touch. The price of refusal can be too high: the destruction of the business premises, or death. Jesus Letona was murdered in Azpeitia in

December 1981 for non-payment, and in September 1983 bar owner Antonio Quintanilla Salas was shot dead in Hernani.

Increasingly, Spanish regional disputes are being over-shadowed by the volume of anti-American activity, and since 1982 targets like the Sears department stores in Barcelona and the Bank of America in Madrid have joined the casualty lists – both bombed in August of that year. Other multinational targets include a Michelin warehouse in Oyarzun, a computer centre of the West German Nixdorf company, the Bank of America in Bilbao, Xerox offices, a Coca Cola factory, and NCR, Pepsi Cola, IBM and 3M offices. After a summit meeting between President Mitterrand of France and Prime Minister Felipe Gonzales of Spain on cross-border and judicial co-operation against terrorists, French interests fell prey to the bombers. Within a few months, $320,000 worth of damage had been done to French car dealerships alone.

International financial and commercial enterprises are a prime target for terrorists, offering large hauls to those who rob them and ideological kudos to those who attack them – particularly in the case of American multinationals, and all the more so if they are part of what Eisenhower called 'the military-industrial complex'. There is a further benefit in the assault on the expensively advertised corporate image of such businesses: it is bad publicity for a company to be identifiably so unpopular as to be the object of terrorist attacks. One Japanese executive admitted that 'if our security people were to carry guns, then visitors would think that we are doing something unusual that attracts terrorists. It would hurt our corporate image.' Just as no state wishes to confine its diplomats to armed bunkers, no corporation wishes to do business behind security guards and oppressive identity-checking procedures, though increasingly they are forced to do so. One major European headquarters building simply does not permit visitors to take their briefcases beyond the entrance hall. There is also the problem that the company must divert its resources to protection measures, which cannot be totally comprehensive, and can be infinitely expensive.

*   *   *

Like ETA, the IRA is also able to support itself from a mixture of community support and local extortion: the former funnelled principally through the organisation Irish Northern Aid, known as NORAID, whose efforts have given rise to the saying, 'Giving money doesn't help Irish widows and orphans, it creates them.' Many detailed investigations have established that Noraid funds have been connected with the IRA's efforts to equip itself with improved or additional weaponry. The best available piece of evidence came from Michael Hanratty, a former electronics purchaser in New York for the IRA, who turned Federal informant.

According to Hanratty's testimony, 'Money supplied by NORAID was sent over to Ireland ... At that point, when equipment was to be purchased, a courier then took some of the money and carried it back to this country.' The circular movement of the funds provides evidence above all of the ease with which weapons – even quite substantial military weapons – can be bought in the United States. The Royal Ulster Constabulary disagrees about the movement of funds back and forth across the Atlantic, but concurs on the use to which those funds are put: 'At least half of what is raised in America stays in the US for the purchase of weapons,' according to an RUC spokesman.

Recently the IRA has found far more lucrative areas of activity close to home, in the shape of old-fashioned criminal racketeering within the Northern Ireland community. At the end of 1983 the Royal Ulster Constabulary established an Anti-Racketeering Unit, to tackle the problem head-on. In the classic style of rackets throughout the century, the focus is on drinking, gambling and the 'leisure industry'. When half of the 500 pubs in Belfast were destroyed by bombs during the 1970s, illegal drinking clubs appeared. Now legalised, a large number are alleged to be run by a syndicate which is closely identified with the IRA. One member was thought to be the Finance Officer of the Provisional IRA in Belfast. Their turnover alone should guarantee profits of several hundred thousand pounds per year.

Protection rackets affect pubs and clubs which are not under direct control, and a novel fundraising exercise involves the enforced introduction of coin-operated pool tables, gambling machines or video games in premises where 'collectors' appear once a week to take away the proceeds. The landlord has no choice, and sees none of the takings.

The building industry everywhere has been susceptible to financial shenanigans – and the IRA has played a part in organising tax-dodges, phantom workers on payrolls, and 'protection schemes' to swell its coffers. The rebuilding scheme for Belfast City Hospital allegedly involved a £1.3 million 'anti-terrorist bonus' to persuade men to come to work. Throughout the province, building costs emerge higher than elsewhere in the United Kingdom, because of the invisible costs of placating and paying-off the terrorists.

Simple theft also plays a part in terrorist fundraising. In nine months from September 1963 to April 1964, the *Front de la Libération Québécois* (Quebec Liberation Front) stole $40,000 in cash, and military and electronic equipment to the value of $55,000. At the opposite end of the spectrum, the late 1980s' most rapid criminal growth industry – computer crime – has begun to feature in terrorist fundraising. It has been suggested that the Colombian terrorist movement M-19 had had some success in this area, being responsible for processing an automatic fraction of cash transfers into its own secret and disguised accounts.

The French terrorist group Action Directe is the source for some revealing information about terrorists' pay. According to Jean-Marc Rouillan, the group's leader, the proceeds of their 'proletarian expropriation' are partly used to pay the terrorists a wage. 'Some of our people underground live on the money that they get from banks, but that's because they are unable to go to work in the normal way,' he explained in 1981. 'It's a sort of salary. They are given money according to their needs, about five thousand francs a month. It's all relative, it's done according to the part they play in the organisation. If they need money to go and do a recce in a big expensive hotel, the militants are given the necessary cash to do so.'

278

Another woman member of Action Directe was more specific: she said the money was used to buy false documents and weapons, and to sustain comrades and international solidarity. 'The armed struggle in France costs a lot, and international solidarity costs a lot, too. There are many comrades in prison in Italy, and in Spain, and in Germany, and we have sent them money.' Asked if the terrorists of Action Directe didn't have fun with some of their huge haul of 16 million francs at Condé-sur-l'Escaut, the woman replied: 'The money didn't belong to the people who carried out the action, or their group, it belonged to the movement, and everyone knew that. Nobody bought a Cadillac or *foie gras*. No one in the movement ever thought the money belonged to him.'

The most extraordinary method of financing terrorism is an inspired Japanese example combining revolutionary politics with the methods of the stock market. The Central Core Faction, the largest and most active student radical group in Japan, issued about 500 million yen worth of 'bonds' (about $2 million) to fund their activities at the beginning of 1985. The six-year bonds, carrying an annual coupon rate of five per cent with a two-year grace period, were sold to the group's sympathisers, who apparently borrowed money from their families or took out bank loans, according to Japanese police. The Faction, which has been prominent in opposition to the expansion of Tokyo International Airport at Narita, was expected to use its funds to develop new weapons and tactics to block the airport development.

The latest presumed source of funding for terrorists is through involvement in drugs. There is no doubt that while the substantial sums that can be made from drug trafficking may attract anyone who is strongly motivated to raise a lot of money, the evidence is so far relatively uncertain. A substantial trade of drugs and weapons passes back and forth between Turkey and Bulgaria, and the rightwing Grey Wolves of Turkey certainly handled the drug trade. So far, however, it seems that the lucrative but risky area of what American officials call 'narco-terrorism' has not developed significantly. The FBI's John Harley, Director of their

Terrorist Research and Analytical Center, describes 'narco-terrorism' as 'a hype – we don't frankly see it'. He distinguishes sharply between drug traffickers who commit acts of violence – '.Most of it could also be called normal criminal activity designed to protect the narcotics cartels' – and the fundraising activities of terrorists – 'We have not seen terrorists get into the narcotics business at all: they do armed robberies, which they call "expropriation from an unjust society". We employ the Racketeering (Influence of Corrupt Organisations) Statute, designed to deal with organised crime like the Mafia, which makes money from criminal methods and employs it in legitimate business to make more. We can act against terrorists because they are engaged in an ongoing criminal enterprise – it works against them pretty well. There's also a forfeiture provision: the effect is to cripple the whole enterprise, more so than just putting a few people in jail.'

The Royal Ulster Constabulary and the FBI both remember the lessons of an earlier age of racketeering: as the RUC points out, the FBI finally caught Al Capone and put him out of business for tax evasion. If it can work against the terrorist racketeers too, they will employ just the same tactics.

Hijacking
Hijacking aeroplanes was a favoured form of terrorist action in the late 1960s; skyjacking hit a high of fifty 'successful' incidents. Through the 1970s the figure first declined to an average of fewer than ten skyjackers a year, then slowly climbed to an annual average nearer twenty. This form of terrorist crime had an impact as long as it was unexpected, and as long as defences were not in place first to prevent, and then to limit, the problem; or as long as special forces had not been created to launch counterstrikes. Indeed, as a terrorist phenomenon it endured not least because the air hijack raised delicate territorial questions, doubts about jurisdiction, and co-operation between unfriendly nations. The London Metropolitan Police Assistant Commissioner for Crime, John Dellow, described the multi-faceted nature of a state's response to a hijacking incident in these terms: 'A hijacking, for

example, can require government involvement and diplomatic liaison with several different countries. It may require the assistance of airline officials, of airline manufacturers (this in itself may require the use of international contacts), of airport officials, of psychologists, of marksmen, of intelligence officers with a knowledge of the political background of the hijackers, of interpreters, of negotiators, and so on.'

As all those preparations, defences, and ultimately counteroffensives became organised and ready; and once states began to develop a slightly more sophisticated response than capitulation when challenged to release hijackers' comrades; then, it appears, the terrorists looked for other methods. The more recent upsurge in incidents seems to demonstrate that terrorists have accepted the much greater likelihood of failure or death.

Just as they are ready to die, they are ready to kill, and no hijack-response team has yet found the clean answer to terrorists who are prepared to murder their hostages systematically to provoke a meaningful response to their demands. The Egyptian troops who stormed an Egyptian Airlines jet at Malta's Luqqa airport proved the impossible odds that the totally ruthless and suicidal terrorist presents to the response team: fifty-seven passengers died, some in the gunfire of the Egyptian troops, others blown up by the grenades that the terrorists threw, finally fulfilling the threat that terrorist hijackers always make.

Identity

If terrorists are to maintain their organisation for any length of time once they have begun to act against their targets, the members of the group need identity papers of every kind. In some countries an identity card is required by law for all citizens, while in others papers can be demanded by police on relatively minor pretexts. Everywhere, terrorists are most at risk when they cross borders – in French, when they are *contrôlé*, which precisely defines the danger. The terrorists need passports, identity cards, social security or employment cards, driving licences, motor insurance certificates, and all the paperwork that is required to prove an individual's legitimacy in modern society.

Marighella pointed out that the urban guerilla who leads a clandestine existence is 'obliged to use false documents', and among the talents he requires of the guerilla is the ability to forge and tamper with official papers 'in order to live within the society that he seeks to destroy'.

Certainly everywhere that police have caught terrorists the paraphernalia of forgery is found, usually alongside large numbers of stolen papers and documents required to support elaborate cover stories and aliases. Willi Voss, a member of the Adolf Hitler Freikorps, and subsequently an unusual German member of the PLO's Black September, had more than fifty aliases during his career as a courier throughout Europe, the Middle East and South America. In retirement, he still goes by at least four names in his various contacts and connections.

The identity of terrorists can be particularly well-concealed in the United States, as the FBI's John Harley remarks: 'They have built new identities for themselves, and some of those people have several different identities. They can get social security numbers and cards. One of the standard techniques, which has also been used by Soviet spies in the USA, is to go through the newspaper columns to find the name of a child which has died in infancy, and assume the same name, and go ahead and get a social security card in that name. Provided you have cash and don't have to get into the credit and banking systems, if you stay out of trouble, and if you don't get into the local police files, you don't exist.'

Action Directe's 'Fairy Godmother', the bookseller Helyette Besse, was tried and convicted in a Paris court for receipt of stolen blank Italian identity cards; and the town hall of Paris's 14th *arrondissement* was raided by Action Directe for identity papers, and the rubber stamps needed to authenticate them. In June 1985, an investigation was launched in Bolivia into the disappearance of no fewer than 30,000 blank passports; and the *Achille Lauro* hijackers had a batch of false Moroccan passports. Equally remarkably, both Armenian and anti-Semitic terrorists who carried out attacks in France had false Cypriot passports with consecutive numbers.

More peculiar is the fact that some terrorists assume the names of notorious historical figures. At the end of May 1972, Kozo Okamoto and two colleagues in the Japanese Red Army staged a surrogate attack for the Palestinian PFLP at Lod Airport in Israel. On his tortuous journey to carry out the slaughter, in which twenty-six people died, Okamoto carried a passport in the name of Daisuke Namba – the real name of the Japanese man who attempted to assassinate the Crown Prince (later Emperor) Hirohito in 1923.

Kidnap

Kidnapping is a classic crime of extortion which has lent itself with particular drama, but little concrete result, to the repertoire of terrorism. Terrorists sometimes kidnap purely for money – which is largely the case in South America – and at other times for political concessions. In the latter case the victim may not be personally rich, but he must be powerful. Thus the first kind of kidnapping has as its targets the relatively anonymous executive of a rich company, or a personally wealthy businessman – like the South American manager of General Motors, or supermarket executive Don Tidey; while the second category produces power-play victims – like Prime Minister Aldo Moro of Italy, General James Dozier of NATO, or Hanns-Martin Schleyer of the West German Federal Employers' Organisation.

The power-kidnap is far more difficult to carry off – and increasingly so, as the powerful are even better protected (at the state's expense) than the rich (who pay for themselves, or have company budgets for security). One thing that is never in doubt is the willingness of the terrorists ultimately to kill their hostage – since they are highly likely to have killed bodyguards and escorts in order to kidnap the hostage in the first place. Aldo Moro's entire guard of five was shot dead when he was abducted by the Red Brigades in Rome's Via Fani; Hanns-Martin Schleyer's driver and bodyguard died when he was taken by the Red Army Faction in West Germany.

The power-kidnap raises the stakes of terrorism: it combines the essential cruelty of hostage-taking with an absolute readiness to 'confront the powers'. This is done by turning the screw harder and harder: by sending messages handwritten by the hostage; by suggesting that some state secrets have been revealed; by sending photographs showing the still-living hostage holding a clearly identifiable current newspaper. Despite the enormous pressure that such devices put upon governments, none has yet openly succumbed to the demands made in connection with the kidnap of such targets. On the other hand, the kidnap-for-money has proved most successful, and a whole new branch of the international insurance business has sprung forth in writing policies for kidnap insurance. It is a growth area in every respect. In Colombia, for example, 1983 saw 113 kidnappings, and the figure shot up to 299 in 1984. In an extraordinary admission, the chief of Colombia's Anti-Kidnapping Corps, Captain Guillermo Benavides, said that 'Routine preventative measures against kidnapping are not very effective in the long term, if someone really wants to kidnap you'. In early 1985 the United States Ambassador to Colombia, Lew Tambs, asserted in passing that he believed his own bodyguards had been bribed to kidnap or murder him. It is estimated that $150 million is paid to kidnappers every year in Colombia, of which perhaps $100 million goes to terrorist or revolutionary organisations.

In the light of such large sums changing hands, a number of specialised companies offer consultation, insurance and negotiation expertise to help minimise the risks. A new service was launched in May 1985 by the American International Group's Special Services Division, described as 'a total corporate extortion package'. The company·brochure is headed 'Special Risk Insurance – Because You Can Be Targeted Anytime'. The insurance covers 'such risks as reward and legal costs, wrongful detention and business interruption'.

According to Commander Churchill-Coleman of the Scotland Yard AntiTerrorist Branch, 'In kidnaps the prime consideration is to save life, so you may have no choice but to pay ransoms.' But in one instance, it appears that a higher priority was detected. When the IRA kidnapped the British supermarket executive Don Tidey in Ireland, the demand of several million pounds' ransom was a sum which could have kept the IRA going for perhaps two years, with no other source of income. According to police sources, the British government's view was that such a prospect was too high a price to pay for a single life, and every effort was made to prevent Tidey's family or company from paying the ransom. Tidey ultimately escaped, though it was not clear whether this was because money had been paid over; certainly a sum of some £2 million was laundered through Irish, Swiss and American banks, and finally confiscated by the Irish government as the property of the IRA.

Links

The assumption and the fear about international terrorism has always been that diverse groups are linked for purposes of arms, training and targeting: the other half of the theory is that ill-motivated states orchestrate the connections. However, while terrorist groups occasionally meet – and the political fronts behind which they operate meet more often – there is little evidence to suggest that links are either particularly common or particularly useful. In the 1960s and 1970s West German terrorists were prominent among the European visitors to PLO training camps; but evidence and firsthand testimony suggest that they were being used by the PLO for local intelligence and propaganda functions rather more than for armed action.

This is not to dismiss the existence of terrorist links, but to underplay the 'Terror Network' theory of the author Clare Sterling, among others. There are so many different species of terrorist, criminal, anarchist, dissenter and mercenary at large in the world, that any neat theory of a network and a master plan invites scepticism. While a press visitor to the Sinn Fein *Ard Fheis* (annual conference) can meet representatives of the marginal political parties of Basque independence, Corsican nationalism, Kurdish resistance and others, the strong impression is that for these comrades there is safety in numbers when whistling in the dark. They are able to display a loose solidarity largely because they have nothing to disagree about.

There is a striking piece of contradictory evidence in the new alliance of Action Directe, the CCC and the Red Army Faction, a Franco-Belgo-German union of terrorists which has a significant strike rate against NATO and American military targets in all three countries. France, Belgium and Germany have somewhat porous borders for the terrorists to cross; yet their further-flung comrades in Portugal, Spain and even Greece have carried out identical attacks against similar targets. In Athens, on 3 March 1985, a foiled terrorist attack on the West Germany Embassy was claimed by the Revolutionary Group of International Solidarity – *Christos Kassimos*. The group claimed to be affiliated with the Red Army Faction – hence the attack on the West Germany Embassy – and to have further links with both Action Directe and the CCC. The alliance has published joint communiqués and joint political programmes, and appears to operate with equal impunity in all the countries it has so far chosen: a fact that is as disturbing to police and security forces in the countries where it has struck as in those where it has not.

Mobility

Terrorism is by definition mobile and elusive. Terrorists prefer to do their travelling by car, if it is at all possible, and (hijackers apart) they avoid flying, as the security checks of airports subject them to the kind of intense scrutiny they would much prefer to avoid. Cars have several advantages to the terrorist: he or she can deliberately cross low-security frontiers; the car itself can be used to conceal weapons, explosives, cash, documentation and disguises; cars are easy to steal and hard to trace quickly if they have false plates; secondhand cars can be bought for cash without raising suspicions; the car itself is a more secure place for the terrorist than the anonymous environment of public transport systems; and different types of car make convincing props for different cover stories. The risks of transnational train journeys, by contrast, were illustrated by the arrest of Action Directe's Turkish explosives courier, Muzaffer Kacir. Having aroused the suspicions of the Belgian border police, he was arrested at journey's end in Paris by the French Border and Air Police.

Surprisingly long journeys will be undertaken by car, not least because terrorists are usually in no great hurry. Known missions for Black September have involved a drive from Madrid to West Germany and another from Beirut, through Syria and Turkey, to Bulgaria. Another case involves a car which became a car-bomb in Paris. A young German woman, Christa Fröhlich, hired a car in Belgrade and apparently drove it all the way to Paris, where it later blew up in the rue Marboeuf, outside the offices of an anti-Syrian newspaper *Al-Watan Al-Arabi*. Fröhlich herself was arrested shortly afterwards getting off a plane in Rome.

An isolated footnote to the style in which the terrorists travel is provided by the fact that when the celebrated PLO woman terrorist Leila Khaled and her comrade Salim Issawi hijacked the TWA 847 Rome-Athens-Damascus flight, they chose to travel first class.

Noms de Guerre

'The Berlin police were looking for hundreds of groups and sects ... when all along it was the same crew, who adopted a new name every week.' Michael 'Bommi' Baumann found the greatest amusement in the antics of the anarchists and revolutionaries who constantly invented new identities to take responsibility for their actions. He went on to describe the tactical idea: 'Ten or twelve attempts were made against judges, prosecutors, prison superintendents and others. Each time a leaflet went out ... And of course each time someone else claimed the action. Overnight there were twenty groups. This was to suggest that suddenly, overnight, a giant people's army had come into being and was now operating – to create confusion among the police and to show the people that we were already a very large circle. In fact, there were only about ten of us.'

Individual terrorists employ false names and aliases as a

INVISIBLE ARMIES

subterfuge, and nicknames or *noms de guerre* to romanticise themselves into the stuff of legend. The Basque 'Tigre', 'Peixoto' and 'Txapela', and indeed 'Bommi' in itself, all exemplify the latter impulse.

There is a very real difficulty for those people trying to assess the actual threat of terrorist activity, which is always at its most difficult when a previously unknown name appears: but the blood is just as red and vital whether it is spilled by a known or unknown group – by ASALA-MR or the Armenian Revolutionary Army; by the PFLP or the PDFLP; by the IRA or the INLA; by the 2nd June Movement, the Revolutionary Group of the 1st October, or the May 19th Communist Organisation.

Until the chance arrest of a Belgian political activist, who turned out to be connected to the CCC group, a theory was gaining currency among European police authorities that the CCC in fact had no real existence, and were simply a front for Action Directe and the Red Army Faction, designed to confuse. It subsequently appears that the CCC is an organisation of some substance, but the terrorists gained a real tactical advantage from the mythology they created around themselves.

Profile

The terrorist needs to be physically unremarkable. He or she must never look like a 'student radical', and the superficial connotation of Arabs with terrorism means that Arab terrorists like to recruit West Europeans who do not seem 'suspicious'. Terrorists must not be unusually attractive or ugly, tall or fat, or tanned – in short, they must not be memorable. One major European terrorist worried throughout his career that his unusual tallness was a risk; but it qualified him to be a member of his country's most prestigious Honour Guard.

Terrorists gain breathing space from seeming to have normal lives, careers and social habits. According to Professor Franco Ferracuti, the stereotype image of the scruffy, unwashed hippy-like terrorist, living in a backstreet commune, is

288

badly flawed. 'They dress like you,' he insists. 'They wear a tie, smart clothes, they could pass for bankers. They rarely live underground. In fact, they have jobs and very normal biographical profiles.'

As a simple example which contrasts with the experience of West Germany or Italy, Irish people in London, though far from rare, are immediately recognisable by their accent. British police sources suggest that because of this Irish terrorists feel uneasily conspicuous and relatively insecure in Britain. Terrorists need to feel comfortable where they are working, able to use the bus or train system, to hail a cab, to go into a pub or bar and order drinks and a meal, without feeling that they are attracting undue attention. It was widely rumoured after the Brighton bombing of October 1984 that the Provisional IRA had employed a 'mainland team' of supporters who were activated by an Irish contact after many years of residence in England – people who were not apparently connected to Ireland at all.

The basic principles of the terrorists' camouflage were articulated by Carlos Marighella, the Brazilian guerilla whose *Minimanual of the Urban Guerilla* is circulated everywhere among underground anarchist and terrorist groups. Under the heading 'Personal Qualities of the Urban Guerilla and How He Subsists', Marighella argues that 'The urban guerilla must know how to live among the people and must be careful not to appear strange and separated from ordinary city life. He should not wear clothes that are different from those that other people wear. Elaborate and high fashion clothing for men or women may often be a handicap if the urban guerilla's mission takes him into working-class neighbourhoods or sections where such dress is uncommon. The same care has to be taken if the urban guerilla moves from the south to the north or vice versa. The urban guerilla must live by his work or professional activity.'

Lastly, terrorists in urban revolutionary groups are young; or they have been young until now. Youth is essential for the commitment that terrorism demands, and for the readiness to break with all other ties. But in the late 1980s the average age is rising slightly, from mid- to late-twenties, as survivors of the student revolutionary movements stick by their radicalism. The *Soixante-Huitards* are also the generation of European terrorists who went to jail for their crimes, or found themselves taking refuge outside their own country. Oreste Scalzone insists that 'the war is only over when the soldiers go home' – and, for that matter, when the 'political prisoners' are allowed out of the jails. When that happens, as in Italy in 1986, will the soldiers and prisoners re-start the war and take revenge for the new injustices they perceive, finding new, youthful recruits for the cause? The answer will emerge in the terrorism that continues into the 1990s.

Recruitment

The recruitment of terrorists varies, but closely reflects the nature of the terrorist group in question. In anarchic-revolutionary urban-based anti-state groups, the move into terrorism comes as a sudden and forceful commitment, often provoked by some particular perceived injustice – whether the arrest and mistreatment by police of the individual or a close friend, or the perceived injustice of a controversial government defence or foreign policy. The new recruit will be someone already active in marginal or extra-parliamentary political circles, already somewhat detached from society and mainstream social values. But the decision to get involved in terrorism involves crossing what is still a very clearly defined line of legality/illegality.

For the nationalist, or the terrorist fighting for independence, there is a far less clear line, and a far stronger sense of a historical tradition of conflict and 'struggle' between the minority group, and the ruling powers. The strength of such a sense of tradition – and its often artificial nature – can be observed in Ireland and Spain. The Provisional IRA speak of seven centuries of struggle with the British colonialists: the Basques of ETA have maintained their hostility to the Spanish government through several decades, despite the transformation of the country from a militaristic dictatorship under General Franco to a Socialist-ruled parliamentary democracy

290

under Prime Minister Gonzales, within a period of less than ten years.

ETA recruits new members through 'contact *etarras*' whose sole job is first to contact, and then draw in, the potential recruit; to guide him through his first relatively undramatic tasks, maintain his commitment and resolve, and lead him on to more serious work. His first tasks may be no more controversial than delivering propaganda leaflets, or helping to spray ETA slogans on a wall: and at that stage the recruit will be privy to very little meaningful information that could leak and endanger the security of the ETA unit. Clark describes the development of the recruit's participation in these terms: 'Once the youth has proven his competence ... the older member may ask him to participate in other operations of increasing danger and complexity such as gathering information on the routine or schedule of bank employees prior to a robbery, for example, or driving a load of weapons to deliver to another ETA member. As the youth demonstrates his ability to carry out challenging assignments, he also invests considerable psychological energy in the operations of ETA, so it becomes increasingly difficult to disengage from the organization.' In effect, the recruit is first seduced, then compromised, however willing a tool he may feel himself to be.

Another study, *Profile of a Terrorist* by Charles Russell and Bowman Miller, draws attention to large Western university campuses, staffed with Marxist professors and Marxist-dominated student federations, as a potent combination for the development of terrorism, and consequently for the recruitment of terrorists. 'For the Japanese Red Army, the universities of Tokyo, Rikkjo, and Kyoto have been very important. In Spain ... the universities of Madrid and Barcelona. Within Italy, the universities of Rome, Turin and Bologna are fertile recruiting grounds ...'

One further aspect of recruitment involves those who lie on the margins of the terrorist group. Sympathetic supporters whose assistance specifically enables terrorist acts to be carried out, though the supporters do not themselves cross the line into violence, are essential to every group. There have been numerous examples, for instance, of terrorists needing to rely upon supporters with medical expertise. Equally, the lawyers who represent terrorists enjoy an uneasy relationship – sometimes they are no more than court-appointed defence lawyers, paid out of public funds, but in other cases they have been alleged to be almost a part of the terrorist group; most notably in the case of Klaus Croissant, the lawyer for the West German Baader-Meinhof terrorists.

Terrorists who need weapons need underworld contacts, used to asking no questions in their transactions; similarly, every terrorist needs his false identification papers, and insiders in the appropriate government offices can be of great assistance. As Billy M. Turner suggests in a paper called 'Demystifying the Terrorist Network': 'The list is only limited by the imagination and operational requirements. Private pilots, prostitutes, professors, sympathetic police, and other persons could all be members of various support teams.'

Surveillance

The existence of terrorism has made most potential victims conscious of the need for precautions. The limited success of terrorism has resulted in the necessity for the terrorists to work harder at observing and researching their victims and targets. They have two objectives; to strike and to escape, so even in the case of random bombings, of which there are in fact very few, the reconnaissance has to establish the pattern of police patrols, security checks, etc. Marighella comments: 'The urban guerrilla must have a great capacity for observation, must be well informed about everything, principally about the enemy's movements, and must be very searching and knowledgeable about the area in which he lives, operates, or through which he moves.'

The counterpoint is the target's awareness of the risk that the terrorist poses: Arnold Campbell of the US State Department includes 'surveillance awareness and personal security' as a central theme of 'Coping with Violence Abroad'. He places emphasis on 'travel precautions as a whole – when you walk out of the house can you see if anything is different? The same thing with your car – you should do a quick check for any signs of tampering. And you did not park the car in a dark area'. The course instructs diplomats to find every way possible to limit the areas of vulnerability, yet Campbell admits that the terrorists ultimately hold most of the cards: 'A terrorist group which is bent and determined to get you will get you one way or another,' he says. 'They may not get a nice clean kidnapping but they can always take you out. We are trying to make people a less intriguing target – like the jerk who is less conscious of the risk and invites a terrorist attack ... It's that person's responsibility to protect himself and increase his awareness.'

Terrorists are all too well aware of the potential surveillance upon their own activities: most of the breakthroughs against terrorist groups in the United States have come through infiltration – not of undercover FBI agents joining the group, but 'electronic infiltration' or wiretaps. This suggests that terrorists have assumed that they were unknown or unlikely to be tapped, but despite the fact that the FBI must show 'probable cause' – i.e., the likelihood of a crime being committed – terrorists have left themselves vulnerable.

Terrorists need access to their targets to carry out an effective attack, which in turn requires detailed knowledge of the lay-out of the target. When Bruno Breguet and Magdalena Kaupp were arrested in an underground garage in Paris, their car contained cash, explosives, false papers, and detailed city maps with town halls clearly marked as targets. In FBI raids on safe houses of the United Freedom Front, Bureau investigators told a court in Cleveland, Ohio, that they had found 'handwritten descriptions of two corporate office buildings bombed in the New York City area in 1984'. The UFF had claimed responsibility for ten such bombs during the year, against targets such as a US Navy research station, Honeywell Computers, the Motorola Corporation, IBM Computers, General Electric and the Union Carbide Corporation. The target-notes related to the General Electric Aerospace division in Melville, Long Island, and IBM in Harrison, New York.

FBI agent James Lyons quoted the notes on the General Electric attack: 'The best place to put it is in the stairwell' – the precise location of the bomb.

A second raid in Baltimore, Maryland at the end of May 1985 linked an apartment to radical organisations suspected of sixteen bombings since 1982, including one inside the Capitol Building in 1983. The prosecutor's office revealed that 'There was a file drawer marked "in progress" and it contained plans and diagrams of a number of Federal buildings, with marks where the bombs ought to be placed.' One such plan was a diagram of the Old Executive Office Building, a part of the 18.5 acre White House complex which houses Administration Offices, an office of the Vice-President, and the Office of Management and Budget.

Terrorists can quite easily research and observe their targets, or their chosen place of operation, by posing as tourists. The layout and the communications in large public buildings can quite plausibly be investigated by an apparently inquisitive tourist, especially when there is a guide to help with questions. But such research efforts can go wrong: when Kozo Okamoto travelled from New York to Paris, on his way to the Middle East and the Lod Massaacre, he was supposed to fly by Boeing 747, to familiarise himself with the internal layout of the plane. When he found that he had inadvertently booked on a 707, and tried to change to a 747 flight, he aroused suspicion – though airline staff only remembered him after the Lod murders had given him massive notoriety.

Targeting

When Action Directe assassinated René Audran, the Director-General of the French Ministry of Defence, they shot him as he got out of his car, in the garage of his house. Security advisers regard the moment when the terrorists' target gets out of his car to open the garage door, or leaves the garage to cross to the house, as the most vulnerable time of all. Arnold Campbell, who organises the US State Department's seminar 'Coping with Violence Abroad', states that 'the highest point of vulnerability is getting from the car into the home. That is where we have seen the highest number of attacks.' While it is an almost insoluble problem, security experts regard the awareness of it as a step towards protection.

Terrorists can strike at anyone or anything, anywhere, any time. They are not so foolish as to attack visibly well-defended targets. Terrorist bombs tend not to explode inside the Ministry of Defence in Whitehall, on crowded aeroplanes or in Parliament buildings, for the reason that they are well-defended and secure to a substantial degree – and for the more important reason that the terrorists can produce the same publicity and reaction by attacking less dangerous targets.

The idea of targeting is governed by two factors: what is possible and what is defensible, within the extremist political view of the terrorists. Despite the predictable horror at the killing or injuring of 'innocent victims', terrorists very rarely kill completely at random. For them, at least, there is always a case to be made for the culpability of the target, whether human or inanimate. Reinhard Rupprecht, the Deputy Director of the West German Federal Police Division argues that the targets of West German terrorists reflect 'the symbolic aims and motivation of the terrorists. Principally the groups acting in the FRG fight against what they call imperialism and colonialism, capitalism and consumism (sic). Most of the selected targets have a symbolic meaning for terrorists; for example, banks stand for capitalism, department stores for consumism, military installations for imperialism, "multis" (multinational businesses) for colonialism in the Third World.'

While the terrorists might like to destroy the communications nerve-centre of an American military base in West Germany, they are far more likely to explode a bomb outside the front gate or in the car park: as they did on 9 August 1985 at the USAF Rhein-Main air base, directly facing another notable terrorist target, Frankfurt International Airport. The bomb killed two people and injured several more, doing superficial damage to relatively unimportant facilities: the far greater casualties that might have been deliberately caused by placing the bomb inside a secure building would have involved far more risk to the terrorists. The attack still got on to the front pages of the world's press, and the claims of responsibility and the political rhetoric of the group were aired in great detail. Terrorism is about headlines, and the headline news reflected that the target was 'the enemy' – the US military.

Thus bombs explode outside minor military installations, or at the pre-security check-in desks of air terminals. If the gleaming plate-glass headquarters of the multinational company is guarded by uniformed security staff, if briefcases are searched at the door or confiscated, and if electronic passes open the lifts, the terrorist leader may decide to fire-bomb the company sports and social club, deserted in the city suburbs between Sunday night and Friday. If the defence contractor is working inside the barbed-wire fences of the military base, the revolutionaries may kidnap him when he is driving his children to the swimming-pool. If the diplomat has an armed guard, his secretary or aide may be shot by gunmen on a motor scooter. The publicity and reverberations are much the same, if the target is resonant enough.

While military officers, and Americans in particular, are a first-choice target, security advisers need to bear in mind that the terrorists may not be very interested in ensuring – or be able to ensure – that their target is relevant to their cause. As Commander Churchill-Coleman points out, 'No matter how hard they may seem on the exterior, the terrorists are always looking for the soft target.' The assassination in Rome of the American General Leamon Hunt is such an example: as the Co-ordinator of the United Nations Multinational Forces and Observers in the Sinai desert, monitoring the restored border between Israel and Egypt, he made a less likely target. But he was quartered in Rome, where a group of terrorists found they could make a hit; and they took their chance. The Red Brigades claimed the murder, though there were later doubts about the authenticity of the claim: the communiqué attacked the installation of American Cruise missiles in Italy, a military matter with which Hunt was entirely unconnected – 'No to all missiles in Comiso! No to re-armament! Italy out of NATO!'

Professor Franco Ferracuti has a pragmatic respect for

terrorists as opponents. As he points out, their dedication to political goals is absolute. In terms of targeting, he makes this observation: 'They are very sophisticated and knowledgeable, with the patience for planning and watching – following a victim over a long period. In terms of attacks on business, with the activities of Action Directe, CCC, the Red Army Faction and Revolutionary Cells, they will certainly be alert for any European companies getting involved in the Strategic Defence Initiative ('Star Wars') research programme of the Reagan Administration. Companies like Alfa Romeo and FIAT might both do so in Italy.'

If one target is too difficult another will arise: as Ferracuti's 'Star Wars' prediction implies, terrorists are not only well-informed about the political world which their enemies inhabit, they are also unlikely to run short of new issues or new targets.

Underground
Publicity is a goal not only in the formal media of the (enemy) state, but also something that serves to inform, mobilise and enthuse political supporters of the cause, usually through underground publications read and distributed informally wherever anarchists, radicals and terrorists gather. These news-sheets are generally produced by hand, on small printing machines and photocopiers, and distributed from post office box numbers or constantly changing accommodation addresses. (*Subversion* magazine, allied to Action Directe and their European comrades, was published from Post Box 1682, Brussels.) *An Phoblacht (Republican News)* is an exception – a full-scale, professionally produced newspaper, openly supportive of the IRA and virulently anti-British, the paper is sold in Republican areas of Belfast and Northern Ireland, particularly in bookshops and Republican Clubs dominated by the influence of Sinn Fein.

One other single example comes from as long ago as the early 1960s, when the *Front de Libération Québécois* (FLQ) organised what they called an 'information service' through their clandestine journal *La Cognée* (The Axe). It contained practical guidance on how to commit acts of sabotage, where to steal dynamite, how to hold up a bank, how to make a bomb, how to start a fire and other useful tricks of the trade. In October 1965, to assist in the production and publication of clandestine materials and communiqués, they stole a Gestetner photocopier and other office equipment and stationery from the Montreal offices of the New Democratic Party.

The language of terrorist communiqués is dense, predictable political jargon, as for example in the Summer 1984 edition of *Breakthrough*, the 'Political Journal of Prairie Fire Organising Committee', a radical relic of the late 1960s 'Days of Rage' on American student campuses:

BOMBING OF IBM OFFICES, N.Y.
Free Azania! Death to Apartheid!

Tonight, March 19, armed units of the United Freedom Front bombed the IBM corporate office building at 3000 Westchester Avenue in a northern suburb of New York City. IBM is a death merchant and directly profits from and supports the fascist South African government, and its war of terror against the Freedom-loving People of Southern Africa.

IBM CORPORATION IS GUILTY OF CRIMES AGAINST THE PEOPLE OF SOUTH AFRICA THROUGH THEIR COLLABORATION WITH THE FASCIST GOVERNMENT!

In the underground press which offers moral support to the terrorists, the names change but the language remains indigestibly the same.

Victims
All terrorism involves victims, and terrorists rationalise the problem in two ways: by arguing that they are fighting a war in which victims are an unfortunate necessity, or that victims are collaborators and thus responsible for their own fate. By and large, most victims of terrorism become targets by virtue of their position or profession, whether as elected members of government, appointed diplomats, professional military officers or career business executives. Probably fewer than five

per cent of casualties of terrorism are 'innocent bystanders', in the sense of falling by utter chance to the violence of a terrorist bomb. Such examples are therefore all the more shocking, such as the bomb at Harrods at Christmas 1983. More recently, however, the fanatical anti-Americanism of militant Shi'ites has blurred the distinction with a good deal of bloodshed: once an individual becomes a target by virtue of being merely a citizen of the USA, all assumptions about relative risk become irrelevant.

A number of terrorist groups make a point of publicly apologising for injuring civilians, and explaining why the government is really responsible for their bloodshed and injuries. John Harley of the FBI quotes the American experience: 'Most of the groups we have had here have been pretty "thoughtful" people. They have almost always been doing bombings, and they set the bombs at a time when people are least likely to be around. They issue warnings, and sometimes even repeat the warnings. In one case they called twice to ask why the police weren't taking their first warning, of a bomb about to explode, seriously.'

Action Directe, in a communiqué that must be noted more for its black humour than anything else, apologised to Parisian residents for disturbing them with the noise of exploding bombs. When Action Directe turned their bombs on French businesses involved in trade with South Africa, they gave a disingenuous warning that members of the public who chose to deal with such companies should 'understand the risk' that they were running. Despite the superficial 'thoughtfulness' of some terrorists, terrorism requires, in Franco Ferracuti's phrase, an 'absolute detachment' from the victim who 'is seen as an object'. Such detachment is the *sine qua non* of the ability to commit acts of terrorist violence, whatever the cosmetic claims and communiqués may suggest.

Weapons
The actions of terrorists require a fairly small amount of 'training', and what little is required is easily passed from member to member of a group. In Italy, most terrorists have

done national military service, in which they gain a grounding in the use of weapons and explosives, among other areas of military expertise. Likewise, in Belgium some 25,000 people a year undergo military service, and in mid-1985 Belgian police were pursuing the theory, based on evidence of explosives expertise in CCC attacks, that one member of the CCC had served in the Engineers or attained the rank of sergeant elsewhere in the army. Two arrested men also had military links, and the Army Training Service was called in to help sift possible suspects from the lists of recruits.

Terrorists have made the Kalashnikov the most famous and effective murder weapon in the world. It is simple to use, dramatic in its firepower, and easily broken down into four pieces which fit in a briefcase or bulky jacket. It is the ultimate weapon in the terrorists' arsenal of essentially unsophisticated, manual weapons – principally pistols, shotguns and hand-grenades.

Terrorists use weapons in two distinct ways – as weapons of strength, and weapons of action: weapons of strength to enforce and enable their activity; and weapons of action to cause death, injury and damage. In the first case, the weapon is the bank robber's shotgun – to assert the strength of the terrorist. Without it he would be a powerless radical, but with it he is a potent and dangerous criminal who can stage a robbery, hijack a car, force his will upon people who can do him some practical service. In the second case, the weapon is still more deadly: it is the machine-gun which kills body-guards protecting the victim of a kidnap, the bomb with a twenty-four-day timer, or the grenade thrown into a bar full of military personnel.

The first use of real weapons occurs in the transition from protest to 'direct action': In Britain, for example, even the activities of the radical Animal Liberation Front, which protests against the use of live animals in scientific experiments, have followed the pattern. Scotland Yard's Anti-Terrorist Branch has found this organisation among its clients: 'The ALF has gone from throwing paint and daubing slogans to placing improvised incendiary devices. It may only be one or two individuals in an organisation, even using it as a front and going on from there to greater things.'

The weapons that terrorists want will come from a variety of sources: some will be bought in underworld circles, some will be stolen to order, and most disturbingly there is growing recent evidence of diplomats functioning as armourers to terrorist groups by the most serious abuse of Diplomatic Bag rules. The varied sources of their weapons means that terrorists always have problems in finding compatible ammunition in sufficient quantities: Marighella defined all the munitions problems: 'The urban guerilla has to capture or divert arms from the enemy to be able to fight. Because his arms are not uniform, since what he has are expropriated or have fallen into his hands in different ways, the urban guerilla faces the problem of a variety of arms and a shortage of ammunition. Moreover, he has no place to practice shooting and marksmanship.' (This is not always true. The rural, agricultural Basque country and Northern Ireland both offer open spaces and farmland where shooting is to be expected, providing cover to terrorists for their training. Croatian terrorists have used the Black Forest for their shooting practice, and Armenians of ASALA made a videotape of their firearms training in the Bekaa Valley in eastern Lebanon.)

Another South American terrorist manual, besides Marighella's, by the Uruguayan Abraham Guillen, goes into great detail about the urban guerilla's arms: they are 'light arms, easily exchanged, usually captured from the enemy, purchased, or made on the spot ... the basic arm of the urban guerilla is the light machine gun ... managed by a good marksman. The other components of the group must be armed with .38 revolvers ... Shotguns can be useful if used at close range and point blank. They are useful even for a poor shot, especially at night when precision isn't much help.'

The ease with which a terrorist organisation can procure weapons is illustrated by the fact that between 1969 and November 1984, a total of 2,843 weapons of United States origin were recovered in Northern Ireland alone. The weapons included Armalite rifles, Garand rifles, M1 carbines and Colt pistols. An apparent theft-to-order occurred in August 1976 of seven M60 machine-guns, stolen from a National Guard armoury in Danvers, Massachusetts. All seven weapons were subsequently found by police in Ireland, three in the Republic and four in the North, the last being recovered in August 1982 in Londonderry. Security forces have ascribed at least 11 deaths and 18 injuries to the seven weapons, on forensic evidence.

Against this background, and against the received wisdom that only 'renegade states' offer training, money, encouragement and weapons to terrorists, it is worth recalling that across America military training camps are run in which any individual can go and get just the kind of expertise any terrorist would find most useful. As one of the 1968 generation of American domestic radicals, Cathy Wilkerson, who was a member of the Weather Underground terrorist movement, observed: 'There are training camps all over this country for right wing groups, that are accepted if not financed by government, training right wing groups from all over the world.' While government involvement is far from obvious, highly liberal American gun laws have allowed such institutions, for example, to give training in irregular warfare to members of the Sikh terrorist organisation, the Khalistan Liberation Army.

Zeal

Terrorism doesn't work, and terrorists cannot be motivated, unless the individuals and the group believe that they can win, and that their vision of victory and the new order that follows it will ultimately be embraced by the majority who presently oppose the terrorists' methods, and usually their purpose as well. As Ferracuti argues, 'They are Utopians, with a total detachment from reality. Terrorists make two traditional mistakes: they commit acts of violence against the proletariat, which undercut potential sympathy for their cause; and they think they have support from trade unions, which they never have.'

In many ways, the two separate pictures – of the patient, sophisticated, politically aware terrorist planner, and the

302

totally convinced devotee who can believe the inherently incredible proposition (for example, that the Turkish government will donate part of Eastern Turkey to the Armenian people as a new national entity) – seem impossibly divergent. Yet it is the intellectual and emotional combination which makes the route to Utopia so dangerous and strewn with casualties.

Without total commitment, the radical does not become a terrorist, and the pressure group does not cross the line into a tolerance for and acceptance of the use of violence as the principal method to pursue the cause. Terrorists and their opponents are united in that view. The Tupamaros of Uruguay rallied around the slogan 'Words divide us, actions unite us.' According to a German rightwinger and Black September officer, the terrorist requires one thing above all – 'To believe in his cause, to believe he is doing the right thing.' John Harley of the FBI accepts that the terrorists' zeal guarantees that the struggle survives individual setbacks: 'You may take out a cell today, and put them out of business, but the cause lives on.' The IRA espouses a saying of Mao Tse Tung's: 'They may kill the revolutionary, but they cannot kill the revolution'. The motivation, in the words of Franco Ferracuti, is simple – 'The belief in an ideal ... The strength of the political credo ... The belief that you can change things through action ...'

Marighella suggests that 'from a moral point of view, the urban guerilla has an undeniable superiority. This moral superiority is what sustains the urban guerilla.' To Abraham Guillen, 'The urban guerilla's reason for existence, the basic condition in which he acts and survives, is to shoot. Shooting and marksmanship are the urban guerilla's water and air.' But perhaps the credo, the motive and the dangerous commitment are best summed up in the simple belief of Marighella, that 'It is better to err acting, than to do nothing for fear of acting.'

The world has no shortage of lost causes or popular struggles, zealously espoused. To act with zeal may satisfy the terrorist, or those whose philosophy endorses violence. But the consequences of such acts, whether justifiable or purely in error, will continue to threaten and oppress all of us. Without conceding anything to the terrorists' blackmailing violence, their fanatical zeal can only be met with a new degree of political realism, diplomatic skill, and public comprehension.

INDEX